T0339731

"At McDonald's, we are committed to feeding and fostering the Hispanic community, and Isaac Mizrahi's book captures the essence of why and how marketers should invest in this segment. I am proud to call Isaac and his alma team partners in the journey of ensuring the Hispanic community feels seen, supported, and empowered."

—Morgan Flatley, evp, Global Chief Marketing Officer and new business ventures, McDonald's

"When it comes to an understanding of how the Hispanic segment can drive business growth to brands and corporations, there are few experts like Isaac Mizrahi. His experience is vast and rich, and his perspective, combining many years on the corporate and ad agency sides, provides an insightful reading experience. This is a must-read book."

—Antonio Lucio, Founder and Principal, 5s Diversity

"A must-read—Isaac Mizrahi uses his decades of experience leading business growth by connecting the U.S. Hispanic segment with clear, direct, and insightful ideas on how corporations should think about doing business in America in this era of enhanced population diversity."

—Marcelo Claure, Chairman and CEO, Claure Capital and Former CEO SoftBank Group Int'l.

Hispanic Market Power

The U.S. Hispanic segment represents the most prominent demographic growth in the country and a huge and untapped business opportunity for companies willing to move away from preconceived notions and market effectively to Hispanic customers. This book shows you how.

Now more than ever, corporations operating in the U.S. should see the Hispanic population at the core of their existing and future strategies, but many leaders believe Hispanic marketing is the same marketing you run for Anglos but translated into Spanish, or that all Hispanics are undocumented immigrants with no purchasing power, or that using Mariachis in their communications is the way to connect with this diverse segment. It's time for a modern approach, and in this book, Isaac Mizrahi, one of the country's leading voices in multicultural marketing, uses his unique experience as a corporate executive, agency CEO, and industry leader to help businesses grow by leveraging the booming Hispanic consumer segment to drive sales.

Filled with straightforward talk, illustrative case studies, and pragmatic suggestions and recommendations, this book counterbalances academic books on the topic with little connection to day-to-day reality and other books with a more political standpoint. This is a business book created by a marketer for other marketers and business leaders looking to succeed in the U.S.

Credit: Fro Rojas

Isaac Mizrahi is a world-class, award-winning CEO with unique experience ranging from working at the corporate side to being an ad agency leader and consultant for the most significant and more relevant brands in the U.S. Born in Latin America, he is a thought leader and industry champion, speaker at conferences and the press, and considered one of the country's most relevant voices for multicultural marketing and DE&I.

Hispanic Market Power

America's Business Growth Engine

Isaac Mizrahi

Routledge
Taylor & Francis Group

NEW YORK AND LONDON

Designed cover image: Daniel Correa

First published 2023
by Routledge
605 Third Avenue, New York, NY 10158

and by Routledge
4 Park Square, Milton Park, Abingdon, Oxon, OX14 4RN

Routledge is an imprint of the Taylor & Francis Group, an informa business

Library of Congress Cataloging-in-Publication Data
Names: Mizrahi, Isaac (Marketing executive), author.
Title: Hispanic market power: America's business growth engine/Isaac Mizrahi.
Identifiers: LCCN 2022052757 (print) | LCCN 2022052758 (ebook) | ISBN 9781032392349 (hardback) | ISBN 9781032392318 (paperback) | ISBN 9781003348931 (ebook)
Subjects: LCSH: Minority consumers—United States. | Hispanic Americans. | Marketing research—United States. | Target marketing—United States.
Classification: LCC HF5415.332.M56 M59 2023 (print) | LCC HF5415.332.M56 (ebook) | DDC 658.8008—dc23/eng/20221104
LC record available at https://lccn.loc.gov/2022052757
LC ebook record available at https://lccn.loc.gov/2022052758

ISBN: 978-1-032-39234-9 (hbk)
ISBN: 978-1-032-39231-8 (pbk)
ISBN: 978-1-003-34893-1 (ebk)

DOI: 10.4324/9781003348931

Typeset in Bembo
by Apex CoVantage, LLC

To the universe, To love, To light,
To my ancestors,
To my parents and family,
To Pabi, Biel, and Karina,
To life

"It is time for parents to teach young people early on that in diversity, there is beauty, and there is strength."

~ Maya Angelou

Contents

Foreword

One of the aspects of the role as P&G's Chief Brand Officer is the wonderful opportunity to speak at conferences, give interviews, and write about views of brands, marketing, and the industry. A consistently meaningful and relevant topic of interest is the importance of multicultural marketing, led by the Hispanic consumer segment, to drive growth and create value on a sustained basis.

For many years, the marketing industry has been talking about seizing the sizable and substantial growth opportunity represented by multicultural marketing. It has been a wake-up alarm that keeps ringing, yet too many in the industry seem to keep hitting the snooze button.

It is concerning that our industry still appears to be missing out on the tremendous potential of marketing to serve Black, Hispanic, Asian, Pacific Islander, Native, and Indigenous Americans—who make up more than 40% of the U.S. population and are growing rapidly. At the same time, we all can be equally as excited too. Because multicultural marketing may be the single biggest source of market growth in our industry now and for the next several years, perhaps even decades. Together, if we put our minds to it, we can make sure we're not asleep at the switch in the coming years and avoid missing the very thing that we want the most in our industry—growth.

According to the 2020 U.S. Census, 100% of the population growth in the past decade came from increases in the Black, Hispanic, Asian, Pacific Islander, Native, Indigenous, multiracial, and multiethnic segments of the population. Multicultural buying power is now worth more than $5 trillion and has been the single biggest driver of market growth for a decade.

Market growth is important because it is the most significant driver of business growth. When markets grow, all brands rise—new users enter the market, product consumption increases, and innovation flourishes with new offerings that drive greater usage and higher levels of value. When done well, this results in increased income and wealth, which translates to more purchasing power.

The opportunity is significant, but it is not new. And that leads back to a concern.

We simply have a lot of entrenched marketing habits, and old habits are hard to break.

They're comfortable, safe, and they've worked for us in the past—all factors when you consider how perilous marketing can be in today's world.

Breaking old habits to build new ones is much harder, so it's easier to keep hitting the snooze button. But if we don't wake up and get moving now, in a few years when multicultural consumers are the majority of the U.S. population, shaping culture, with the majority of purchasing power, and driving more market growth, they'll leave brands that kept snoozing in the dust, wishing they had done a lot more, a lot sooner.

How do we break the old habits and build the new ones needed to seize the tremendous multicultural market growth opportunity in front of us? Take an objective view of our current behavior, change, and grow.

That's what makes this book by Isaac Mizrahi so timely and powerful. Isaac's leadership in our industry has been respected and revered for many years. He has worked firsthand on brands. He has been an outstanding advertising agency executive at the legendary alma advertising agency. He has led the industry as the chair of the Hispanic Marketing Council. And he has been one of P&G's valued and trusted partners when it comes to multicultural marketing.

Isaac has brought that long line of experience and wisdom into the contents of this book. While some talk about the Hispanic market opportunity from a theoretical perspective, this book brings a pragmatic perspective, based on Isaac's significant industry experience, enriched by case studies, and expanded upon by the expert opinions of several storied guests.

This book can become a resource to all of the leaders and practitioners in our industry, from the entry-level students that are considering their careers in marketing to C-suite executives and their board of directors. I hope you enjoy reading it, but more importantly, applying its lessons. If we all do that, we can help the Hispanic segment and all multicultural segments achieve the enormous potential as perhaps the single most important driver of business growth for years to come.

Marc Pritchard, Chief Brand Officer, Procter & Gamble

Acknowledgments

Writing a book is a long and arduous journey and one that I am happy I had the opportunity to experience. During this process, many people helped me directly, supporting the creation of this book, or indirectly, by nurturing my ideas and providing the necessary help to shape who I am and my professional development.

Here is a tentative way to express my gratitude to at least some of them.

First, I'd like to express my gratitude to my grandparents (in memoriam), who left behind the tragedies of war and religious intolerance in their home countries to find a new life as immigrants in Brazil. Their life stories inspired me to start my immigrant story in a different country.

To my parents, Fani and Jacob, for teaching me the importance of education, hard work, and perseverance. To my brother Andre, for always being one of my biggest supporters.

To Karina, for being this wonderful mom to our kids and for keeping me grounded and focused.

To Patrick and Gabriel, for giving me the best gift in the world: the opportunity to be their father. I have so much fun with you; thanks for picking me as your father.

To Chiqui Cartagena, thanks for giving me the incentive to write this book and offering to be my editor. I couldn't have written this book without you.

To Rubens Campos, thanks for offering me my first job, setting the bar very high, and being my friend until today.

To Omar Rodriguez, for being my boss, my mentor, and my friend. And for showing me a more human side of a corporate executive. Also, thanks for providing your input on this book's first manuscript.

To Chuck Fruit (in memoriam), Scott McCune, and Rebecca Messina, for, together with Omar, being the reason I moved to the U.S. and for all support received through the years.

To Fabio Coelho, who helped me in a crucial moment in my career and remained a friend since then.

To my friends, the ones from my teenage years back in Rio de Janeiro and the ones I made in the U.S. When you are an immigrant, friends become your family. I am blessed to have many friends in my life.

To colleagues from past jobs, at Souza Cruz, Coca-Cola, BellSouth, Sprint Nextel, especially my team members. Thanks for your constant support.

To Luis Miguel Messianu, for opening the way for a different aspect of my career, one that I've never dreamed about, and for treating me not as a subordinate but rather as a friend and partner. Moreover, thanks for giving me the incentive to start writing my first articles and for providing your suggestions and input on how to make them better. Not many writers have the privilege of being coached by a talented copywriter.

To Angela Rodriguez, for being my informal editor in most of my articles. When you say you liked something I've written, that's when I know the content is ready.

To Alvar Sunol, Angie Battistini, Michelle Headley, Leo Peet, Mike Sotelo, Carola Chaurero, and all other current and past alma colleagues.

To Ana Banos and her team, who always helped me with proofreading my articles. To Candy Cabrera, who helped with the book cover image licensing.

To alma's clients, my gratitude for believing and investing in the Hispanic market and for understanding that creativity has the power to drive growth.

To my colleagues at DDB and Omnicom. Thanks for your trust and support.

To Avi Dan who opened the door at Forbes and to the Forbes team. To all those who read my articles, shared them, liked them, and commented on them. Each of these actions gave me the confidence to keep writing.

To John Santiago, Felipe Korzenny, and Robert Rodriguez, for all advice given when I approached you to discuss the idea of writing this book. Felipe, your work inspired me to become a better marketer. John, your enthusiasm was contagious; I am lucky to have you as a friend.

To Daniel Correa, for his brilliant and generous art for the cover.

To Marta Insua, for her support throughout my career and her patience in reading an early manuscript of this book.

To Marc Pritchard, for his support of this book, and to Antonio Lucio, Morgan Flatley, and Marcelo Claure, for their generous words of praise.

To the team at Routledge, and Taylor & Francis Group to Meredith Norwich and Bethany Nelson, for believing in this book and getting it published. To Sophia Levine, who accepted an unsolicited message sent via LinkedIn and made the right connections so my book's idea could be heard.

To Howard Koning, for the fantastic work with data checking. To Charles Knull, for his legal advice. Thanks to Fro Rojas, for my picture portrayal. Thanks to Mark Lopez and Tanya Arditi at the Pew Research Center for your support.

To Horacio Gavilan and the Hispanic Marketing Council and my multi-cultural marketing industry colleagues, for your support, help with the case studies, and mostly for working hard to create and grow a whole industry.

To J. Balvin, Jennifer Healan, Veronica Thompson, Elizabeth Campbell, Kelly Frailey, Lina Shields, Monica Morales, Greg Lyons, Esperanza Teasdale, Rita Rodriguez, Jeronimo Escudero, Andrea Schoff, Trish Cox, India Boulton, Peter DeLuca, Melody Macaluso, Greg Knipp, Issac Morales, Marisstella Marinkovic, Ross Daron, Maria del Pilar Casal, Sebastian Preciado, Diana Delgado, Raquel Meza, Silvia Rodriguez, Adam Silverman, Michelle, St Jacques, Marcelo Pascoa, Chris Steele, Marcia Flynn, Marisol Pelaez, Jason Coochwytewa, and Fabio Acosta. To my alma colleagues Bea del Amo, Cristina Lage, Jose Hawayek, and Madeline Perez-Velez. Your support in getting all case studies reviewed and approved for publication was invaluable.

To the leadership and employees from Dieste, Urias Communications, TelevisaUnivision, and Inspire Advertising, for your generosity in supporting this book with your clients' case studies.

To Josy Rodrigues, who gave me an important incentive for me to decide to write this book.

To my ancestors, to my guides, to my guardians, to the Creator.
Gratitude.

About the Author and Contributors

Isaac Mizrahi is a world-class, award-winning marketing executive who spent his 30+ years of career working with brands such as BAT, Coca-Cola, BellSouth, Nextel, and Sprint, in several different functions covering multiple geographies.

Isaac has been a speaker in several multicultural marketing conferences and has been featured in *The New York Times*, *San Francisco Chronicle*, *PBS*, *Ad Age*, *AdWeek*, and other industry publications. In 2006 he was recognized as U.S. Hispanic Marketer of the Year by Ad Week's "Marketing y Medios" for his work at Sprint-Nextel. In 2021 he was recognized by *AdWeek* as one of the top 50 marketing executives of the country.

Over the past decade he has transitioned from the client side of the business to the agency side, as the CEO of alma advertising, a leading multicultural strategy and advertising agency, working with corporations like McDonald's, PepsiCo, Molson Coors, CVS Health, Lilly, Google, and Intuit among others.

Isaac also served on the board of the Hispanic Marketing Council, the organization that represents our industry, and has a monthly online column on Forbes.com, where he writes about Multicultural Marketing in America for thousands of readers.

He was born in Rio de Janeiro, Brazil, immigrated to the U.S. in 1999, and lives in the beautiful Miami with his wife, his two sons, and his dog, Ollie.

Chiqui Cartagena is a Hispanic media and marketing thought leader on the Latino community in the United States. She currently serves as the Interim Executive Director of CUNY TV, a non-commercial, educational channel that is part of the City University of New York, and she served as editor of this book and is herself the author of two business books about the importance of the Latino Community in the U.S.

Daniel Correa is a multi-awarded Brazilian designer and creative director. His work in advertising has helped global brands overcome their challenges and find their place in pop culture. In 2022, Daniel was named by *AdWeek* as one of the 100 most creative and innovative people in the world. He was the author of this book's cover design.

Preface

August 12, 2021, was an important day. That's when the U.S. Census Bureau released the first official data from the 2020 Census. For the first time, it confirmed what some experts had predicted: that the absolute number of the White Caucasian population in this country is declining for the first time.

Moreover, the Census also reported that 100% of the country's population growth during the past decade came from the minority ethnic populations, led mainly by the three major segments: Hispanics, Blacks, and Asian American Pacific Islanders.[1]

For some observers, this was just another curious piece of information that comes and goes in this constant news cycle we live in nowadays. Others perhaps interpreted this news as an exciting trend that can shape the future of the country's political and social discussions. And a few may also study this report as an interesting academic or anthropologic experiment on a large scale.

However, for anyone doing business in the United States of America, this is one of the most transformational forces that will significantly influence who will be the winners and losers in the country's dynamic marketplace in the upcoming years and decades.

I decided to write this book with three main intentions in mind. First, I want to help corporations grow their businesses by tapping into the power of the Hispanic segment and doing so by sharing my experience of more than two decades working with the top brands in this country and observing how they succeeded or failed in their efforts.

Second, I hope my experience can inspire the current and the next generations of marketers in this country, making this multicultural specialization not only better understood but also more in demand for years to come.

Finally, and extremely important to me, I want to convey a positive message around the idea of diversity. Often I hear criticisms such as "focusing on diversity divides us, makes us separate; we need to focus on union," or "we should focus on our similarities, not on what makes us different."

As a matter of fact, I think the opposite is true. I believe that we will only achieve a more just and fair society when we learn how to respect our individualism. I believe that we should be more tolerant and that we need to celebrate what makes us unique.

Being part of a collective shouldn't happen at the expense of celebrating who we are as individuals. That's for me one of the most important lessons of this century, and the business community can and should contribute to spreading this message.

I believe it's time to evolve, to embrace the idea that diversity (of people, of races, of religions, of backgrounds, of genres, of ideas, you name it!) is what makes us better, and that by incorporating new and different ideas and traditions, we progress toward a better future.

My observations are derived from a unique vantage point, which has helped me throughout my career: to view and take part in the evolution of multicultural marketing and to be witness to the best and worst marketing practices available in today's marketplace.

Unfortunately, in my experience, very few organizations truly understand how these demographic changes can positively impact their businesses. Even some business leaders, who seem to have a sense of the multicultural growth opportunity, tend to be reluctant to take the necessary steps to leverage it effectively.

My goal with this book is to help business leaders understand why Hispanic marketing is critical for their future growth and business success. I want to share with you what effective brands are doing to capture the lion's share of this business opportunity and what are the risks and mistakes associated with inaction or missteps.

In this book I will discuss some ideas and concepts covered partially by some of the articles I have written over the past few years, mainly the ones published at Forbes. I hope this book can be used by a broad spectrum of business stakeholders, including board directors, c-suite executives, and marketing professionals. Moreover, I hope this book can also be relevant to other professionals that are part of the U.S. marketing ecosystem, including media advertising agencies, consultants, research executives, and aspiring marketing and business leaders at academic institutions.

Multicultural or Hispanic?

While I have worked on many multicultural marketing projects involving multiple ethnic populations throughout my career, this book will be mostly focused on the U.S. Hispanic consumer segment for a few reasons.

First, it is the largest minority segment of this country, with more than 62 million individuals according to the latest Census data, and a healthy growth rate.[2] U.S. Hispanic consumers also represent one of the most significant untapped business opportunities for companies and brands doing business in the U.S.

Second, this is the segment that I have the most extensive experience and personal connection to, given my background and professional journey. This doesn't mean that other ethnic segments are not important for marketers across America. As a matter of fact, when appropriate, I will mention some cross-learnings that can be applied to other segments based on my experience.

For example, the Black consumer segment is experiencing a renaissance from an investment standpoint and it is an essential component of any marketer's multicultural marketing considerations. The influence of the Black segment in our country's business and culture is vast and well documented by so many great books, and I encourage you to learn more about that through other experts' books. For example, I like David Morse's books, including *Multicultural Intelligence* and Steve Stoute's *The Tanning of America*.

It's important to mention that there are also other segments that are becoming more relevant from a diverse perspective, even if they don't represent a culture-based segment, like the LGBTQ+ segment, or People with Disabilities.

Trying to cover all multicultural segments at once not only increases the complexity of the discussion but will also not do justice to the importance of these other relevant multicultural or diverse segments. In the end, this was a decision I made based on a desire to have more focus and depth on Hispanic marketing.

Hispanics, Latinos, or Latinx?

In her book *Latino Boom II: Catch the Biggest Demographic Wave since the Baby Boom*, Chiqui Cartagena, one of the leading experts on the Hispanic segment in the U.S. and editor of this book, wrote:

> I prefer to keep things simple and go by the dictionary. According to Merriamsss-Webster's Collegiate Dictionary, Latino refers to people who come from a Latin American country (there are twenty-two of them), or a person of Latin-American origin living in the United States. Hispanics is a more comprehensive term that applies to the peoples and cultures of Spain and Portugal.

According to the Pew Research Center,

> Pan-ethnic labels describing the U.S. population of people tracing their roots to Latin America and Spain have been introduced over the

decades, rising and falling in popularity. Today, the two dominant labels in use are Hispanic and Latino, with origins in the 1970s and 1990s respectively.

More recently, a new, gender-neutral, pan-ethnic label, Latinx, has emerged as an alternative that is used by some news and entertainment outlets, corporations, local governments and universities to describe the nation's Hispanic population.[3]

However, the study conducted by Pew in December 2019 revealed that only 3% of U.S. Hispanics used the term "Latinx" to self-describe themselves. The Pew Research Center traces the roots of Latinx in their 2019 report as follows:

The emergence of Latinx coincides with a global movement to introduce gender-neutral nouns and pronouns into many languages whose grammar has traditionally used male or female constructions. In the United States, the first uses of Latinx appeared more than a decade ago. It was added to a widely used English dictionary in 2018, reflecting its greater use. Yet the use of Latinx is not common practice, and the term's emergence has generated debate about its appropriateness in a gendered language like Spanish.

As Chiqui points out, while there's a difference between Hispanics and Latinos (and as a Brazilian-born person, I know this difference very well), for the sake of simplicity and standardization, this book will adopt "Hispanics" as the preferred term not only because it is the official way the population is referred to in today's government communications, like the U.S. Census, but also because it is gender-neutral. Sometimes in this book, I kept the reference to Latino or Latina as part of a reference to an organization's name or to honor a quote from one of the people I interviewed featured in the book.

My Journey

I believe it may be worth sharing a few words on my journey to better contextualize my background and how I ended up working in multicultural marketing.

I was born and raised in Rio de Janeiro. My parents were first-generation Brazilians; their parents were Jewish immigrants who left their respective countries to find refuge and an opportunity for a better life after suffering religious persecution in Turkey (paternal side of my family) and the impact of Nazism and the Holocaust in Poland (maternal side of my family).

I think my ancestral background helped shape my professional experience because I understood innately the fundamental characteristics of ethnic minority populations in America. All immigrants are driven to leave their home countries because they have a sense of "betterment." Immigrants are just trying to provide a safer present and a better future for the next generations compared to the past generations.

I studied economics, mostly because I wanted to balance the rational, quantitative, and objective side of the business environment with the human, emotional, and subjective parts of it. During my teenage years, Brazil experienced significant economic and financial turmoil, and for a curious kid like me, who loved reading the news and following the political debate of a country that was just emerging from 21 years of military control towards democracy, economic-related topics were as popular as Brazil's amazing "fútbol" or our famous soap operas.

An internship at the local office of British American Tobacco turned into my first full-time job, and for five years, I had the opportunity to get a crash course in marketing. At that time, marketing and advertising for cigarette products were still legally approved by the local government, and I had the opportunity to work and learn the trade by rotations in many areas like business analytics and planning, competitive intelligence, brand management, sports and events, and media planning and buying.

In 1996 I was approached by The Coca-Cola Company, who was looking for a head of their Marketing Services team in Brazil, a job which included media planning and buying, sports marketing, managing the company's advertising agencies relationships, and the development of special trade marketing merchandising materials. This was my dream job as Coke Brazil was probably one of the ultimate advertisers in the country. Little did I know that that decision would change my life significantly.

At that time, Coke operated under a very interesting approach of regional and global networks of subject matter experts. That meant that I was directly connected to other Coke executives who also managed similar functional areas in Latin America and other Global networks. That was the first time I was exposed to other Latin American markets from a business standpoint, traveling to regional summits and listening to peers about their challenges and opportunities.

A few years later, I was invited to join Coke's Latin American Marketing team based in Atlanta, Georgia, and in 1999 I immigrated to the U.S. to be Coke's regional media services leader, working with the same colleagues I had already interacted with for a few years. The move from Brazil to the U.S. was supposed to be temporary, a three to five-year assignment with probably a return to Rio de Janeiro, where I would take a new position at Coke's Brazil division—at least that was the plan initially presented to me.

So, January 8, 1999, became the day I officially immigrated to the U.S. as a temporary resident (or alien resident to use the official lingo). That's the day I became a "Hispanic" in the eyes of other Americans. While my name or skin color could easily misrepresent me as a regular Anglo, White Caucasian of Jewish origin, my broken accent and my cultural differences quickly made me fully aware that I was not exactly "from here."

This experience of being an immigrant and starting a new life in a different country was also significant to my work as a multicultural marketing expert and gave me a degree of empathy that is important for this job.

To say that the Hispanic culture is fascinating is redundant. Working with countries so rich in their own culture, but at the same time with so many things in common at the macro level, was an experience of a lifetime. For someone like me, raised in the Brazilian culture, shaped by a Portuguese colonization process (that was so different from the vast majority of Latin American countries which were colonized by Spaniards), it was a kind of a wake-up call because many Brazilians from my generation tend to completely ignore their Latin American neighbors and the amazing things they can offer.

During my tenure at Coke, I was able to witness how challenging it is for global brands to balance the need to seek efficiencies with one single global positioning and communication strategy, with the requirements and expectations of local marketers, who, based on insights and knowledge from their local consumers, wanted to create opportunities for local ideas and local customizations that may cost more, but also could be more effective and yield higher returns on invested marketing dollars.

It was at Coke that I was introduced to the U.S. Hispanic segment for the first time by working as an internal media consultant for Fanta, a brand with strong sales in Latin America that saw the growing Hispanic segment as a sales opportunity.

After a few years at Coke, I became a permanent U.S. resident. I chose to become a permanent resident because Brazil's political and economic situation in the early 2000s made me consider adopting the U.S. as my permanent home. Shortly thereafter, I received an invitation to join a Telecom company in Atlanta called BellSouth, which owned a wireless division in Latin America, with operations in ten countries.

My stint at BellSouth was short because the Latin American operation was soon sold to Spain's Telefonica. So in 2004 I saw myself looking for a new job after only five years in the United States. But the wait was short, and I was blessed to have a few opportunities to choose from and decided to accept an offer from Nextel, a national wireless operator based in the Washington, D.C., metro area. Nextel was famous for its walkie-talkie-like feature (called "push to talk") which was very popular among business owners of many sizes and especially with Hispanics.

The reason for the popularity among Hispanics? Unlimited and free walkie-talkie communication between the U.S. and selected Latin American countries, including Mexico, which was obviously the most significant of them. So basically, Nextel users in the U.S. could speak as much as they wanted with family, friends, and business connections in Mexico as part of their regular wireless plan without having to pay the astronomic calling rates that were normally charged by existing international calling plans or having to purchase international calling cards which came with lower costs, but also lower call quality and a complex calling process, involving memorizing numbers and long pin codes.

Getting the job was surprisingly easy, despite my limited experience working with U.S. Hispanics. Of course, I brought a recent hands-on experience working with Latin American consumers in a wireless company. So after trying to update myself on what was key for the segment, I found myself working full-time exclusively on the U.S. multicultural segment. The job was mostly focused on the Hispanic segment, but I also managed an Asian American Pacific Islander (AAPI) program targeting Chinese-Americans, Korean-Americans and Filipino-Americans in key markets like Los Angeles, San Francisco, and New York. Initially, my work was on branding and marketing communications, but after a few months, I was asked to manage the whole business program, including their sales efforts.

Approximately a year after I arrived at Nextel, the company was acquired by Kansas-based Telecom giant Sprint and I was invited to stay with the newly merged company, now managing both brands, Sprint and Nextel, with a much larger scope and budget.

Building My First Multicultural Marketing Model

Working as a multicultural marketing leader at any organization is a constant battle for resources and attention. Most of my time at Sprint was split between frequent traveling to visit local markets, meeting sales teams, wireless dealers, local media, and, of course, the local consumers. The other big part of the job was spent on the process of internal selling: explaining what we were doing and, most importantly, why we were doing it.

Unfortunately, neither company had a solid track record of supporting the Hispanic segment, and many still viewed the Hispanic market opportunity as an "extension of cause marketing" or corporate marketing outreach. Moreover, the little activity that had been done "targeting" Hispanic consumers was based on translating messages from English to Spanish, following a decentralized approach, where each department head had the freedom to choose any approach they wanted towards the segment.

My first and most important challenge was to create awareness of the Hispanic segment as a business opportunity and to implement a new integrated model where departments would collaborate on one single plan that also leveraged the segment's uniqueness, idiosyncrasies, and opportunities. All of this needed to be accomplished while still working with the company's overall marketing objectives and strategies.

Did I have any benchmark or any guidance that helped me implement this complex plan? Not really. I was guided mainly by a tremendous amount of optimism and energy combined with intuition. I was blessed to have my previous manager, Nextel's chief marketing officer, Mark Schweitzer, appointed as the marketing leader of the newly combined company. During the initial stint at Nextel, he knew my work, and he was happy with the initial results. Besides, his style gave his team members autonomy and he always positioned himself as someone to help remove obstacles.

For the internal selling process, I did what every salesperson does. I had my sales pitch under my arm and I met almost every single manager of Sprint's marketing operations and other related areas. For these meetings, I came prepared with three principles that guided our approach.

First, a picture of the country's demographic trends at the national and local market levels.

Second, a set of business key performance indicators, broken down between the Hispanic and non-Hispanic consumers, like sales, churn rate, average revenue per user, market share, and much more.

Finally, during these meetings, I presented a simple model to explain to my colleagues what our approach towards the Hispanic segment was, represented by three fundamental dimensions we needed to incorporate in our approach in order to succeed.

First, that (Spanish) language was the foundation of our strategy. Therefore, Spanish needed to be reflected across all consumers' touchpoints (physical and virtual stores, customer service, billing) and not only advertising.

Second, that our approach towards the Hispanic segment understood, celebrated, and leveraged critical cultural aspects of the Hispanic consumer's lives. For instance, at that time Sprint's consumer marketing was anchored by a major sponsorship deal with NASCAR, and there was an expectation that the company's Hispanic program would completely "mirror" the promotional calendar the company was following.

Fortunately, we were able to convince management that NASCAR was not culturally relevant for our segment, and we looked for other culture-based platforms like soccer (fútbol) and music to more effectively reach Hispanics.

Finally, as a company, we looked at specific product usage behaviors from the Hispanic consumer and addressed them as we built our marketing plans.

Aligning on these three principles may seem trivial for some readers, but these principles were almost the opposite of how Sprint and many other brands saw marketing to Hispanics in the early 2000s. At that time, marketers mainly treated Hispanic marketing as an advertising-only activity, with messages in Spanish available in advertising creative, translated from the same advertising messages that had been specifically designed for your average White consumer.

Moreover, the marketing plans for Hispanics mainly reflected the same plan and calendar of the general market, i.e. White Americans. In summary, marketing to Hispanics in the early 2000s was relegated to translating ads from mainstream consumer marketing plans into Spanish.

During my tenure at Sprint, our Hispanic marketing program was considered an enormous success and an industry-wide benchmark. Despite having fewer resources than the competition and some chronic network quality and customer services issues, Sprint at one point achieved leadership in market share among Hispanics. Moreover, by the time I left, other operational key performance indicators were stronger among Hispanics consumers when compared to non-Hispanic ones.

In 2009, after five years at Sprint I moved to the advertising agency side of the business and joined alma advertising, one of the most successful and influential multicultural advertising agencies in the country.

Switching to the agency side allowed me to be exposed to many more organizations in different stages of their search for growth by leveraging the multicultural segments. In the past 14 years I have been able to work directly or indirectly with organizations like McDonald's, Procter & Gamble, PepsiCo, Google, Molson Coors, Wells Fargo, Lilly, CVS Health, Intuit, Amazon, PNC Bank, and Clorox, among many other companies from different sizes and industries. Partnering with them gave me a significant perspective and I am thankful for the opportunity to learn from amazing clients.

Since 2017, I have also written about our industry's development in a monthly column on multicultural marketing for Forbes.com, and I am an active member of the Hispanic Marketing and Advertising Association (called Hispanic Marketing Council), where I served on its board of directors. This is not only a great way to give back to my industry, it also helps me get perspectives from other agencies and media executives while keeping me closely connected to the latest trends in our industry.

This Book's Structure

This book is based on my articles published on Forbes.com since and in other outlets since 2014. Each article was reviewed, updated with the latest data, and edited to build a cohesive narrative for the reader to get a deeper understanding of how individual topics connect. In addition, I have added original content and some of the industry's most effective case studies.

Given its origins, the book was not written in a linear way, like a novel, and I envisioned it being read in different ways, either from beginning to end or even being consulted by relevance, depending on what aspect of the book the reader prefers. Either way, given its nature the reader may perceive some repetition in a few themes as they were written on different periods of time, but I used my judgment to keep them when I felt necessary to reinforce some of the book's messages.

In Part I of the book we will review the fundamentals of the U.S. Hispanic segment and show the incredible growth opportunities they represent for companies or brands as well as the evolution of the Hispanic consumer marketing segmentation. In Part II, we will debunk a few myths and barriers that get in the way of the proper implementation of these programs. In Part III we will cover how the minority-majority demographic shifts in America will potentially reshape some of the largest industries in the country. In Part IV, we will discuss how to move from theory into action, creating and implementing your own Hispanic marketing program, and finally, in Part V we will review a few additional considerations associated with effective Hispanic marketing programs.

Case Studies

An Example on How Culture Can Drive Business Results (Chapter 2)

An Example on How a Brand Can Implement an Integrated Marketing Program without Adopting a One-Size-Fits-All Approach (i.e. Total Market) (Chapter 4)

An Example on How Even Smaller Brands with Limited Budgets Can and Should Consider Multicultural Marketing as Part of Their Strategy (Chapter 5)

How a Brand Can Be Connected to Social Causes on a Relevant- and Diverse-Oriented Way (Chapter 6)

An Example on How Culture Can Drive Business Results (Chapter 8)

Financial Services Brands Leveraging Hispanic Cultural Insights to Drive Results (Chapter 10)

How Brands Can Provide Grassroots and Community Support with a Sense of Purpose (Chapter 13)

How a Brand Can Leverage a Sport Passion to Convey a Relevant Diversity Discussion (Chapter 18)

Most Pharma Companies Have Historically Ignored Diverse Segments in Their Marketing Programs. One Company Is Changing That (Chapter 20)

An Example on How Brands Can Grow Their Business Even after a Hiatus on Hispanic Marketing Investments (Chapter 40)

Notes

1 U.S. Census Bureau, 2010 Census, 2020 Census.
2 U.S. Census Bureau, 2010 Census, 2020 Census.
3 About One-in-Four U.S. Hispanics Have Heard of Latinx, but Just 3% Use It by Luis Noe Bustamante, Lauren Mora and Mark Hugo Lopez. August 11, 2020. © Pew Research Center.

Part I

Fundamentals of the
Hispanic Market

Chapter 1

Is Your Brand Ready for the 2030 Census?

Imagine you're a CMO from a giant U.S. Corporation, and you just received a message from your boss. She just got an email with two questions from a member of the board of directors of the company and wants you to help her craft a response. The two questions are: Have you seen the latest Census data? And most importantly, are we ready to compete in this new diverse marketplace?

Ideally, any CMO wouldn't have much problem answering these questions. However, the reality is that many CMOs in America today would not be able to articulate their strategies towards a more multicultural consumer.

Some CMOs may refer to their DE&I efforts; others might repeat the failed theory that "one strong message should unify all of us." However, none of this will be enough to keep your brand relevant for years and decades to come. Frankly, for some marketers, if you were not ready to compete when the 2020 Census results were released, your brand may become irrelevant by the time the 2030 Census comes around.

According to TelevisaUnivision, a leading Spanish-language media and communications conglomerate in the United States, there are approximately 1,500 brands that regularly advertise on English-language TV networks that completely ignore advertising in Spanish in order to connect with a significant share of the Hispanic population that consumes culturally-relevant content in Spanish.

In spite of all the hoopla around the gathering of the Census data during the COVID-19 pandemic, the Department of Commerce was able to release the results of the 2020 Census in August 2021. Here are a few key takeaways every business leader must know off the top of their head and ask their senior leadership teams to start assessing:

1 Non-Minority Population Growth Was Negative:

The 2020 Census results revealed that, for the first time, the non–Hispanic White population decreased by 5.1 million people or 2.6% between

DOI: 10.4324/9781003348931-2

2010 and 2020.[1] This trend is expected to continue for the next several decades as the majority of White Baby Boomer generation ages.

2 Multicultural Population Growth Is Exploding:

The country's population growth was 100% dependent on diverse/ethnic population segments. The Hispanic population in the U.S. accounted for the largest population gains of all diverse segments, reaching almost 19% of the country's total population, with 62 million people. Just two decades ago, The Black population was roughly the same size as the Hispanic population but now the Hispanic population in the U.S. is over 50% larger than the Black population, which according to the 2020 Census accounts for 40 million people and equals about 12% of the total U.S. population. Meanwhile, the AAPI (Asian American Pacific Islander) population continues its fast growth trajectory, accounting for 20 million people in 2020 which is about 6% of the total population.[2]

Together these three population segments are referred to as multicultural consumers as opposed to non-Hispanic White segment which is commonly referred to as the "general market" or "mainstream" consumers. But make no mistake, these multicultural consumers should not be seen or treated as one group but rather as distinct segments, each requiring specific marketing approaches.

3 Multicultural Consumers Are Everywhere:

While the diverse population growth was more concentrated in urban areas and in the western and Southern regions of the United States, most counties in the country experienced an increase in Hispanic population.[3]

This has not always been the case. Up until the 2000s the growth of the Hispanic population was seen mostly in the southern and western states and with large concentrations in northeast (New York, New Jersey) and in Illinois in the midwest. But the growth of Hispanics in "non-traditional" areas of the midwest has exploded ever since 2000. The 2020 Census shows us that this trend continues to be true. The Hispanic population grew 148% in North Dakota in the past decade, 68% in Louisiana, 62% in New Hampshire, and 56% in Kentucky![4]

While in the 1970s, 1980s, and 1990s marketers could replace a national Hispanic marketing strategy with a regional one, now marketers need to build on national Hispanic approaches supplemented by regional heavy-ups.

4 Minority-Majority Is Becoming a Reality:

Approximately 53% of Americans who are 18 years old or younger are of ethnic/diverse backgrounds.[5] Furthermore, six states (California, New Mexico, Nevada, Texas, Maryland, and Hawaii) and the District of Columbia already have a minority-majority status, meaning the majority of the total population in these markets are from diverse segments.

Ideally, no one should be surprised with any of this. All this data about the growth of diverse segments has been available for a very long time. What we are witnessing is a trend that has been building up for decades.

So, if you are a business leader and feel you're a bit out of touch with the minority-majority transformation of the country, here are a few actions you can implement in the next 30–60 days to start your journey towards a better understanding of your multicultural marketing opportunities.

Reach Out:

Start implementing a process to listen to your diverse employees, existing customers, and past customers, focusing on how their experience and perspectives are similar or different from your own, or from your average non-Hispanic White employee or consumer. Ask lots of questions; ask what they would do differently.

But don't stop there. Put together an advisory council with subject matter experts to help your organization on its journey towards more equitable and intentional multicultural investments.

Learn:

Develop a learning plan, starting with data, insights, and information gaps that your organization may have, and commit the necessary resources to a multi-year research plan to close this gap. Effective multicultural marketing is managed best based on high-quality data and consumer insights.

Integrate:

Set a modest and achievable multicultural marketing goal and then make your multicultural marketing goals a company-wide effort, integrating them into your overall growth plans, your DE&I plans, your R&D processes, your sales and distribution strategies, and your community outreach. Ideally, multicultural marketing should "reside" with your marketing team, but the whole corporation should own it.

Find a Champion:

Many multicultural marketing programs fail for lacking a champion that can protect it in its infancy and support it as it grows. A CMO can be a great champion; I had a few great CMOs helping me when I led multicultural marketing programs in the past.

But ideally, the search for a champion should go even higher in the organization; it should be at the CEO level. This executive should make it a clear goal for all to see and share the program's status in every company update meeting and every town hall. Ultimately, the organization will understand that if multicultural marketing is a priority for their bosses, it should be a priority for their employees as well.

It's time to move from a discussion about multicultural marketing towards action, and this action should be backed up with resources and consistency. The cost of doing nothing grows every single day, and it may reach a tipping point soon. If as a business leader you don't act decisively and adequately now, you may risk losing an important, and for many, the only source of significant growth you will have in the U.S. for years to come.

Notes

1 U.S. Census Bureau, 2010 Census, 2020 Census.
2 U.S. Census Bureau, 2010 Census, 2020 Census.
3 U.S. Census Bureau, 2010 Census, 2020 Census.
4 U.S. Census Bureau, 1990 Census, 2000 Census, 2010 Census, 2020 Census.
5 U.S. Census Bureau, 2010 Census, 2020 Census.

Chapter 2

When It Comes to Multicultural Marketing, Doing Nothing Has a Cost

As a marketer focused on multicultural marketing in America for the past two decades, I am still surprised when I see a brand that has the potential to capture substantial sales and profits by connecting with the Hispanic consumer but is doing very little or nothing at all to seize this opportunity.

A few months ago I spoke with a CMO at a large retail company, one that historically hasn't leveraged the Hispanic segment and asked him why his organization was not focusing on this consumer. His answer was very straightforward: "We are doing relatively well in our industry and to be honest, with all the budget cuts and pressure we have been facing, I don't have the resources to do it properly."

That's the typical answer most CMOs give when asked the same question. He continued with a compelling narrative, "If you add up the amount of media, production, research and ad agency fees associated with a Hispanic marketing program, a company my size would be investing at least $30 million a year."

Naturally, as an experienced CMO, he had the numbers at his fingertips, all itemized, detailed, and precise, and he was probably right! But then I asked him a question he wasn't expecting: "I see you have the cost of doing Hispanic marketing all figured out, but have you ever calculated the opportunity cost?"

He gave me a puzzled look, so I continued my rationale. "I looked at MRI-Simmons data on consumers who shopped at your stores in the past four weeks, and I noticed that at the national level you had approximately 20.6 million shoppers. That is impressive! More impressive is that it represents two successive years of shopper growth," I added. "Well, I told you we were doing well," he replied with a proud smile.

"Yes, you are indeed," I said, "but I also noticed that your share of shoppers coming from the Hispanic segment was meager, just 9%, while the national average for all retailers was at 16%. This is almost half of the national average," I said. "Moreover, I looked at your market share among Hispanic shoppers these past four weeks, and you were at a 5% level, way below some of your competitors who have a double-digit share." At that point, his smile was gone, and a curious look was the incentive I needed to keep on talking. "Imagine

DOI: 10.4324/9781003348931-3

you can close this gap among Hispanic shoppers and get to the national average your competitors already have. This could represent almost 1.3 million incremental shoppers in any given period. That's your opportunity cost, that's the cost of not actively executing a Hispanic marketing strategy."

When I was ready to continue, he interrupted me by saying "Seventy-five million dollars." And I said "What?" He then added, "1.3 million incremental shoppers would bring in approximately seventy-five million dollars of incremental revenue, without counting the repeat visits these incremental shoppers could have within a year. This amount could be doubled, or even tripled, in a given fiscal year."

Bingo! He was starting to realize what the cost of doing nothing really is. Simply put, $75 million was how much the company was leaving on the table by ignoring this important segment.

The Hispanic population in the U.S. grew by 23% in the past decade alone while the non–Hispanic White population actually declined 2.6%[1] during the same period. However, don't jump to the conclusion that you can simply add a media buy and translate your message to Spanish and voila you have a strategy! More and more studies have demonstrated that reaching Hispanics with an Anglo-driven message is not an effective way to drive strong ROI. You can reach Hispanics with your existing Anglo-centric plans, but you may not be connecting with them without a strong culture-driven approach led by experts in this segment.

And while there are companies that are paying the "cost of doing nothing" every year, there are also many companies that have historically invested in this consumer segment, but may not be fully capturing their fair share of the Hispanic consumer.

For example, I looked at another national retail brand, one with a consistent track record of Hispanic marketing investments, and I noticed that while their gap to fair share was smaller than the previous example, they were still below the 16% benchmark. For them, the monetary benefit of closing the gap to fair share was estimated at 3.7 million incremental Hispanic shoppers, which could bring more than $200 million of incremental sales per year in the most pessimistic assumption.

So, investing in multicultural marketing shouldn't be looked at as pure cost since, when properly executed, its benefits may far outweigh the investments. Moreover, it's important to start comparing the returns of implementing a multicultural marketing program with the correct benchmarks: comparing the cost of doing nothing or, worse yet, watching your competitor reap the sales that otherwise should be yours. When it comes to multicultural marketing, a company's victory is another company's loss. Since this is truly a zero-sum game, the inertia to act may give your competitor not only a short-term sales edge but also a chance to create loyalty with this growing customer base that will certainly cost you more to win back in the future.

It's time to start calculating the cost of sitting out and watching how other companies are capturing a disproportionate share of the Hispanic consumer, one of the only sources of growth in our current marketplace. Doing nothing is not an option.

Why Should You Focus on Hispanics?

There are three simple reasons why you should consider the Hispanic consumer as a key focus area in your multicultural marketing efforts:

- The demographic trajectory of our country won't change in the years to come.
- In this cluttered environment, brands need to find a relevant voice to stand out and grow their business more than ever.
- There is more research and ROI analysis affirming the effectiveness of Hispanic marketing than ever before.

Let's just look at the basics:

The Hispanic population in the U.S. today is over 62 Million strong, representing almost 20% of the country's entire population. Furthermore, the latest Census projection shows this population will continue to increase at a faster rate than the non-Hispanic White segment, making the absolute and relative number of Hispanics even larger in the years to come. Besides, there are additional reasons to be focused on this segment. For the past decade, Hispanics have been graduating from high school at higher rates than in the past two decades and have been enrolling in college at record levels[2]— progress that is reflected in the average Hispanic household income, which has increased to $55,658 in 2019, growing faster than the general population's growth rate (39% vs. 31%).

According to the Latino GDP Report 2021, a study published by the Latino Donor Collaborative in collaboration with the Center for Economic Research & Forecasting (CERF) and the Center for the Study of Latino Health & Culture (CESLAC)[3]:

- Total economic contribution of Hispanics in the U.S. was $2.7 Trillion in 2019, up from $2.1 Trillion in 2015 and $1.7 Trillion in 2010.
- Since 2010, real Hispanic GDP has grown 57 percent faster than real U.S. GDP and 70 percent faster than non-Hispanic GDP.
- From 2010 to 2019, Hispanic real consumption grew 123 percent faster than non-Hispanic's, driven by large gains in personal income, which flow from rapid gains in educational attainment and strong labor force participation.
- The median age of the U.S. Hispanic population is 28, which is 10 years younger than the U.S. population which has a median age of 38.2 years old.

- This means that the effective buying power of Hispanics is also higher, a whopping 20 years more! Hispanics have 56 years of effective buying power versus only 36 for the non-Hispanic White segment.
- In terms of workforce participation, Hispanics have the highest workforce participation rate at 66.4% according to the March 2022 report from the U.S. Bureau of Labor Statistics[4] and will account for 82% of net new growth across the entire U.S. workforce.
- And finally, Hispanics are America's fountain of youth. One million Hispanics turn 18 every year (and will continue to do so for every year over the next two decades) and Hispanics represent 26% of millennial Americans and 28% of Alpha Gen Americans.[5]

The bottom line is that Hispanics are growing in number and influence and spending power more than ever before, representing a large share of corporations' current and future growth.

Moreover, Hispanics tend to stay connected to their culture. According to data from MRI-Simmons[6] seen in the following table, connection to Hispanic culture remains strong regardless of generation (with around 75–80% of all segments agreeing to the statement "MY CULTURAL/ETHNIC HERITAGE IS AN IMPORTANT PART OF WHO I AM").

Hispanics are connected to their Hispanic culture, and almost 75% of third generation have a strong connection to their heritage, in spite of the loss of language fluency. These results demonstrate that the relevancy of the Hispanic culture is strong and will remain even stronger for decades to come, despite perceived acculturation by some marketers.

	1st Generation Foreign Born	2nd Generation U.S. Born	3rd Generation Parents U.S. Born	All U.S. Hispanics
My cultural/ethnic heritage is an important part of who I am—Agree Completely	39%	36%	30%	36%
My cultural/ethnic heritage is an important part of who I am—Agree Somewhat	40%	44%	45%	43%
Total	**79%**	**80%**	**75%**	**79%**

Source: 2021 Fall MRI-Simmons

	1st Generation Foreign Born	2nd Generation U.S. Born	3rd Generation Parents U.S. Born	All U.S. Hispanics
Language respondent personally speaks at home (only Spanish/ mostly Spanish)	79%	38%	10%	51%
Language respondent personally speaks at home (any Spanish)	96%	90%	51%	83%

Source: 2021 Fall MRI-Simmons

Let's briefly go back to *Merriam Webster* to define the word "acculturation," which is often misused and misunderstood.

Definition of *acculturation*

1   cultural modification of an individual, group, or people by adapting to or borrowing traits from another culture

ex: the *acculturation* of immigrants to American life

also: a merging of cultures as a result of prolonged contact

2   the process by which a human being acquires the culture of a particular society from infancy

All immigrants to the U.S. go through this process of acculturation, not just Hispanics. However, acculturation is a very personal journey and one's rate of acculturation is determined by many factors, including geography, age, level of education, and socio-economic status, not to mention how technology and media fragmentation has increased one's ability to stay connected to one's culture regardless of the distance to our homeland.

After years of trying the same formula based on reaching Hispanics via English media (instead of truly connecting with Hispanics) with one-size-fits-all strategies and creative development managed by general market agencies (that may have hired a few token "Hispanics" for their teams) maybe the time has come for brands to recognize the failure of a model that denies CMOs of their most important role: to help their brands grow again.

It's time to bring Hispanic marketing plans back to the 21st century. It's time to celebrate the Hispanic segment opportunity. It's time to use the power of marketing and advertising to grow businesses again. In today's environment that should be music to any CEO's ears!

Case Study—An Example on How Culture Can Drive Business Results

Sprint—"Greatest Hits"

Executive Summary

Hispanic consumers engage with the wireless category differently—they count on their wireless phones more than non-Hispanics do. Their smartphone is more likely their only access point to the internet.

Hispanics see their phone as a vital connection to their social world. In short, they *love* their phone and what it provides. And this love further extends to shopping, the category which is distinct from rational and price-driven general market consumers.

The Business Challenge

In 2018 Sprint was focused on using robots in their advertising to convey the simple logic of switching to Sprint and saving. But while the robots were performing well for the general market, Sprint needed to find a better way to motivate Hispanics to switch to Sprint. Hispanic wireless consumers are younger than non-Hispanic consumers and have a stronger attachment to technology. They cannot live without the internet or imagine life without new electronic gadgets, but more importantly, their hunger for new technology translates to hunger for new wireless services, benefits, and devices.

The Insight and Strategy

Sprint's research made it clear that the biggest barrier to winning new Hispanic customers was the skepticism that switching would result in better service and cost savings. They simply were not convinced by the current, rational reasons that Sprint (and their robots) were giving them. They were not willing to risk losing their current service in order to try Sprint, even if they weren't completely in love with their current wireless service provider.

But they had the perfect way to rekindle that love for their wireless phone and service. Sprint not only promoted their unlimited service, newest devices, and lowest prices but they also brought in the one thing that every new relationship needs—a money-back guarantee! The reassurance many would need to be confident they would be gaining more than what they were leaving behind with their current carrier.

And to ensure we were connecting directly and successfully with Hispanics, Sprint stepped away from logic and connected with Hispanic consumers in a heart-to-heart way, by exploring a more emotional way, playing to the love they feel for wireless in a fun and engaging way, supported by our highly competitive and reassuring offer.

Idea/Execution

Adding Emotion into Sales Promotion

Their approach was to utilize elements of storytelling and humor to build emotional appeal and engagement. Sprint knew that they could build trust and entice Hispanic consumers to make the switch by going beyond just telling them why Sprint is the risk-free choice.

The fully integrated campaign spanned four original TV spots with digital, social and retail extensions, all filled with humor, using characters such as friendly singing ghosts, a lounge singer, a merman, and a flying cupid who would sing Sprint love songs to consumers.

1 Remixed Love Songs

Sprint hijacked a few famous Spanish love songs and rewrote the lyrics to tell people about the benefits of Sprint's network. For example, they took the song "Vuelve," by Ricky Martin, which means "come back," and modified the lyrics to tell people exactly why they should come (back) to Sprint. Building on these popular Spanish ballads with a unique twist that's unmistakably Sprint was a distinctive and engaging TV approach in a category that is otherwise bland and somewhat confusing.

2 Love Therapy

The "fall in love" concept was extended through segments on the daytime TV show, *Un Nuevo Dia*, which initially focused on help with relationships, and then naturally pivoted to Sprint with the show's host giving advice on falling in love again.

3 The Love of Fútbol

To really spread the "love," Sprint extended the elements of the campaign to their sponsorship of the Concacaf's Copa Oro soccer tournament. A gold, heart-shaped soccer ball trophy anchored the campaign throughout digital and retail, to make the love of fútbol an intimate part of falling in love with Sprint.

4 Heart Emojis

Entertaining GIFs on social media focused on our fun characters and also leveraged the same Copa Oro soccer themes to maximize the relevance of their messages to both soccer fans and non-fans alike, because everyone deserves a chance to fall in love (again).

All of these efforts were aimed at creating more awareness and consideration of Sprint among potential Hispanic switchers. And to entice them to take action and make the switch, Sprint leveraged their whimsical and lovable characters to promote the most popular phones everyone wants to upgrade to—the phone they want on a network they will love. What's not to love about that?

Results

Overall, "Fall in Love with Sprint" spots stood out from the category. "Fantasmas" was the top performer in the category with a score of 8.6 (on a 1–10 likeability scale) along with "Roadside Bar" (8.3). These were excellent scores considering that the industry average was at 5.0 and the highest the "Robots" campaign scored was 7.4 (source: iSpot TV).

This campaign successfully connected emotionally with Hispanics and rekindled their love of wireless, resulting in a marked increase in positive brand sentiment and a 22% lift in weekly sales.

Author's Commentary

This Sprint case study demonstrates how culture can be leveraged by a brand to create an authentic connection between the consumer and the brand based on a demonstration of culture fluency: that the brand understands their consumer target and acknowledges the importance of the Hispanic culture in their lives.

This connection helps break the clutter, increases the probability of advertising awareness and consideration, potentially improves the perceptions the consumer has of the brand, and ultimately increases the probability of sales. All of this is achieved by overcoming budget limitation versus competitors with deeper pockets, meaning that creative effectiveness helps overcome smaller budgets.

Notes

1 U.S. Census Bureau, 2010 Census, 2020 Census.
2 2010 American Community Survey, 2019 American Community Survey.
3 2021 LDC U.S. Latino GDP Report, www.LatinoDonorCollaborative.org.
4 U.S. Bureau of Labor Statistics, Labor Force Participation Rate—Hispanic or Latino [LNS11300009], retrieved from FRED, Federal Reserve Bank of St. Louis; https://fred.stlouisfed.org/series/LNS11300009, April 12, 2022.
5 Latinos in America, An Inside Look Into America's future. ©Latino Donor Collaborative 2020
6 2021 Fall MRI-Simmons.

Chapter 3

The End of Total Market— It's Time to Try a New Approach

In the aftermath of George Floyd's death, many of us are still trying to understand how to honor this critical moment in our country and evolve. The consequences are many and will continue to impact us as individuals, and as business leaders.

There's little doubt in my mind that progress will mean a combination of actions and behaviors alike, including better education and understanding of the realities faced by minority groups in the ad industry, better hiring practices, and more representation at all agency levels.

One additional aspect that has started to get more attention is the importance of consistency and commitment to targeting multicultural consumers as part of a brand's marketing plans. This is an important debate, since over the past decade, the advertising community, driven mostly by short-term efficiencies, has adopted what they call the "Total Market" approach.

According to Total Market advocates, cultural and ethnic background nuances are not necessarily proper segmentation parameters. Instead, everyone should be targeted based on their shopping behaviors, and a single message and media plan should be sufficient to reach everyone. When they present their arguments against Total Market, multicultural marketing experts are accused of either "trying to divide people, instead of uniting them" or trying to "complicate things, with more meetings, more agencies, more work," or ultimately, "create a parallel, separate marketing plan for our brands."

Advocates of "Total Market" say that this approach is a natural evolution of the demographic changes in America, where brands no longer should focus on Hispanics as a "unique target" but rather integrate them into one single, comprehensive (hence "Total") platform.

While at first glance the foregoing description may seem very reasonable, a deeper analysis easily shows some of the pitfalls of the Total Market approach that I consider crucial:

> First: The idea that one insight can be strong enough to apply to all ethnic segments.

DOI: 10.4324/9781003348931-4

In my experience, there are few unique and universal insights that can create differentiated and relevant communication ideas across different segments. Chances are the broader your insight, the more generic, less differentiated your message will be perceived by the diverse segments, undermining the probability of creating relevancy above the norm. It is what we call the "We All Love our Moms"-type of insight.

A Total Market approach attempts to create work that's inclusive of all segments, but ironically it can only work by excluding ideas that appeal to the segments individually.

Market segmentation was created to achieve higher effectiveness by addressing different target audiences' knowing and respecting their own sets of expectations, idiosyncrasies, wants, and values. The more specific you are about the target's insights, the more authentic your message will be and that will increase the probability that your message will be more relevant and more effective.

Second: Forgetting that in advertising, the *delivery* can be as important as the insight.

One of the reasons Hispanic advertising tends to resonate more with its target audience goes beyond insights and is also related to execution. According to an important study conducted by Nielsen,[1] the usage of the Spanish language is important, but nuances like context, style, and humor are crucial to be able to really resonate with Hispanic consumers. That means that even a strong, insight-based creative idea can flop with Hispanics if the execution doesn't provide cultural cues that can increase empathy and affinity.

Many in the multicultural marketing industry believe that the "Total Market" approach is being used as an excuse to cut budgets on behalf of short-term potential synergies and efficiencies. I believe that while we all should be responsible for looking for efficiency in our day to day, we can't ignore the fact that brands are built and growth is only achieved through higher effectiveness. What advertisers save by reducing Hispanic fees and production budgets is a relatively small savings when compared to what can be gained by crafting a truly relevant strategy to address Hispanic consumers. The question you should ask yourself is: how much money are we leaving on the table?

This Nielsen study demonstrates that Hispanic consumers show stronger response (Recall, Likeability, Consideration, and Purchase Intent) when exposed to a creative message developed with Hispanic relevancy (both in Spanish and in English) than to a general market message based on universal insights.

The reality is that during the past decade many companies have tried the "Total Market" approach but what has happened with "Total Market" approaches is the potential creation of a more sophisticated form of stereotype-based messages, where casting and the usage of generic insights (plus maybe someone saying "Hola" or another word in Spanish in an English ad) may provide a false sense of comfort to marketers, who thought they were truly crafting a modern 21st-century messaging while they inadvertently were just moving "forward to the past."

The irony is that most of the companies that prioritize short-term savings versus marketing effectiveness tend to think of themselves as consumer-centric organizations. Ultimately, brands that adopted the "Total Market" approach started to be negatively impacted. Moreover, they concluded that any savings or efficiencies achieved were short-lived and not replicable in the following years. In fact, they experienced declines in brand attributes, sales, market share, and margin among the fastest-growing segments in America: multicultural consumers.

The time has come for our industry to abandon the "Total Market" trap, reject the one-size-fits-all approach, embrace America's multicultural consumers as segments to be acknowledged, and respect these consumers' unique culture and characteristics. A more modern and contemporary approach towards our minority-majority marketplace is needed—a new approach that values multicultural marketing professionals and multicultural media as partners on this journey.

Furthermore, we need to recognize that expertise matters and that differentiation and authentic connections come from embracing our differences. Besides, there's a need to reinvent the models, processes, and paradigms created decades ago when multicultural marketing was mostly an afterthought and treated as an appendix or supplement of a mostly non-Hispanic White-focused marketing plan.

I spoke with Carlos Santiago, president of Santiago Solutions Group and co-founder of the Association of National Advertisers' AIMM, Alliance for Inclusion and Multicultural Marketing, who conducted a comprehensive study on this subject, and here's what he had to say,

> Total Market is another legacy monument that runs a blind eye at the value of cultural richness. As validated by AIMM's Cultural Insights Impact Measurement™ in 2019, Total Market efforts rarely appealed with strong cultural relevance to all the segments under "total," and it didn't serve advertisers to boost purchase intent. In fact, in nine out of ten ads Total Market under delivered authentically to each segment.

This new approach will create opportunities to converge messages towards a broader target at times and diverge towards more segmented targets at others. It will consider multicultural opportunities beyond Black History Month, Hispanic Heritage Month, and Pride Month. Besides, it is very important to emphasize that this new approach will not make minority segments compete against each other for a limited size of the investment pie.

Instead, they will consider redistributing the whole pie according to the growth opportunity each segment represents to a brand and our country's changing population composition.

Let's all embrace these changing times with humility. We don't have all the answers, and we need an open mind to break with the dominant practice of lumping all consumers together when crafting messaging strategies. Breaking with the status quo will require significant collaboration, optimism, and courage. But as DDB's founder and ad industry icon Bill Bernbach once said, "The people who are going to be in business tomorrow are the people who understand that the future, as always, belongs to the brave."

Note

1 "The Secrets to Higher ROI in Spanish Language TV," Nielsen 2017.

Chapter 4

Why Are Some Marketers Still Lost in Translation?

One of the aspects of my career I like the most is the opportunity to mentor young professionals, and a few months ago, I received a request from someone asking for my advice. She had been asked to help her employer, an ad agency, translate a creative idea created for the "general market" (which means Anglo White Caucasian consumers) from English into Spanish to target Hispanic consumers with it.

The task itself was not a problem. While she is not a translator and her current job description doesn't include translating materials to Spanish, the work was relatively simple for someone who is a native Spanish speaker, as she is. What concerned her was the fact that the idea itself was not something that would be relevant to Hispanic consumers, and no matter how well she could do the translation task, the ad would still be ineffective, and she might be blamed for it.

Based on my experience, I can share that this scenario happens almost every day across agencies. What is behind it? Sometimes, the excuse is that there are not enough funds to hire experts (agencies) to do the "right" job; you know, "budgets are very tight." In other instances, it's the fact that old misconceptions are still prevalent, such as the one that confuses Hispanic marketing with marketing in Spanish.

Either scenario can be reinforced by a General Market agency desperate to increase or retain revenue, telling their clients that their ideas work for all consumers, and a translated version of their ads could be generated for free, thanks to a great Spanish-speaking creative team they just hired.

Unfortunately for clients, translation strategies based on efficiencies and cutting corners may ultimately sacrifice effectiveness. While on paper they may seem to deliver savings, the cost is greater, as this strategy tends to use the bulk of the budget on media plans that will be airing subpar and less relevant ideas that may even damage the brand's reputation. Most clients that use translation as a strategy may end up achieving little, or even negative ROI on their investments.

Here are a few reasons why translation is not a viable strategy when approaching diverse segments:

DOI: 10.4324/9781003348931-5

1 Translation Doesn't Reflect a Different Culture

Most translated executions reflect the environment and culture of the target for which they were created. Most ads in America are created by and for White Caucasians, and they tend to reflect a world seen from a White Caucasian perspective.

That doesn't mean that this world is better or worse than a different reality lived by a diverse consumer; it's just a different reality and could be reflected in a choice of casting, dialogues, music, and even the story narrative. This gap between experiences and marketing messaging may create a perception that the brand in question "doesn't get" the consumers they are trying to reach.

Also, it is important to mention that the opposite is hard to achieve, as sometimes clients ask their agencies to create "the most inclusive and representative creative idea ever," running the risk of making an ad that doesn't resonate with anyone, as it looks artificial and unauthentic.

2 Diverse Segments May Offer a Different Business Opportunity

When brands automatically assume that their existing creative campaigns may be effective with diverse segments by just translating them, they may be making the dangerous assumption that diverse consumers perceive and use their products and services the same way White Caucasian consumers do.

For instance, many brands may have a marketing objective of increasing the frequency of consumption, while household penetration among diverse consumers may still be below the national benchmark. Hence, a translated ad focused on increasing frequency towards diverse segments may not work well, not because the ad is not good but because it was created for the wrong business opportunity.

3 Translation May Not Capture Humor Correctly

One of the most underestimated aspects of communications to diverse segments is how relevant humor can be to create authentic narratives and increase the probability of higher effectiveness. Humor is compelling as a catalyst of cultural subtleties and offers a range of possibilities that varies from a more traditional to a more contemporary and fresh approach.

4 Translation Ignores the Contextual/ Situational Aspect of a Creative Idea

Also underestimated when crafting a creative message to diverse segments is how effective the nuances of a creative idea can be in creating a stronger connection between message and consumer/prospect.

A simple example could be a creative idea that requires a small family gathering at home. If you want to feel more authentic in the eyes of a Hispanic consumer, this family gathering wouldn't be that small and would probably showcase at least ten different people, including multiple generations of a household and some extended family members (and some other non-blood-related friends we are used to calling "tío" and "tía").

5 Translation Is about Efficiencies, Not Effectiveness

For all the foregoing reasons and many more, it's been documented by different market studies like Nielsen[1] that translating an ad from the general market to diverse segments may be three to four times less effective than crafting original ideas.

While budget restrictions may make a translation approach viable or acceptable, they may only make it harder for brands to capture the full potential of marketing to diverse segments since the limited budget would have a low probability of a positive ROI. Worse, this failed experience may fuel the negative perception that marketing to diverse segments doesn't work.

For years, marketers were concerned about being "lost in translation" and failing on a campaign because they used the wrong words in their translation. But it's 2023, and gone are the days when campaigns could be translated to Spanish as an effective way to connect the Hispanic segment. Nowadays, a marketer is lost by just considering translation as a strategy.

Case Study—An Example on How a Brand Can Implement an Integrated Marketing Program without Adopting a "One-Size-Fits-All" Approach (i.e. Total Market)

McDonald's—"Dorado"

Executive Summary

In 2020 McDonald's launched a successful marketing program called "famous orders," where celebrities present their favorite McDonald's meals. When McDonald's decided to follow up with a Hispanic version of it, instead of adopting a copy-and-paste approach, they decided to make it more relevant, more specific to Hispanic consumers. This is an example of a client who fully understands that the one-size-fits-all approach towards marketing is over.

The Business Challenge

The fast-food category has been growing over the past five years, with much of this growth coming from Hispanic consumers. The majority visit a fast-food restaurant at least once a month and these numbers are only growing. Notably, by 2060, 32% of those under 18 will be Hispanic.[2]

However, McDonald's was no longer capturing their fair share of business, specifically from young Hispanics, due to decreasing brand relevance.

The writing was on the wall. McDonald's had to take action to again become a brand young Hispanics want to be seen with. The challenge was to develop a cultural moment big enough to get young Hispanics talking about McDonald's in a new light, setting the stage for more innovative brand connections, ultimately driving them to the restaurant.

The Insights/Strategy

One way that they did this was through music from their culture—Latin music. According to Pandora, in 2020, Hispanics were turning to Latin music more than ever, for relief and as a way of staying connected. Music was the perfect vehicle to share a meaningful message.

But, it was in the unique Hispanic brand of optimism, unwavering in the face of adversity and strengthened by cultural roots, that we found direction. The pride that Hispanic youth have in this optimism shines through even in the hardest of times. This truth spoke to us and grounded our thinking:

There is no stronger source of pride to Hispanics than the optimism of their culture.

Idea/Execution

A musical love letter from McDonald's to Hispanic youth.

The idea was inspired by the generations of Hispanics who have brought the optimism of their culture through the doors of McDonald's restaurants across the country. From the young athlete passing through, alongside the older gentleman sipping his McCafé, to countless crew members, every Hispanic has been a part of McDonald's history and still is today.

The company partnered with a global Hispanic artist who embodies optimism, J. Balvin, to create a music video experience that would speak directly to young Hispanics. The brief was simple: write a letter to young Hispanics via an original music video, recognizing how their optimism and culture have impacted the McDonald's experience and culture at large.

The lyrics of *Dorado* were crafted by J. Balvin to deeply connect with the cultural pride of young Hispanics. The song echoes "donde hay Latino, hay fiesta" (where there is a Latino, there is a party), celebrating the positivity that follows every Hispanic. The prideful words continue with "gracias mamá por hacerme Latino" (thank you mom for making me Latino). In essence, it is a love letter from McDonald's to young Hispanics.

The brand leveraged J. Balvin's multi-platinum album, *Colores*, as the context in which to launch the music video. The album, which was made up of songs, each titled with a color of the rainbow, did not include the color most associated with optimism and with the McDonald's brand: "Gold." It was meant to be.

And we had a name for the music video; *Dorado* (Golden) was born.

The campaign started the journey of *Dorado* by teasing fans on Twitter of a possible music collaboration happening between J. Balvin and McDonald's. While the world was trying to figure out what was coming, they made sure his biggest fans had the inside scoop. When it was finally time for the world premiere, they did it during the Latin Grammys, a night when all eyes were on J. Balvin, and they turned everyone's attention to the McDonald's app, the only place to see the video.

Linear TV and pre-show support from Univision amplified the idea, while news outlets across the country picked up the story. After the initial launch of the video on the app, the company posted the video on both McDonald's and J. Balvin's YouTube channels to expand their reach. The content continued with J. Balvin dropping a video about the meaning behind the lyrics, amplifying the conversation and generating interest.

On the night of the Latin Grammys, the music video was only available to the public via the McDonald's app. This strategic choice was made to (1) provide a sense of exclusivity to the audience and (2) encourage app downloads that serve as a long-term reminder of the brand on their device. The company measured app downloads among Hispanics compared to the same time last year.

The day after the Latin Grammys, the video was released on both J. Balvin's and McDonald's YouTube channels, without paid support, to increase reach among the target audience. The *Dorado* video earned more organic views than years prior versus other McDonald's content.

Results

During launch, 70% of those who engaged with *Dorado* content on the McDonald's app placed an order. The video then earned 35 times more views and 137 times more engagements than the average on the McDonald's YouTube channel in 2020. Social engagement surpassed all benchmarks.

Author's Comments

This case study received an Effie Award for effectiveness in 2021 and it's undeniably a very comprehensive and strong case study. While it also reinforces the importance of culture as seen in the previous Sprint case, there's one aspect of this case I'd like to highlight.

This Hispanic-centric campaign was more than a continuation, or an adaptation, of an innovative idea McDonald's launched a few months earlier. The idea was to allow consumers to buy the same meal combo of their favorite artists.

The Hispanic execution could have taken a "Total Market" approach, by either using creative translation into Spanish or by adopting a creative strategy that just featured J. Balvin's favorite meal. Either execution would have cost the client less and could have achieved some positive results.

However, McDonald's, one of the most relevant advertisers in the multicultural space, understood that the potential was much bigger. They leveraged this campaign to create unique content that resonated with their Hispanic consumer (creating a song that paid homage to the target's culture) hence making a promotional idea also a true branding idea.

Furthermore, McDonald's also smartly connected the exclusive content created with their 1:1 program, offering the newly created song "Dorado" first to customers who downloaded the brand's mobile app.

So suddenly, an idea that could be easily adapted using a smaller budget became a fully integrated branding, promotional, and 1:1 idea, delivering significant results for the business.

This is an example of a brand that understands that the concept of "Total Market" no longer serves the business needs of a more diverse and fragmented population.

Notes

1 "The Secrets to Higher ROI in Spanish Language TV," Nielsen 2017.
2 U.S. Census Bureau, Population Division (revised release date: September 2018).

Chapter 5

Every Brand Is Already Involved in Hispanic Marketing

In today's U.S. market landscape there are two types of companies: those who actively try to connect with multicultural consumers, and those that leave it up to chance whether they appropriately connect. The latter group's inaction is mostly driven by their perceived lack of resources or a belief in a one-size-fits-all strategy, also known as "Total Market." However, one can argue that it may be more accurate to say that the divide lies between companies that recognize the country's demographic reality and leverage multicultural consumers' contribution as a driver of growth to benefit their bottom line, and those who risk sales, growth, and profits due to inaction.

Think this is an exaggeration? Not really, if you consider that close to 10% of all national sales for several categories were made by the Hispanics living in three states alone[1]: Florida, Texas, and California. The sheer size of these three states' population is worth noting, and they are getting larger and larger every year.

These states have reached a point where the Hispanic population is no longer a niche; instead, they represent a significant portion of their population. In other words, even when you don't target Hispanic consumers as a segment, your sales are probably impacted by decisions made by Hispanic consumers.

To better illustrate this point, I pulled MRI-Simmons 2021 data for three different categories: consumers who purchased a new TV set in the past 12 months, consumers who purchased a pair of jeans in the past 12 months, and overall individual yogurt consumption.

As you might expect, the results showed a strong correlation between population size and consumption rates. Florida, Texas, and California together represented 27% of all TV sets purchased in the past 12 months in the entire country, 27% of all pairs of jeans bought in the past 12 months, and 26% of the yogurt consumption.

Furthermore, the analysis demonstrated the importance of the Hispanic segment in these particular states. For TV sets, Hispanic consumers were responsible for 40% of all sales; for yogurt consumption, the number was at 37%; and for jeans, the Hispanic share of sales was at 40%. So, as I said at the beginning, around 10% of these categories' national sales come from Hispanics who live in Florida, Texas, and California.

DOI: 10.4324/9781003348931-6

Another impact derived from a strong presence of multicultural consumers in any given market is that they do not live in a vacuum. In fact, they also tend to influence the non-ethnic population just as much as they are influenced by mass culture themselves. This is what I like to call "mutual influence."

One category where we see this "mutual influence" clearly is in America's evolving beer consumption patterns. Did you know that 18% of non-Hispanic consumers who live in Florida, Texas, and California are regular buyers of imported beers? Imported beer is a category that over-indexes with Hispanic consumers, with an outsize number of Latin American brands available for consumption. Outside of these three states, this percentage drops to 16%. This difference may seem small, but these 2 percentage points represent tens of millions of dollars.

The idea of "mutual influence" goes beyond just consumption behaviors, it also shapes non-ethnic Americans' attitudes in a broader sense. For instance, one of the statements from the aforementioned MRI study is "I like to learn about foreign cultures." Nearly 77% of non-Hispanic respondents in these three states agree with the statement, while 71% of non-Hispanics in the remainder of the country say they also agree.

I believe that a new wave of business opportunities will be created in the next few years for multicultural marketing experts. We will move beyond regional market strategies, to leading our industry in assessing the process of the "mutual influence" of cultures, by helping corporate America understand the consequences and opportunities associated with it.

There's an expression that says that "everything communicates." This means that everything you say, but also everything you don't say, conveys a message. Similarly, in business, everything you do and, more and more, everything you don't do impact your business. Don't you think it is time to act and do Hispanic marketing for real?

Case Study—An Example on How Even Smaller Brands with Limited Budgets Can and Should Consider Multicultural Marketing as Part of Their Strategy

Desert Botanical Garden—"Las Noches de Las Luminarias"

Executive Summary

Located in Phoenix, Arizona, Desert Botanical Garden (DBG) is a compelling attraction and desert conservation pioneer, offering worldly plants, world-class exhibitions, festive events, and much more. The Garden attracts visitors from all over the world and they are constantly developing experiences that are relevant to their guests.

The Garden has had a long-standing commitment and partnership with the Hispanic community in the valley through the presentation of experiences like the Dia de Los Muertos, Ofrenda, Margarita Cabrera exhibit, and many more.

The Garden understands that authentically engaging new audiences is crucial to sustaining the Garden and that building cultural capacity through diversity, equity, and inclusion initiatives is the key to success. The Garden is a good institutional citizen with a spirit of volunteerism and recognizes the importance of community collaborations. The Garden is focused on the pillars of its mission that connect to new audiences through fun, play, and social celebrations. One example of this commitment was the 2019 creation of the La Posada.

For nearly 45 years, Desert Botanical Garden has held a holiday tradition called Las Noches de las Luminarias, attracting thousands of people each night. During this event the Garden is illuminated with more than 8,000 luminaria bags along its trails accompanied by various musical experiences. In 2019, the Garden expanded on this program during the Christmas holidays, by incorporating a traditional Mexican "Posada," a reenactment of the pilgrimage to Bethlehem by Mary and Joseph, a strong tradition among Hispanics.

The Business Challenge

How could a botanical garden attract more Hispanic visitors during the Holidays?

The Insights/Strategy

To create an authentic experience based on traditions, celebrating Hispanic roots and heritage.

Idea/Execution

The creation of La Posada at Desert Botanical Garden is a true example of community effort. On the one hand, the Garden, supported by its team and agency partners, had the cultural expertise, partnership recommendations, and entertainment options for La Posada. On the other hand, the Garden had a Latino committee and partnered with the Mexican consulate to gather additional insights about this beloved tradition.

During the event, Garden guests were welcomed with small poinsettias for children and candles for adults. The mariachi started singing *villancicos* (Spanish Christmas carols) and led the way to three stations that included Alan Ponce from The Voice as well as members of the Mexican Consulate and the Arizona Hispanic Chamber of Commerce. Additional event elements included piñatas, a burrito sabanero, Noche Buena flowers, and tamales. This event brought back childhood memories for many and allowed younger Hispanic generations to be part of their parents' traditions.

The event was promoted through social media, public relations efforts, a media campaign, strategic partnerships, and word of mouth. The Garden does not receive a large number of Hispanics during weekdays on Las Noches de las Luminarias. However, creating an event that spoke directly to Hispanics' hearts made this event sell out in its first year of promotion.

Results

Since 2019, the Garden has increased Hispanic visitors to the Garden by 4% and is continuing to look for ways to connect with the community.

Author's Comments

One of the biggest misconceptions of our industry is that only brands with large marketing budgets can benefit from effective multicultural programs. In this case we saw a local brand leveraging authentic insights with limited budgets, through an experience, rather than a traditional awareness-driven marketing campaign.

Note

1 2021 Fall MRI-Simmons.

Chapter 6

The Path for Growth Is Towards the Multicultural Youth

If you ask a CMO, "Who is your target consumer?" there's a high probability the answer will be "millennials or Gen-Zers."

One of the characteristics that distinguish these two demographic cohorts is that these are the most multicultural generations we have ever seen in the U.S. It is estimated that almost half of all Gen-Zers and 45% of millennials are from a multicultural background. Together, these two groups represent over 40% of the country's population.[1]

Unfortunately, some marketers are still trying to understand the consequences of this younger demographic transformation into a more diverse and multicultural consumer set. Most of them tend to bundle these diverse consumers into a single homogenous group, hoping to grow their businesses while achieving their efficiencies and synergies.

What these marketers don't realize is that by bundling these consumers under a single spectrum of behaviors and attitudes defined by their age, they ignore the importance of culture and the unique sense of identity these millennials and Gen-Zers bring with them. And this generalization towards these younger consumers creates the risk of developing ineffective marketing plans with low/no ROI on marketing initiatives.

But the challenge for CMOs is significant. First, the pressure for budget efficiencies is the norm in most companies. Second, it is natural to assume that Hispanic millennials, Black millennials, and non-Hispanic White millennials have a lot in common. After all, they share their status as the first digitally native generation who have lived through similar life stages as they reach adulthood, including professional aspirations, relationships, jobs, and children.

But multicultural millennial consumers also have much more nuance and richness for marketers to understand. Tapping into these nuances opens up significant opportunities to engage in more authentic conversations and differentiation for a brand.

For example, Hispanic millennials differentiate themselves by demonstrating a significant connection with their Hispanic culture. They are trendsetters who mash up mainstream influences with Hispanic music, food, and

DOI: 10.4324/9781003348931-7

culture. They see themselves as fortunate to follow their dreams thanks to the hard work of their parents and family, so they seek to "pay it back" by striving to be agents of change within their neighborhoods and aim to make their families proud. This is also very true of AAPI millennials.

As they have for several decades now, Black millennials continue to shape American mainstream culture while experiencing a Black cultural renaissance, embracing and celebrating their African roots in new ways. They are experiencing a new wave of successful Black entrepreneurship and the dominance of cultural institutions beyond music and sports.

A recent study commissioned by the Hispanic Marketing Council, a national trade organization of marketing, communications, and media firms with Hispanic expertise, sheds some light on this topic, sharing insights into the similarities and differences between Gen-Zers and millennials across generations and ethnic backgrounds.[2]

The study, conducted in early 2020, was based on 2,418 interviews, plus 54 in-depth qualitative discussions with non-Hispanic White (NHW), non-Hispanic Black (NHB), and Hispanic consumers aged 13–49, plus the parents of kids aged 8–12. It covered a wide range of topics, including cultural and societal issues, identity, politics, brands, technology, and media content.

While reading the study, one thing became apparent. There's a gap that separates young multicultural consumers from their Non-Hispanic White peers of the same generation. Understanding this gap may be essential for marketers to better succeed in the marketplace today and in the years to come. This gap can be expressed in what some call "the small things," which, in my opinion, are anything but small, as they tend to illustrate a set of core beliefs and values that multicultural families have.

For instance, one of the questions that I loved to read about was the one that covered the attitudes of families towards allowing their kids to have sleepovers at their friends' houses. Black and Hispanic families have long been reported to be stricter, with broader family definitions and tighter reins on independence with their children. The data shows this is still the case, and when it comes to Hispanics, the centrality of parents and family has not loosened with the passing of time.

Among Non-Hispanic White families, 81% of 8 to 12-year-olds were allowed to sleep over at their friends' houses, while only 61% of Hispanic and Non-Hispanic Black families allowed sleepovers, a 20-point gap. Interestingly enough, the gap is almost identical for the 13 to 17-year-old age group. Furthermore, the study's qualitative part found that virtually all of the Black and Hispanic families' sleepovers were with cousins and other family members, not other friends as was normal with the Non-Hispanic White family's respondents.

Another question from the study that illustrates the values gap was about the percentage of kids that verbally disrespected their parents. While 46% of Non-Hispanic Whites respondents said that their kids between the ages of

8 and 12 had disrespected them before, less than a third (32%) of Hispanic and Non-Hispanic Black households said that they had experienced verbal disrespect from their kids.

Nancy Tellet is a well-known multicultural research specialist, who was commissioned by the Hispanic Marketing Council (HMC) to lead this research. When I asked her what her most significant learning from the study was, she said,

> In HMC's 1st multicultural study a few years ago, the most significant learning was the sheer power of in-culture digital content in Black and Hispanic lives and the significant amount of time spent in these deep culture environments. In HMC's 2020 study on 13–17 aged members of America's 1st multicultural majority generation, the most significant single learning was the sheer power of race and ethnicity in the brands that Hispanics and Blacks choose to embrace or quit. The #1 reason to quit a brand was racial/ethnic disrespect for their segment or someone else's, and even a respectful ad adjacent to disrespectful content was enough for 31% of 13–17 year-old's to have already quit a brand.

On the surface, these behaviors may seem to be mere curiosities, but underneath, what it demonstrates is that millennial and Gen-Zers' attitudes towards family are heavily influenced by their culture. Unlocking these nuances and understanding how they can shape and influence these consumer behaviors is the challenge for all modern marketers who are living in a diverse and multicultural marketplace.

Case Study—How a Brand Can Be Connected to Social Causes on a Relevant and Diverse-Oriented Way

Pepsi—"Unmute Your Voice"

Executive Summary

Pepsi strives to be at the forefront of culture as a business growth strategy. In a year of strong civic engagement among young Hispanics—a group crucial to Pepsi's long-term growth—they launched a call to action for young Hispanics to register to vote and, by doing so, "unmute their voice," a phrase that has become ubiquitous in global vernacular.

The Business Challenge

Among Hispanics, Pepsi was losing the battle against the leading cola competitor. Their Likeability was 16 points lower and purchase intent was 12 points lower than their leading competitor.

Even worse, brand linkage showed that their marketing efforts were promoting the category, *not* Pepsi. At just 35%, linkage was 28 points lower than the category norm and 23 points lower than its main competitor.

It was clear that Pepsi was *not* on track to drive Hispanics' preference over their rival and needed to go back to its big-in-culture-through-music ways.

The Insights/Strategy

Young Hispanics care about their communities but do not think their vote or voice matters.

Our target was young Hispanics, who make up 27% of Pepsi's 18–34 consumers and are essential to their long-term success. These young Hispanics are bilingual, bicultural, and culturally influential.

They tend to appreciate when brands play a positive role in their communities. They will be "more favorable" to that brand (84%) and "more likely to be a customer" (81%).

Younger Hispanic voters want to see a change in their communities but lack knowledge of the electoral process, making it difficult for them to participate in democracy.

- They feel that their vote won't make a difference.
- Casting a ballot can be complicated—especially for first timers.
- For young minorities, it's not a topic discussed at home, which creates additional disengagement.
- Too many forms/deadlines make the process unclear.

Despite gains in 2008, multicultural voting declined in 2016. Hispanic voter turnout was just 47.6% versus 65.3% of non-ethnic voters. This fact made voter registration in 2020 even more important.

Pepsi realized that a nonpartisan message focused on their issues and the importance of voter registration was a perfect aperture to connect with young Hispanics.

The Idea/Execution

Talking without voting is like speaking on mute. Useless.

Pepsi flipped the meaning of the unmute button by turning it into a symbol for the power of being heard.

They turned the unmute button into a symbol that shows the power of being heard and inspired voter registration. They leveraged Pepsi's rich history in music and entertainment in order to connect with our audience across media touch points.

Knowing their target lives with phone in hand, they took the campaign to the platforms they love most: Facebook, Instagram, Twitter, Snapchat, and Pandora. Spreading the vote registration message and getting them pumped for what we did next.

Delivering Big in Culture

Pepsi took over the most iconic night in music: MTVs Video Music Awards. And our young Hispanic target was there for it. The creative ran in the show and across digital channels.

During the show, Sofia Carson presented H.E.R. the Video for Good Award for her song "I Can't Breathe." To demonstrate the power of using one's voice, Pepsi donated $100,000 to H.E.R.'s chosen organization, the *NAACP Legal Defense Fund*. Following H.E.R.'s acceptance speech, Sofia Carson went on to encourage viewers to hit the polls in the upcoming elections: "Make a difference in your community's future, in our country's future, unmute your voice, and speak up about what you believe in. Register to vote because your vote is your voice."

As voter registration deadlines were approaching across the country, Pepsi and Rock the Vote brought together Demi Lovato, Chance the Rapper, Chloe x Halle, Saint JHN, Brett Young, and Ava Max to encourage their fans to make their voices heard on popular music platforms Triller, YouTube, and Twitch. Pitbull got into the action and encouraged even more fans to vote with a concert on *LiveXLive*.

As part of the concerts, each artist would "unmute" his/her voice during the performances and encourage music fans to unmute their voices by registering to vote.

Results

- Ninety-one per cent of young Hispanics were more likely to register to vote in the general election after seeing Pepsi's campaign.
- Unmute Your Voice outperformed Spanish Language TV Norms as the Pepsi brand resonated with viewers, leading to a purchase intent 19 points higher than the norm.
- Hispanic Penetration increased +1.1% versus the prior three months, leading to a share increase of 0.2% versus prior three months. (Seems small but it means *millions* in sales.)

Author's Comments

As our country shows signs of strong political division, getting involved in an effort to incentivize young consumers to register to vote could be perceived by some as something outside the role of a brand, or worse, there was a risk to be perceived as partisan.

However, research shows that consumers, mainly the ones from generations Z and millennial (most of whom are from a diverse background, led by Hispanics), expect brands to be more involved in social issues and causes.

Balancing these two facts represents a tough challenge for brands. In this case, Pepsi successfully achieved its goals because (1) it recognized that not every single idea should gravitate around itself, (2) it understood that as a mega brand, Pepsi could lend attention to this issue through its marketing investments and partnerships, and (3) it found a contemporary, fresh and authentic way to deliver the idea.

Notes

1 2019 American Community Survey.
2 https://hispanicmarketingcouncil.org/race–culture–identity/

Chapter 7

The Six Learnings Every CEO Needs to Understand

As we come to the end of Part I, I want to spend some time reviewing what learnings these different chapters have in common and, most importantly, how business leaders across the U.S. are applying them.

The demographic changes we face as a country bring challenges and opportunities for corporations as new consumption patterns emerge, especially after the COVID-19 pandemic subsides. Today's consumers have different communication needs as well as distinct attitudes and behaviors. Understanding and, ideally, preempting these transformational changes will require a new set of skills for CMOs across America, who will need to become "fluent" in multicultural marketing.

1 Multicultural Marketing Is Not a Niche Anymore

Treating multicultural marketing as a niche discipline has, over time, led many organizations to deprioritize marketing to multicultural segments. After all, once a program is considered niche, it automatically becomes optional or dependent on the notorious search for "incremental budget."

Multicultural marketing as a discipline deserves the same status as other important marketing disciplines already have like media, shopper marketing, and PR.

"If you're not growing with multicultural consumers today, you're not going to grow. The under 18 population in the U.S. is already a multicultural majority with GenZ as the most racially and ethnically diverse generation. As marketers, we should always re-evaluate whom we are trying to reach and build deeper empathy and connection with people to ensure they're feeling seen. Marketing today means marketing in a multicultural world."

(Brad Hiranaga, Former Chief Brand Officer, General Mills)

DOI: 10.4324/9781003348931-8

2 Total Market Is Over, but a New Model Is Still in the Works

If you still believe that one-size-fits-all when it comes to consumer marketing in the U.S., you're probably three to five years behind where the market has gone. The idea of Total Market as one single approach towards consumers has failed miserably and has denied many corporations a shot at one of the few growth opportunities in the marketplace—the multicultural segment.

However, a new model is still in the works. There won't be a model that will work for just any company type. I have seen successful brands orchestrating a calendar that combines moments of mass-reach messages with stronger moments with a segmented focus.

"One of our key values at McDonald's is that we open our doors to everyone. As marketers, it's our responsibility to understand our multicultural consumers intimately and keep them at the center of our growth plans. In the last year, we've walked away from Total Market. Today, we kick off all our projects with a round-robin grounding in the insights from all of our different segments. This has brought specificity and inspiration to our marketing and is helping us connect in relevant and authentic ways."

(Morgan Flatley, evp, Global Chief Marketing Officer and new business ventures McDonald's)

3 Expertise and Specialization Are Required to Avoid Improvisation

The era of improvisation and lack of investments in dedicated specialists to lead multicultural marketing efforts is over. CMOs need to surround themselves with executives, agencies, and consultants that have the experience and the know-how to properly support them. Having one employee from a multicultural background and/or the company's ERG group leading multicultural marketing efforts will probably fail, and this failure will cost companies millions of dollars.

"We are also re-thinking how we staff, hire, partner with agencies to fund, and build our plans. This has been driven by a clear expectation from me that our business requires this shift to lead with the multicultural consumer for the future. We are pleased with the steps we have taken, but we will need to continue to evolve in order to stay relevant to this changing customer landscape and the minority-majority shift. I see this as part of the challenge of marketing, the constant evolution and curiosity of staying connected with our broad consumer base."

(Morgan Flatley, evp, Global Chief Marketing Officer and new business ventures, McDonald's)

4 Multicultural Marketing Requires a Robust and Comprehensive Plan

The days of multicultural marketing being expressed by a few ads during Black History Month or Hispanic Heritage Month are over. CEOs need to lead the process of creating goals that put multicultural consumers at the center of their growth targets and include business aspects beyond communications, including product development, distribution, employee recruitment, pricing, product mix, and packaging, among other needs.

Moreover, these plans need to be properly funded, proportionally to the size of the opportunity and the importance of these consumers to the company's overall goals.

"At P&G, we fundamentally believe that building our multicultural business is good business. As such, we are building multicultural marketing into the fabric of how we build brands vs. bolting it on as a separate effort. Our intent is to make these efforts part of our winning strategies—to help widen our advantages across the vectors of superiority which will improve productivity and strengthen our organization. That's how we lead constructive disruption across the value chain."

(Jeronimo Escudero, Senior Director Brand Innovation, P&G)

5 Culture Is the New Marketing Currency

For decades, multicultural marketing has been reduced to marketing in Spanish, Mandarin, or stereotypical ways to approach the Black segment. Today, multicultural marketing must be more sophisticated as the stakes are much higher from a business standpoint.

Marketers require a more in-depth understanding of how culture shapes multicultural consumers' attitudes and behaviors and, more importantly, how multicultural consumers shape the country's broader cultural scene.

6 The Minority-Majority Demographic Shift Is Real

Today, the majority of America's population under the age of seventeen years old is already from a minority background.[1] Moreover, this demographic trend is projected to continue for years to come, reaching a moment in the early to mid-2040s, according to the Census projections,[2] when the majority of the country's population will be from a minority background. This is not some political statement or wishful thinking but this is a reality, and business leaders need to set their personal views aside and prepare to deal with this entirely different marketplace.

"America is in the middle of a demographic revolution. These are major, transformative changes in the demography of our country that fundamentally reshape our economy, society, and American identity. Diverse communities are leading this change and reshaping how we communicate, how we consume content, and what defines American culture. As brands come to the table, "reaching out" isn't enough. Brands must be authentic, develop relationships based on trust and a unique understanding of the diverse consumer experience. That takes time, focus, and effort. Diverse consumers are your next best consumer, your biggest fan in social media, and your winning strategy as our American demography evolves."

(Stacie de Armas, SVP Diverse Consumer and Insights & Initiatives DE&I Practice, Nielsen)

I sincerely hope that these simple (but deep) learnings will help CEOs in one way or another across corporate America become more versed on what could turn out to be the largest source of growth for your brand and consequently your company's bottom line.

Notes

1 U.S. Census Bureau, 2020 Census.
2 U.S. Census Bureau Population Division (revised release date: September 2018).

Part II

Myths and Barriers

Chapter 8

Seven Myths about Hispanic Marketing

The COVID-19 pandemic literally brought the world to a screeching halt in 2020 and changed everything, from the way consumers behave to how we work. Among the many challenges facing companies across all industries today are higher consumer expectations around e-commerce, a renewed scrutiny around sustainability, and a ton of pent-up demand for everything! Based on my personal survey with clients and prospects, most predict that the next couple of years will be filled with many post-pandemic challenges, with any gains from a potential higher GDP growth being eaten up by historically high inflation, channel disruptions, and a more-than-ever empowered consumer ready to make the switch to competitive brands.

I also see brands that are still timid about taking the plunge into the Hispanic segment as a growth driver, mostly because of misconceived notions or simple misinformation that have created a series of "myths" around the Hispanic segment.

In this chapter, I will try to tackle the most important myths that need to be addressed for marketers to unlock the power of Hispanic growth in America.

1 Behavioral Segmentation Makes Cultural Segmentation Irrelevant:

This is probably one of the most important myths and one of the least debated.

In this paradigm, individuals are basically reduced to consumers instead of people, and what matters is the ability to use big data to assess and predict consumption behaviors, and then try to influence their future purchasing patterns by offering the right product, at the right time, for the right price, and use consumption behavioral data as the driver of any segmentation model.

This Behavioral Segmentation model advocates that a consumer's cultural and ethnic background don't have a major impact when it comes to influencing sales. The advocates of this approach claim that "Hispanic consumers don't make their purchase decisions on buying brand A or B based on their

DOI: 10.4324/9781003348931-10

ethnic background, but rather based on their individual needs as consumers. Therefore, there's no need for a multicultural marketing approach."

While Behavioral Segmentation models are an important part of strategic marketing, I believe ignoring or reducing the importance of culture-based segmentation is a big mistake CMOs can no longer afford to make for one important reason: while behavioral segmentation tends to focus on what consumers do, cultural segmentation focuses on *why* they do it and, most importantly, on what are the triggers that can make a Hispanic individual more connected to a brand or a message.

Recent marketplace studies prove that brands achieve a higher ROI when using culturally oriented, emotionally driven creative messages. These studies have confirmed what many of us already knew intuitively: that a successful, culturally driven Hispanic creative approach doesn't create a new "reason-to-believe" or a new functional attribute, but rather, it helps to break through the media clutter we live in and it can also create an emotional layer that increases relevancy in the eyes of a Hispanic individual.

Behavioral segmentation focuses on the rational, while culture-based segmentation brings to the mix the power of emotions on brand building. The modern market challenge is to recognize how both should play a role in building a brand's strategy and what's the right balance between the two of them. Ignoring this will help to commoditize established brands, and it will make it harder to create new ones.

2 Adopting a One-Size-Fits-All Approach Is the Right Thing to Do:

Progressive brands figured out long ago that Inclusive Marketing is about being flexible to capture the Hispanic segment opportunity in order to increase relevance rather than concentrating on false efficiencies. Given that when efficiencies are achieved at the expense of effectiveness, any savings will be washed out by lower market share and sales performance.

In my experience, the secret is to keep one brand positioning and DNA, while looking at opportunities to compare Hispanic and non–Hispanic similarities or differences for dividing the analysis business, consumer insights, and creative execution, asking at every step whether the segments should converge or diverge based on the relevancy of the data.

3 General Market Agencies Can Handle Hispanic Marketing:

Right before the pandemic hit, there was a wave of Hispanic professionals being hired by General Market agencies, and while we applaud this trend, we should also be clear that this doesn't mean that your agency is now ready to manage Hispanic marketing.

First, just because someone may speak Spanish, comes from a Latin American market, or has Latino heritage doesn't make him/her an expert in

Hispanic marketing. Sometimes they have never worked directly with the Hispanic segment, but have the cultural background, their recommendations may be completely biased towards their personal experiences, which could be dangerous for any brand.

Second, even when agencies hire professionals with a background in Hispanic Marketing their voices are seldom heard. Why? Because the internal processes are designed to unify messages and ideas under one single direction—the "one-size-fits-all" marketing mentality. In my experience, key decision makers in Creative, Planning, Digital, and Account Services tend not to be from a minority background, and their answer to proposals from their minority employees tend to be "What is not Hispanic about this idea?" So, the bar moved from trying to develop an idea that can best work with Hispanics to maximize effectiveness to working on adaptations and translations that should minimize the risk of alienating Hispanics to maximize efficiencies only.

Recently, I spoke with a Hispanic professional who expressed her frustration with the above situation and she summarized it best:

> I currently work for one of those "One-Size-Fits-All" agencies and it's just exhausting. Coming from a Hispanic agency shop, I accepted this job with the promise that I will "manage" an entire team dedicated to adapting General Market work into Hispanic Market. So far, I'm the only Spanish-speaking executive and overall the creative is extremely hard to adapt (no wonder our clients' shares keep falling).

4 Hispanic Marketing = Hispanic Advertising:

Different from regular advertising agencies, a great multicultural ad agency goes beyond marketing communications and should help your organization have a broader marketing perspective from a multicultural angle. For instance, when it comes to Hispanic marketing, a great agency should be able to support the creation of an annual business plan that includes market prioritization, measurement tools, distribution footprint analysis, sales force training, and so on. Moreover, a strong multicultural agency can also support a client when it comes to benchmarking organizational design and structure as well as provide the client's employees with multicultural training.

In the end, while we live in an era when consulting companies are starting to behave like ad agencies, when it comes to multicultural marketing, the opposite is also true, as clients have been leveraging their agencies beyond their creative needs. A great multicultural ad agency is also a multicultural consulting partner.

5 Incremental Budget Is Needed:

I've heard this one several times: "Isaac, I hear you, I see the data, I see the growth, if I just get this incremental budget approved to fund the Hispanic initiative I would be able to start the program right away."

My answer is always the same: "Why do you think the Hispanic segment requires incremental funds? Why can't you simply reorganize and rebalance your resources to allocate them proportionally to the growth opportunity that you have?"

Nine out of ten times their answer is: "It's hard to change our culture, budgets have been created the same way for many years, we have to fund several programs, etc."

I know this. I've been there. I worked on the client side for more than 18 years of my career. The reality is we don't live in normal times anymore. It's been harder than ever to find any incremental growth, and CMOs' tenure has been at the lowest point in many decades.

Hispanic marketing leaders shouldn't be asking for any kind of special allocation system, they should only ask for the same level of scrutiny and validation as any other marketing regardless of the segment. I am convinced that once marketing dollars are allocated based on a mix of sales growth, share growth, margin, and customer long-term value (CLTV), Hispanic marketing allocation would double from the current industry average of 7% to at least 15%–20% of marketing budgets.

6 There's Not Enough ROI Research to support the Investment:

This is far from being true. While there are some possible limitations on measurement, Hispanic marketing has come a long way over the past decade. Consumer goods companies have access to a myriad of studies ranging from IRI, MRI-Simmons, Claritas, Scarborough to Nielsen.

In addition, there are plenty of studies that can help track your brand and advertising health among Hispanics (and compare them with non-Hispanic executions), like the ones from Nielsen and ANA's AIMM.

All these sources, combined with your own primary data sources, driven by your own transactional data and websites, mobile apps, store trackers, and social media, can help you draw a pretty accurate picture of the consumer's response to your Hispanic marketing investments.

Lastly, companies like Nielsen, Millward Brown, and even some media companies are now also capable of building marketing mix modeling studies that can estimate the ROI of your Hispanic marketing efforts over time.

7 The Number of Spanish-Language Users in the U.S. Is Down:

Wrong. That's it. This statement is as false as a three-dollar bill. According to the U.S. Census Bureau between 2010 and 2019 Spanish-language usage at home has grown from 34 million to 39 million, a 14% growth!

Now, it is important to mention that the incidence of Spanish speaking at home has decreased during the same period from 75% to 71%. However, if you're a marketer making decisions about language usage, the reality you must face is that there are 5 million more people speaking Spanish at home in this country than nine years ago.[1]

Some may say that "knowing how to speak Spanish doesn't mean people are speaking it often." Fair comment, but it's important to note that the study didn't survey Spanish knowledge, but actual usage of Spanish at home. When one is home, you are close to family and friends and that's when a lot of content and media consumption happens—in other words, when many emotional and cultural connections are made.

Tackling these seven myths, or at least openly discussing them with your teams, will help your agencies take the first step towards a stronger marketing plan.

Case Study—An Example on How Culture Can Drive Business Results

Kia—"Give It Everything"

Executive Summary

Kia America, the automaker that for years was thought of as just a value brand, is evolving in more ways than one. The vehicles themselves are now built better than ever before and their advertising is maturing. As part of the coming of age, this case study is focused on deeply connecting with the consumer. By identifying that both Kia and Hispanics are undervalued and underappreciated they were able to tell a three-part compelling campaign.

The Business Challenge

For many years Kia was viewed as a manufacturer of affordable cars. One customer said, "Kia was an inexpensive car, something that came with limited options." Kia's cars were not particularly stylish and there were concerns about quality. Without abandoning its roots of being affordable, Kia was evolving to quality craftsmanship, dedication, and continuous improvement. Yet some customers still thought of Kia as a value-for-money carmaker.

The Insight and Strategy

Kia and young Hispanics have something in common. For many years, Kia has been evolving its proposition from an affordable carmaker to true craftsmanship in automaking. It has made more attractive, better performing cars and has made cutting edge technology available for a broader consumer base. Despite this, some people still view Kia as a value-for-money proposition.

Something similar happens to Hispanics. Although there are countless examples of how Hispanics are a key part of the fabric of American society, Hispanics still take a backseat in many roles while others take the credit. As a famous chef once said, "Your favorite French chef is probably Hispanic."

No matter how much work Kia and Hispanics put in, they're both undervalued and underappreciated. They may even be delivering better products than others who leverage yesterday's success. When that happens, they believe it's best to let the work speak for itself.

Idea/Execution

Despite putting in the work to make great vehicles, Kia rarely got the credit it deserved. Like Hispanics, the automaker was undervalued and underappreciated. Both don't give it everything for the credit or the fame but for something bigger than themselves.

The first part of the campaign told a true story about a Chef who gets all the credit for his dishes. Instead of praising him, Kia praises all the hands that make his food possible. Hispanics are the backbone of the restaurant industry anonymously and, like Kia, prefer to let their work do the talking.

The second part told the story about being behind the spotlight. While Hispanics are underrepresented in Hollywood, they're in the middle of it, doing the risky stunts for celebrities that get the credit. Hispanics, and Kia, don't work to get the credit, they work because they can.

When Hispanics do get attention, it's often for the wrong reasons. Therefore, the third part of the Kia campaign was about Hispanic weather girls being more than just the stereotypical pretty face. Instead, the campaign looked for the brains supporting weather reporting weather reports—the storm chaser.

Results

Goal # 1. Grow visits to kia.com/espanol by 10%
Results: Traffic reached 1MM by EOY, growing 29.9% YOY

Goal # 2. Maintain 2019 sales numbers despite COVID.
Results:

- At the end of 2020, Kia's sales in the Hispanic segment had grown 27% (Dec '19 vs. '20). Auto sales in Hispanic segment had only grown 22%.
- At the end of the 2-year campaign, Kia's sales in the Hispanic segment more than doubled, growing 101%. (Mar '20 vs. '21) outperforming the Hispanic segment. In that same period, Seltos sales grew 175% and is at parity with Sorento and the Telluride in terms of sales.
- Kia achieved record volume of sales in America.

Goal # 3. Maintain 2019 volume share despite COVID-19.
Results: At the end of 2020, Kia's share grew 20 bp, growing faster than the category, being one of the few brands that grew the year.

Author's Commentary

In a highly competitive category, where several marketers are still focusing on synergies and efficiencies, by approaching the Hispanic segment through translations and transcreations, Kia was extremely successful by tapping into relevant and authentic Hispanic insights.

Moreover, Kia achieved these results despite not being the largest Hispanic advertiser in the category. Which reinforces to me the idea that most advertisers should dedicate more focus and attention to the message they deliver through their media investments.

What is the point of spending millions of dollars on marketing campaigns to Hispanics and not trusting true experts to create authentic ideas that have a higher probability of effectiveness and higher ROI when compared to "one-size-fits-all" ideas?

Note

1 2010 American Community Survey, 2019 American Community Survey.

Chapter 9

Is Marketing in Spanish Still Relevant to Hispanics?

By now, we know all about the dangers of "fake news," but there's another form of false information, the concept of "fake trends," that marketers should be aware of since these can have a negative impact on business strategies. We are witnessing one of them right now when it comes to Hispanic marketing.

The "fake trend" goes like this: Since the Hispanic population growth in the U.S. has been shifting from immigration-based to U.S.-born-based, the need to reach out to this segment from a marketing standpoint should also shift, because young Hispanic millennials and Gen-Zers tend to culturally assimilate to the broader general market target. As a result, brands may not need to create culturally driven and Spanish-language campaigns to connect with Hispanics any longer. Right? Following this logic then, one strategy, one message, one language would fit all. Correct? No, this is completely false.

On the surface, the foregoing narrative makes sense, since we know that Hispanic immigration has indeed slowed down, and we all have seen data that shows that young Hispanics are speaking more English and consuming media in English. Given that CMOs are always under significant pressure to cut their budgets and find efficiencies, the idea of limiting or simply eliminating multicultural marketing efforts in favor of a one-size-fits-all approach is certainly tempting.

But Is It True? Is It Better for Business?

First, let's tackle the idea that there are fewer Spanish speakers in the U.S. than a few years or decades ago. This is simply not true. According to the U.S. Census Bureau, the number of Spanish speakers in the country has been continuously growing since 1980, from an estimated 11 million to 17 million in 1990, 25 million in 2000, and 34 million in 2010, and by 2022 it had exceeded 41 Million in the United States.[1]

So, while the relative number of Spanish-speaking Hispanics may be decreasing due to the growth of U.S.-born Hispanics, the absolute number of Spanish-speaking Hispanics keeps on growing.

DOI: 10.4324/9781003348931-11

Second, is advertising in Spanish relevant or effective? Over the past few years, we have seen further proof of the power of the Spanish language to drive higher effectiveness within the U.S., especially with Hispanic marketing efforts.

In October 2016, Facebook released the results of their "Facebook IQ"[2] study conducted by the Collage Group. The in-depth study surveyed 500 Hispanics from different language usage backgrounds (English-dominant, bilingual, and Spanish-dominant) and complemented their quantitative findings with in-depth interviews.

The study reached several conclusions, of which I want to highlight the following:

- Eighty percent of U.S. Hispanics don't feel they need to stop speaking Spanish to be part of American culture.
- Eighty-six percent of respondents believe the Spanish language helps them remain connected to their culture.
- Ads targeting Hispanics in Spanish significantly increased their interest in purchasing products.
- When online, more than 80% of Spanish-dominant Hispanics use Spanish at least half of the time when they read, write, or watch videos.
- Seventy-nine percent of Spanish-dominant, 82% of bilingual, and 60% of English-dominant Hispanics surveyed on this research think brands should reach out to consumers in both English and Spanish.
- Fifty-eight percent of Spanish-dominant Hispanics and 48% of bilingual Hispanics think that brands that reach out to them in Spanish demonstrate they value the Hispanic community.

Furthermore, the Facebook IQ study also mentions that Hispanic consumers don't want to be exposed to mere translations of messages from English to Spanish; they want to receive messages that reflect their culture, and these messages should also make sure they cast actors who speak Spanish well, using humor, and reflecting situations that Hispanic consumers can relate to from a cultural standpoint.

Finally, something that many would find very surprising, was the fact that when it came to bilingual Hispanics, 62% used Spanish at least half of the time when reading online, 66% when writing online, and 69% when watching videos online.

This study has significant importance, as it debunks the idea that the more acculturated the Hispanic consumer is, the less relevant Spanish language becomes. That is simply not true. In addition, the study challenges the common perception that while some Hispanics still prefer to consume some traditional media in Spanish, English was the best way to reach Hispanics online and on social media.

Moreover, the source of the study is also important as Facebook is considered a neutral media company since it doesn't have any preference on whether advertisers use English or Spanish on their campaigns; they are just interested in helping their clients maximize their campaigns' ROI.

Nielsen, another heavyweight when it comes to advertising effectiveness, released another study in 2017 where it analyzed the ROI of hundreds of Spanish-language TV campaigns and compared their effectiveness to their English-language general market TV ads. The study[3] was authored by Matt Krepsik, Nielsen's head of Marketing, ROI Analytic Products, and included results across the marketing efforts of more than 50 projects with clients in a wide variety of categories. Nielsen assessed the campaigns on several dimensions, including creative quality, execution pattern, spend, category, and brand indices among Spanish-speaking consumers, existence of cross-channel media efforts, and return on investment.

The Nielsen study started by comparing the ROI of general market English-language ads and Spanish-language TV ads and saw a gap. Whereas English ads had an ROI of $1.10, Spanish ads showed an ROI of only $0.80. Trying to understand the reason behind this gap, the study conducted an in-depth analysis of the Spanish-language TV ads and concluded that not all Spanish-language TV ads were created equally. In fact, 54% of these Spanish-language TV ads showed equal or higher ROI than their general market counterparts.

So what made these Spanish-language ads more effective? What were the common characteristics that significantly increased their ROIs? Stronger creativity.

Ads with higher ad memorability, brand memorability, message memorability, and likability tend to have a higher ROI. Furthermore, the study called out what made these higher ROI Spanish ads stronger from a messaging standpoint.

The Nielsen study identified five key factors that drive high creative resonance scores (as measured by Nielsen Brand Effect) among Spanish-language campaigns:

- *Use original Spanish content:* Ads developed in Spanish that are culturally tailored to the U.S. Hispanic market outperform ads that are simply translated into Spanish.
- *Spanish dialogues matter.* Ads with on-screen dialogue in Spanish help enhance cultural relevance.
- *Incorporate a narrative storyline:* Engage with a story, particularly one that highlights family bonds.
- *Use humor:* Leverage the universal human desire for a good laugh, but make sure the humor is culturally relevant.
- *Make it relatable:* Feature relatable characters in familiar, real-world settings.

The study also reported that major CPG brands that followed the above direction have seen ROI returns up to four times higher than general market ads.

The study highlights additional ways to increase Spanish-language TV ads' ROI, including recency and frequency of media flights and the usage of richer media mix to complement TV, mostly with the inclusion of digital executions.

It is worth noting that similar to the Facebook IQ study, Nielsen also doesn't have a preference when it comes to clients' advertising language strategies, as their sole focus is to support their clients in increasing the effectiveness of their campaigns.

Historically, Hispanic marketing has been seen with skepticism given its limited measurement and ROI analysis, but over the past few years, a series of studies have been shedding much more light into what works and what doesn't with this segment, so clients can make marketing allocation decisions based on facts, not myths.

While most experts on Hispanic marketing agree that the Spanish language alone is not enough to create an effective campaign, we know now that abandoning Spanish to focus only on cultural nuances may not be enough. You need both. *Los dos*.

Notes

1 U.S. Census Bureau, 1980, 1990, 2000 Census and 2010, 2019, 2020 American Community Survey.
2 www.facebook.com/business/news/insights/gains-in-translation-what-your-language-choices-say-to-us-hispanics
3 The Secrets to Higher ROI in Spanish-Language TV, February 2017 Copyright © 2016 The Nielsen Company. www.nielsen.com/wp-content/uploads/sites/3/2019/04/the-secrets-to-hispanic-roi-feb-2017.pdf

Chapter 10

Don't Suffer Multicultural Myopia

According to the official U.S. Census Bureau, 2020 was the year when, for the first time, the majority of our country's population of 17-years-olds and under came from a minority background, most of them from a Hispanic, Black, or AAPI ethnicity.[1]

Moreover, according to Census projections,[2] what started with our younger population in 2020 is a trend that will continue over the next two decades, age group by age group, culminating at some point between 2040 and 2050, when the entire nation will become a so-called minority-majority country.

Ironically, even before the COVID-19 pandemic hit, we were witnessing a backlash to the idea of a multicultural America, with its most visible expression being the attacks on the value immigrants bring to this country. This is truly sad, given the fact that this country was founded by immigrants whose values of resilience, hard work, perseverance, optimism, and the search for a better life have always shaped the fabric of the American experiment.

As a business leader and multicultural marketing expert, I am frequently asked how corporations should navigate the balance between catering to the new demographic changes in the marketplace while avoiding getting caught up in the heated political debate and the divisiveness we are experiencing in our society today. My answer is this: while we must pay attention to what's happening in the short term, as business leaders it is imperative that we plan for the next 5, 10, 20 years. The demographic changes we are experiencing today won't change in the next two decades, no matter which political party is in power.

In fact, the demographic forces shaping the changes we are facing today are less driven by immigration policies, as they are by the organic population growth, mostly from the Hispanic and AAPI segments. While we expect the population growth rate from minority groups to slow down over the next few decades, their growth rate will still be significantly higher than the White Caucasian population growth rate, which in 2020 saw declines for

DOI: 10.4324/9781003348931-12

the first time, following a pattern seen in some countries in Western Europe and in Japan.

Not recognizing the transformational power of these demographic changes in almost every aspect of our society and the impact they will have on business is what I call "Multicultural Myopia," to paraphrase an expression coined by Professor Theodore Levitt's work to explain a short-sided approach to marketing that doesn't focus on consumers.

Research has already shown that multicultural consumers have demonstrated somewhat different behaviors, preferences, and attitudes towards brands and services in a vast array of industries, including consumer goods, healthcare, and financial services, to name a few. These behaviors may offer opportunities for different products and services, changes in packaging, sales channels, customer service, distribution, and pricing, among other areas.

Consumer research studies conducted by industry leaders like Nielsen, Kantar, and MRI-Simmons have all confirmed that the new generation of multicultural consumers does not adhere to the old assumption of "natural assimilation," which entails fully adopting a monolithic Anglo culture as was the case with many immigrants that came to America from parts of Northern Europe like Scotland, Ireland, Germany, and Poland in the early 20th century. As a matter of fact, we are seeing signs of the opposite trend: not only are younger, U.S.-born, multicultural consumers seeking to retain important aspects of their cultural heritage—like language and culture—they are also exerting significant influence and power in shaping America's mainstream culture. This can be seen in their choices of food, music, fashion, and sports, for instance. Can you guess which is the number one music genre watched on YouTube? It's neither Pop nor Country music; it's Latin music.

Why is this meaningful? Similar to changes in our business environment driven by technological advances over the past two decades, the changes we are witnessing—and will continue to observe at an even faster rate in the years to come—will create a fertile environment for growth, innovation, and, most importantly, changes in the current competitive positioning of several corporations and brands in America. In short, leading corporations and brands may see significant shifts in their market share positioning and sales growth trajectory. These movements will be tracked closely by Wall Street, and analysts will start to assess a brand's value based on their ability to navigate these new demographic changes.

How should your company prepare for this new multicultural marketplace? Leading companies have been successful by following a few useful strategies. First, by getting alignment at the senior leadership level on a plan that addresses this tremendous opportunity by investing consistently over the years versus approaching the opportunity as a tactical short-term project. Second, by recognizing the need for a holistic approach to capitalize on the multicultural opportunity that includes investing in consumers; building and maintaining good community engagement; and building a strong recruitment, retention, and DE&I advancement program for minority employees and suppliers.

As a friend of mine, the author and business expert Rishad Tobaccowala, recently stated when discussing the topic of America's demographic changes, "If you don't like change, you may not like irrelevance either." The stakes are high, and the time has come for corporate America to consider multicultural marketing as a growth strategy. The victors will reap the benefits of a young, loyal, and vibrant set of new consumers; the markets will penalize the losers. This is a long-overdue conversation that board of directors and C-suites across our country need to have. Just ask yourself: Who is taking the lead on the race for market leadership in the decades to come?

Case Study—Financial Services Brands Leveraging Hispanic Cultural Insights to Drive Results

Prudential Financial—"Cuéntame Más"

Executive Summary

A partnership between Prudential Financial and Univision with the goal of educating Hispanic consumers in New York on the importance of life insurance and driving traffic to Prudential's Spanish-language site.

The Business Challenge

The main challenge was to engage the New York Hispanic consumer around the topic of life insurance in-culture and in-language and to position the Prudential brand top of mind. Another challenge was dealing with a topic (life insurance) that involves tough conversations around death and planning, which can be taboo for Hispanics.

The Insights/Strategy

Based on a proprietary study conducted in 2020 (Prudential Financial Wellness Census), Prudential found that 56% of Hispanic Americans are worried about their financial future.

The program's concept had two key tenets: first, to inform audiences about the financial benefits of life insurance, and second, to empower them to use life insurance to secure their finances.

Idea/Execution

For this program Prudential partnered with Univision to develop a custom, cross-platform, campaign to engage Hispanic consumers and empower this audience with information and resources to better understand life insurance. They also worked on an influencer activation that helped provide personalized rationalization, showing audiences practical uses of life insurance and empowering them to take advantage of it as well.

The creative platform included three key mediums and distribution points: Social media, Digital media, and Radio. Social media and Digital media are excellent tools for engaging the Hispanic audience that over-index in social consumption across platforms and in mobile and video consumption. Terrestrial and streaming radio is an equally effective medium for driving messaging and recall, as the Hispanic population remains loyal radio listeners.

Content formats were tailored to the platform, to create unique content for each medium that reflected consumers' behaviors on those platforms. For social, content was executed in a two-prong approach: (1) utility based, informational, content to educate audiences and (2) influencer-created content to drive shareability and build authentic connection. Content was distributed across Univision's and influencer's Facebook and Instagram channels, geo-targeted to the client's key market. Targeting and regionalized messaging is key to driving performance with this specific subgroup of the Hispanic population.

Digital media leveraged brand spots to complement the social engagement with a harder sell and delivery of brand messaging points. These assets drove to Prudential Financial's site where consumers could find more information on the subjects and view the social videos.

Radio leveraged custom-created spots in the voice of the influencer, and they were distributed via a frequency schedule to ensure consistent messaging to the audience.

Results

Campaign over-delivered across all KPIs. Total delivery across all platforms:

> All metrics were delivered in the NY market and so figures represent hyper-targeted results; we were able to deliver a significant portion of the Hispanic population in NY.
> Results:
>
> * 10M Impressions
> * Over 600K Video Views
> * More than 75K Actions taken by consumers, including clicks to client site and "Saving" of Instagram posts, one of the deepest measures of consumer connection on social media

Author's Comments

There are several aspects to call out on this case study. First, local/regional marketing. While Prudential is a national advertiser, they decided to laser focus this effort on the NY DMA. This is something I often see and recommend to clients. If your resources are limited, or if your business challenges in specific markets require special attention, local marketing programs can be very effective.

Second, it is important to recognize the fact that several financial institutions still see Hispanics as an unattractive target due to the misperception that all Hispanics are low-income consumers, with limited to no interest in financial products like life insurance.

Finally, I'd like to also mention the fact that this program was created in partnership with Univision. In my experience Hispanic media outlets tend to offer more flexibility to create tailored solutions to advertisers and their agencies, versus just offering them exposure through existing programs.

Notes

1 U.S. Census Bureau, 2020 Census and 2010–2019 American Community Survey.
2 U.S. Census Bureau, Population Division (Revised Release Date: September 2018).

Chapter 11

DE&I and Multicultural Marketing Are Not the Same

Over the past few years, we have witnessed an uptick on the debate around the importance of diversity, equity, & inclusion (DE&I) for corporate America, and this is excellent news. After all, we live in the most diverse and multicultural society America has ever seen. Furthermore, for the next two decades, we are on the path of becoming a "minority-majority" country. Any effort to enhance this debate and make our business environment more reflective of the societal changes we are witnessing should be welcomed and supported.

The not-so-good news is that for some corporations, DE&I may be competing or, worse, replacing existing multicultural marketing programs, at least from a resource allocation perspective. Don't get me wrong; I believe both concepts are equally important, and I understand they may be considered related. But the risk of treating them as the same thing is what may hurt a brand's bottom line.

In my experience, a strong DE&I program is necessary for corporations to build an organization that reflects the society and marketplace they operate in. Diversity helps in bringing the right representation, and inclusion is a must for having these voices heard at the decision-making level. An effective DE&I program can serve as a springboard for an inclusive approach across all stakeholders, including not only employees but also suppliers, retailers, and consumers. And precisely because retailers and consumers should be engaged in this effort, the multicultural marketing discipline and its expertise are required.

The fact is that DE&I efforts are not truly complete without a multicultural marketing strategy. And multicultural marketing strategies may be incomplete and ineffective if developed without people who understand the new demographic paradigm of America.

I spoke with Gonzalo del Fa, president of GroupM Multicultural, a leading multicultural media planning and buying agency, and chairman of the Board of the Hispanic Marketing Council, the association that represents

DOI: 10.4324/9781003348931-13

multicultural advertising experts. This is his opinion on the relationship between DE&I and multicultural marketing:

> Some marketers believe that having a DE&I corporate program can replace having a multicultural marketing strategy. Unfortunately, that is not true. DE&I is an internal effort that a corporation commits to encouraging a work environment that inspires diversity of representation and thought, promotes and celebrates inclusivity, and provides equitable opportunities to all.
>
> Multicultural Marketing is an external effort for a corporation to promote and sell products or services, including market research and advertising to one or more audiences of a specific ethnic background.
>
> We have proof that DE&I is a source of tremendous benefit for organizations because differences in background, experiences, and thinking lead to increased innovation and insight. However, those innovations and insights need to be communicated to multicultural consumers in a relevant and authentic way, and that is only possible by having a proper multicultural marketing strategy.
>
> A DE&I program is always welcome for a corporation to create an inclusive working environment, but a multicultural strategy is imperative for a business to grow.

I also talked about this topic with industry leader Monique Nelson, from Uniworld Group, a leading multicultural ad agency. Here's her take on this topic:

> "Establishing value-driven, inclusive leadership programs that are branded and recognized both by employees and leaders as value-creation activities allow for an inclusive journey that will truly yield results," said Nelson, "It can shape our opinions of ourselves and the people around us for better or worse. To ensure that advertising is truly representative means that businesses—when engaging consumers, suppliers, distributors, and employees—must understand and share a common goal, that we all exist together in our communities, in our companies, and on this common planet," she concluded.

When thinking about this important topic, I like the simple and on-point definition given to me by one of my mentors and managers, Luis Miguel Messianu: "DE&I is about values, and multicultural marketing is about driving value." It's time to bring these two together in a meaningful way. It's time to connect internal and external efforts in an aligned and synchronized fashion.

Chapter 12

Seven Reasons Why Your Multicultural Marketing Plans Didn't Work

When I sit down with marketers who claim their multicultural marketing efforts didn't work, I try to dissect the underlying reasons for this potential failure, and curiously enough, most marketers don't even know these reasons themselves. In this chapter, we will discuss what separates successful multicultural marketing programs from unsuccessful ones in an attempt to break down the most common barriers to entry.

1 Marketing Means More Than Advertising

This is probably the most common mistake marketers make when they plan their multicultural marketing programs: reducing an entire strategic plan to a single advertising flowchart, possibly featuring a creative message that is not fully relevant to the target, usually supported by a restricted media mix and a bare-minimum amount of continuity, reach, and frequency.

A strong multicultural marketing plan starts by assessing the state of your business from a multicultural perspective and analyzing the brand purchase funnel, distribution gaps, adequate sales channels, and customer service levels, as well as cross-selling and upselling strategies. A successful multicultural marketing plan includes relevant messaging strategies based on true consumer insights and ideally also touches on important aspects such as community partnerships and employee recruitment and engagement.

Learning: A multicultural marketing program includes a strong advertising plan, but it is not exclusively based on advertising.

2 Short-Term Focus

Frequently, when I ask why a certain brand doesn't have a strong multicultural marketing program, I hear the same answer: "We have tried it

DOI: 10.4324/9781003348931-14

before; it didn't work." However, when we assess these past programs, most of the time we realize that this conclusion was reached after reading a few weekly, maybe a few quarterly, data results.

When a brand decides to invest in multicultural segments with a focus on short-term results, there is a high probability that it will fail, since success in marketing tends to be the result of a consistent level of investment measured in years, not weeks or months, because any marketing program requires constant adjustments and fine-tuning, regardless of the segment being targeted.

Moreover, marketers tend to ignore the fact that brands may have different life cycles for different targets, meaning that multicultural consumers may not have reached the same level of awareness or experience with your brand like other consumers who have been exposed to your brand for many more years.

Learning: When it comes to multicultural marketing, long-term consistency is key.

3 The Investment Level Was Not Adequate

When multicultural segments in America represent over 40% of the country's population,[1] a significant percentage of your sales, and, in several cases, most (if not all) of your incremental sales growth will come from multicultural consumers. Nevertheless, when many companies only "invest" 10% or less of their marketing funds in multicultural marketing, they are not expecting ROI; what they are looking for, really, is a miracle.

In my experience, the majority of the brands investing in multicultural marketing under-invest when compared to the contribution these segments have on a brand's potential growth. This under-investment is mostly driven by an inability to reframe your current marketing resource allocation.

Most brands allocate their marketing funds based on plans from previous years, with room for small fine-tuning adjustments. This is an approach that protects the status quo and avoids transformational changes.

Given that multicultural marketing investments already start from a small base, chances are they probably will not reach their optimal investment level. This fuels the famous "incrementalism" illusion, which creates the perception that when marketers "find" incremental resources, they will definitely appropriately fund multicultural marketing programs. This is the wrong approach.

Learning: Your multicultural marketing investment should be proportional to the size of your opportunity, measured by either existing purchasing power or future growth projections.

4 Leadership Turnover

Most multicultural programs in the marketplace are connected to a passionate leader in the organization who is able to gather the minimum amount of resources to get the program started. Once this person leaves the position or the company, most multicultural programs tend to lose momentum, and resources tend to be reduced or completely eliminated until a new champion brings the idea back to life.

This cycle tends to repeat itself every four to five years, and it costs corporations a significant amount of money and energy, as most of the time they keep trying to reinvent, re-learn, and re-test what their predecessors have already done and learned, years ago. Leading organizations in multicultural marketing protect themselves from this cycle by imbedding the need for a robust and relevant multicultural marketing approach to the company's future growth strategy at the board level: CEOs and CFOs need to champion these programs, and CMOs and their teams need to implement them and make them part of their performance objectives.

Learning: Effective multicultural programs have longevity and have mechanisms to protect themselves from constant executive turnover. A top-down approach starting with the board of directors and C-suite is recommended.

5 Reaching Is Not Connecting

Most marketers believe that reaching multicultural consumers through a sophisticated media plan is enough. In reality, it does not necessarily mean that you're actually connecting with these consumers. Just because you are reaching someone does not mean you're connecting with them; it only means that they have an opportunity to see your ad. Recent studies on the topic of multicultural marketing commissioned by leading companies like Nielsen, MRI-Simmons, and Kantar have reached similar conclusions regarding the best approach to connect with ethnic consumers. It is fundamental to focus on culture, to understand the best context for your message, and to make your marketing message relatable, never stereotyped, never complacent to the target.

It is curious to see how some marketers invest a significant amount of money and time in understanding their media choices, but little attention and rigor is given to understanding what effective multicultural creative can really do. A great media plan with mediocre creative strategy and low production value will not improve your brand's performance. On the other hand, a great creative idea, based on meaningful insights and produced with craft, may not require a significant amount of media dollars to deliver great results.

Learning: When it comes to multicultural marketing, reaching the target is not enough. Building cultural affinity is more important than the quality of your media plan. The best-in-class marketers invest properly to develop effective multicultural creative messages.

6 Your Measurement Plan Is Not Adequate

Any measurement plan may have limitations, and understanding these limitations is key for assessing your results and acting on them. Measuring the effectiveness of multicultural marketing programs can be very challenging, as existing tools tend to have a limitation on their sample size or distributions. The lack of awareness of these limitations by most marketers, and how much they rely on these limited sources to make their decisions, surprises me.

In my experience, leading brands in multicultural marketing have invested in a combination of external and proprietary measurement tools, ranging from sales and market share performance to consumer attitudes and behaviors, social media listening, and messaging trackers. All of these measurement tools should be supported by robust data representation, including the size of the sample and composition breakdown, language preference, country of origin, generation, household income, educational level, and so on.

Learning: Having an understanding of your KPIs and, most importantly, how to measure them is key before implementing any multicultural marketing effort.

7 True Experts Are Not Involved

Sometimes decisions are made based on either stereotypical thinking or recommendations from executives who claim to understand the latest trends and opportunities around multicultural segments.

Almost every single day I read about a brand that messed up when it came to multicultural marketing even though most of them had "good intentions." In almost every case, it is clear that early involvement from truly seasoned multicultural experts could have prevented the troubles faced by the brands and, most importantly, minimized the negative impact on the brands' reputation and saved these companies money.

True experts are those who have significant experience in creating and executing multicultural marketing programs and can be either internal (i.e. employees) or external, like consultants, research companies, and communication companies (like ad agencies). For years, most organizations trusted their diverse employees to handle their multicultural efforts. However, while being from a minority background can be helpful, it's not enough to make an individual expert in multicultural marketing.

Learning: Effective multicultural marketing requires expertise, which can't be confused with having a diverse set of people around you. If they don't have experience in multicultural marketing, their views may be biased.

Effective multicultural marketing programs should be built with a combination of learnings, successes, and failures. Early obstacles can be discouraging, but avoiding this list of mistakes can help your company get back on track. We are reaching a point in our country when not having a multicultural marketing plan is no longer an option, but having an effective one still is.

Note

1 U.S. Census Bureau, 2010 Census, 2020 Census.

Chapter 13

If You Want Your Hispanic Marketing to Fly High, Upgrade to Business Class

As part of my work, one of the most common questions I get asked, either by clients or prospects, is "What is the best way to structure my multicultural marketing efforts from an organizational design perspective?" This is an important question, as this marketing discipline has evolved over the past decade, and today it requires a much higher level of expertise and specialization.

Here are some of my observations based on several years of experience at the client and agency sides.

First, it is important to note that the vast majority of corporations in America don't have a dedicated approach towards multicultural marketing; consequently, they have no formal strategy or structure in place to capture this segment's growth opportunities.

Some companies leave it to the people responsible for diversity and inclusion (who in most cases may have limited marketing background since most come from the HR sector). Others ask their existing brand teams to manage and informally "handle it" on a reactive basis. Often, this is assigned to an employee with ethnic heritage irrespective of this person's actual experience in the area—"Isn't your last name Martinez? Great, you're now leading our company's Hispanic marketing efforts!"

Multicultural marketing segmentation has been around for almost 50 years now, and of course, the companies that have been doing a better job (probably representing 30% of active marketers) have some sort of multicultural organization in place. While some organizations function with a Center of Excellence structure, also known as COE, others prefer to have multicultural experts embedded in their existing marketing organizations or brand structures.

Recently, however, I have noticed a slightly different type of structure, one that approaches the multicultural opportunity from a more comprehensive business standpoint, and that entails the creation of a stand-alone Business Unit exclusively dedicated to the multicultural marketing opportunity. Consider it a Center of Excellence on steroids!

This is an exciting development, one that makes much sense in my opinion. First, because it elevates the multicultural marketing opportunity

DOI: 10.4324/9781003348931-15

beyond advertising, avoiding one of the biggest mistakes companies make with this segment. Advertising is essential, of course, but a comprehensive approach like this one also helps companies treat their efforts as a business imperative, bringing with it the discipline that other business decisions are exposed to, such as the creation of a business case, specific actions to address eventual opportunities and vulnerabilities, allocation of resources on a multi-year perspective, and the alignment of key performance indicators, just to name a few.

It is remarkable to me the number of companies in corporate America that support multicultural marketing efforts but don't have a detailed business plan behind it, often reducing their efforts with this important growth sector to an advertising flowchart instead.

I am privileged to work closely with two brands that are leading the way on this new trend of structuring their multicultural marketing efforts as a Business Unit.

One of them is Pepsi. After several years of trying different approaches when it came to Hispanic marketing, in 2018 PepsiCo. decided to create a dedicated Hispanic Business Unit, with its own general manager, Marissa Solis, a PepsiCo veteran, who now is working at the NFL, as the league's SVP Global Brand and Consumer Marketing.

I asked Marissa why Pepsi decided to elevate the Hispanic opportunity to the status of a Business Unit, and she said,

> It all started with a very strong business case. When you see the actual numbers of what Hispanic growth represents for our food and beverage categories, it would be crazy to ignore it. However, developing a business case was not enough. We had to ensure that there was a commitment to this cohort across the entire business from our CEO to the front line. Having a dedicated business unit signals to our organization, our consumers and our retail partners that we are serious about rolling up our sleeves to both engage authentically and meet the growing needs of this diverse and dynamic community.

One of the aspects of this new structure that is very different from other companies is the fact that Marissa had a dual reporting structure: she reported to her company's CMO and their head of sales. This strong connection to sales in my experience helps to push the multicultural business opportunity to the top of an organization's agenda.

Another company that took a similar approach is Sprint. In early 2015 the then CEO, Marcelo Claure, had the vision to reinvest in the Hispanic segment. He established a new Hispanic Business Unit with its own general manager, putting Roger Sole to lead their efforts. Later, in recognition of his leadership, Sole was promoted to be the company's CMO.

After four years of continuous support, Sprint's Hispanic marketing efforts brought significant results across different performance indicators and contributed significantly to the company's turnaround story.

Whether your organization can benefit from this approach or you think your company is too small to create a whole new business unit dedicated to the multicultural segment, there are a few learnings almost any size organization can benefit from:

- Start with a business case; estimate how much the multicultural consumers bring to your organization, and ideally, how much more they could bring in the future.
- Multicultural marketing is more than multicultural advertising, and a comprehensive plan across all marketing functions is the best way to create lasting and effective results.
- Make these efforts a top priority at the C-level suite, starting with the CEO, preferably with strong support from the CFO and the sales organization.
- Leave multicultural marketing efforts to experts and seasoned executives. If you don't have one within your organization, consider hiring one.
- Invest according to the opportunity. Do multicultural consumers bring 50% of your sales? Why only invest 10% of your budget on multicultural marketing then?
- Play for the long term. Short-term results are welcomed, but real winners in this segment are based on how consistent their efforts are, measured in years, not quarters, and how resilient their programs are to changes in their company's leadership.

As we start a new decade, facing strong headwinds regarding our economy, the takeaways from this chapter may be a great way to "take off." Makes no sense to get on the "standby list" if you can upgrade to Business Class, spread your wings, and make your brands soar.

Case Study—How Brands Can Provide Grassroots and Community Support with a Sense of Purpose

P&G—"Hispanic Progress Is a PRO for America"

Executive Summary

This is the story of how P&G strengthened its reputation as a force for good among Hispanics and invited all society to recognize that Hispanic success equals American success.

Over the years, P&G has taken great pride in supporting Hispanic communities through education, social impact, and relief efforts. That's why, in celebration of Hispanic Heritage Month in 2021, the brand introduced a new comprehensive initiative to accelerate the progress of Hispanic communities across the U.S.

A core element of this effort was P&G's partnership with the "Hispanic Star Alliance." With the support of Hispanic Star, P&G and P&G brands like Always, Tampax, Vicks, Gillette, Old Spice, Crest, and Oral-B are creating and helping expand programs to provide Hispanics with access to better education, better health, and better jobs; fight discrimination; and promote equality and inclusion.

Within this context, the purpose of this campaign was as follows:

1   Strengthen P&G's reputation as a force for good among Hispanics
2   Drive awareness and recognition of the Hispanic Star Alliance

The Business Challenge

Countless studies and stats prove that Hispanics are helping drive prosperity and reinvigorating the culture and the economy in the U.S.

- Hispanics represent $1.9 trillion in purchasing power in the U.S.
- The U.S. Hispanic GDP is $2.7 trillion.
- If U.S. Hispanics were a standalone economy, they would be the third fastest-growing economy in the entire world after China and India.
- Sixty percent of new homes are bought by U.S. Hispanics.
- The federal, state, and local tax revenue generated by Hispanics is $215 billion.
- Latinos are job makers, business leaders, and entrepreneurs. Eight out of ten new businesses are started by Hispanics. One out of every five entrepreneurs is a Hispanic.
- Hispanic women create small businesses six times faster than any other group in the U.S.

But despite these and many other contributions, there are still people in the U.S. who see Hispanics as "takers." They see Hispanic gains as their loss in a zero-sum game. In fact, some high-profile media personalities explicitly say that Hispanics are taking away jobs and don't contribute to society.

The Insights/Strategy

Challenge stereotypes, while celebrating all the positives of Hispanic progress, and boldly call for all society to recognize that Hispanic success equals American success.

Idea/Execution

Showcasing "Hispanic progress is a **PRO** for America." With this concept, P&G showed that Hispanic progress fuels America's progress, which is why P&G joined forces with the Hispanic Star Alliance to empower Hispanic communities through better jobs, better education, and better health.

The campaign was structured in an owned and paid media ecosystem where P&G built several pieces of content spread across the three months of the campaign. This included a series of videos, audios, billboards, retail activations, social media content, and multiple digital formats to present all the "Pros" Hispanics bring to America.

Results

- Neuroscience research conducted by "Nielsen Neuro" showed that our Powering Progress campaign had an emotionally motivating narrative resonating strongly with all viewers, irrespective of race/ethnicity. The spot delivered strong action intent, in line with P&G's norms, and above-average emotional engagement.
- Qualitative research also showed that the message gave Hispanics an overwhelming sense of pride and inspiration. Non-Hispanics felt the message was positive, progressive, and relevant.
- Research also shows that our Powering Progress, 30-sec film, significantly improved the perception of P&G as a brand that's celebrating and "empowering" Hispanics.

- Finally, the campaign has also helped the "Hispanic Star Alliance" gain traction and visibility in the corporate world and local communities. After P&G joined the alliance and launched the campaign, the number of companies participating in the Hispanic Star program has grown around 30% (which has resulted in new funding that allowed the program to feed over 2 million Hispanic families in need and provide hundreds of scholarships to Hispanic youth).

Author's Comments

P&G is one of the leading advertisers in the world, and whatever direction is taken with their marketing efforts has a significant impact on the whole industry, given their size, scale, and importance.

By signaling the importance of investing in grass-root support, the company demonstrates a strong understanding of the Hispanic segment, as most Hispanic consumers expect marketers not only to advertise in a relevant and culturally meaningful way but also to invest in activities that support their community.

More companies should consider connecting their advertising with relevant community-focused efforts, creating a new and more human marketing approach. P&G's "force for good" approach is an instant industry benchmark.

Part III

The Minority-Majority Shift—The Impact on Business

Chapter 14

Two Decades That Will Change America

There is no doubt that demographic changes in America and the evolution towards a minority-majority population will have profound and transformational consequences on the business environment for years and decades to come.

While the premise of demographic shifts is not new, one of its less-discussed consequences does require special attention, namely how this demographic trend is reshaping the population and makeup of cities and states across the country, and how this process will create unique challenges and opportunities for marketers.

At a National Level

Let's start with the basics. Based on the latest data from the U.S. Census Bureau, the country's population has grown by 7% in the past decade. However, all of this growth was driven by the minority populations, since the non-Hispanic White Caucasian population actually decreased by 3% during the same time period.[1]

In the last decade, the country added close to 28 million new minority residents to its population.[2] To better understand this number's magnitude, consider that Australia, the world's 13th economy,[3] has a total population of 26 million.[4]

Why is this important? Consider the fact that countries without population growth have a higher probability of economic stagnation. Just look at the economic and demographic trends from countries like Japan and Italy over the past decades.

Since 2010, the AAPI population has grown at an incredible 35% rate, six times faster than the population growth rate of the Black segment, reaching a total of 6% of the country's population, while the Black population share stayed relatively stable at 12%.[5]

Furthermore, the Hispanic population continued its high growth trajectory with over a 20% increase, adding 12 million new residents to the country and

DOI: 10.4324/9781003348931-17

reaching 19% of the country's population share. These three major minority segments together represent close to 40% of the U.S. population.[6]

Negative Growth Is Pervasive across the Country

According to the Census data, three states (Mississippi, Illinois, and West Virginia) have experienced total population declines during the past decade. Moreover, five additional states (Connecticut, Michigan, Ohio, Pennsylvania, and Wyoming) have experienced stagnant growth, with a population growth rate below 2%.[7]

While there are several reasons to explain these declines, one thing they have in common is the fact that their minority population hasn't grown faster than the White Caucasian population.

In total, 35 states have experienced a decline in their White Caucasian population in the past decade[8]—all but three of them still grew their total population thanks to the much faster growth of their minority populations.

The Minority-Majority States and the Path Forward

In the U.S. there are six states: California, Hawaii, New Mexico, Texas, Nevada, and Maryland plus the District of Columbia, representing 25% of the country's population, that already have a minority-majority population composition.[9]

Over the next decade a number of additional states will likely join them, including Georgia (49.9% ethnic minority population), Florida (48%), New Jersey (48%), New York (48%), Arizona (47%), Mississippi (45%), and Louisiana (44%).[10]

Some Potential Consequences

Coupled with COVID-19-induced population shifts away from big city/urban centers that are still being tracked by economists and demographers, these changes in population dynamics across the states will be consequential and will impact several aspects of our lives, including both the public and private sectors. Three of them are listed:

1 Business Footprint Will Reset

What part of the footprint you ask? All of it. From where to produce and distribute products and services to where their suppliers are located and what kind of physical or virtual experience businesses will offer in the future—they will all be heavily impacted by post-COVID-19 business practices and these population shifts.

Marketers will have to reimagine the way they compete at the local level. For example, from recruiting the right mix of employees to better reflect the market you're targeting to offering multi-language capabilities online and in-store, or assessing the best merchandise mix offered in specific zip codes. These are just a few decisions organizations will have to rethink over the next few years.

2 Cities Will Compete to Attract Multicultural Residents

After the "Great Resignation" wave that started in April 2021, it is very likely that over the next decades, cities and states will have to compete for talent in order to drive growth, as they try to stay relevant from an economic, social, and political perspective. Some cities and states will understand that creating an environment that welcomes and promotes multiculturalism among other values may be the key to their success.

3 Redefining Political Myths

The traditional concepts of Red State/Blue State also seem to be changing. Of course, this is not something that will happen over a few election cycles, but if you consider the next two decades, there is no doubt that the U.S. will experience a significant disruption of these old concepts. Look no further than the growth of "Blue" values candidates in typical "Red" states like Texas and Georgia.

As in anything related to the country's shift towards a minority-majority population, the flow of population changes within cities and states will be the equivalent of "reshuffling" the deck of cards for many companies and brands. The time has come for marketers and business leaders not only to monitor or assess the consequences of these changes but also to put plans into action. Real competitive advantage will be based on the ability to transform your business before it is too late.

Notes

1 U.S. Census Bureau, 2010 Census, 2020 Census.
2 U.S. Census Bureau, 2010 Census, 2020 Census.
3 International Monetary Fund (IMF), 2022.
4 U.S. Census Bureau, International Database 2022.
5 U.S. Census Bureau, 2010 Census, 2020 Census.
6 U.S. Census Bureau, 2010 Census, 2020 Census.
7 U.S. Census Bureau, 2010 Census, 2020 Census.
8 U.S. Census Bureau, 2010 Census, 2020 Census.
9 U.S. Census Bureau, 2010 Census, 2020 Census.
10 U.S. Census Bureau, 2010 Census, 2020 Census.

Chapter 15

The Surge of Multiracial Families

As we have already discussed, over the past few decades America's population growth has been fueled by minority segments. Still, one less discussed consequence of this demographic change is the significant increase in multiracial households. While there's not enough quantitative research on this, the data from the 2020 Census report shows that the number of non-Hispanic Americans who identify as multiracial has jumped by 127% over the past decade.[1]

For people who identified as Hispanic, the increase was even higher, according to the same Census data and changes in the way the Census tracks race and ethnicity have helped many Americans fully embrace their multiracial roots like never before. For Hispanics in particular, the numbers are impressive as can be seen in the following table.

In addition to self-identification, another reason why more Americans are embracing their multiracial roots is because the number of interracial marriages in America has also increased significantly in the past two decades. A 2018 Census[2] report on interracial marriage says that the number of interracial couples in the U.S. grew from approximately 7% in 2000 to at least 10% in 2016, the most recent year for this data.

A variation of the 3% points in 16 years may not seem like much, but when we analyze the data from an absolute standpoint, one can assess its magnitude. In 2000, these multiracial/multiethnic couples were estimated at approximately 4 million, and in 2016, this number was almost 6 million, which represents almost a 50% increase! And I believe this trend will only accelerate in the years to come.

According to the "Growth in Interracial and Interethnic Married-Couple Households" report, the vast majority (40%) of the biracial couples were comprised by non-Hispanic Whites (NHW) and Hispanic couples, followed by 14% of couples comprised by non-Hispanic Whites and AAPI individuals, and 8% of interracial couples between non-Hispanic Whites and Black individuals.

The *New York Times* article[3] "Behind the Surprising Jump in Multiracial Americans, Several Theories," by Sabrina Tavernise, Tariro Mzezewa, and Giulia Heyward, discusses the growth of multicultural Americans in the 2020 Census:

DOI: 10.4324/9781003348931-18

Hispanics	2010 Census	2020 Census	% Var.
White	26,785,713	12,579,626	−53%
Black	1,243,471	1,163,862	−6%
Asian/PI	267,565	335,278	25%
American Indian/Alaska Native	685,150	1,475,436	115%
Some Other Race	18,503,103	26,225,882	42%
Two or More Races	3,042,592	20,299,960	567%
Total	**50,477,594**	**62,080,044**	

Part of the rise in people identifying as multiracial was simply the growing diversity of the American population. As the newest immigrants, largely from Asia and Latin America, have children and grandchildren, and those Americans form families, they are much more likely to marry outside their racial or ethnic groups than their parents were. Among newlywed Hispanic people who were born in the United States, about 39 percent marry someone who is not Hispanic, according to the Pew Research Center. For the AAPI segment, that number is about the same.

Looking beyond the numbers, one of the crucial aspects of this trend for business leaders to understand is how these biracial families retain both cultural backgrounds while still navigating the mainstream Anglo culture.

To get some further guidance on this topic, I reached out to David Morse, author, speaker, and CEO of the New American Dimension, a research company that studies topics like this one. Moreover, David also lives in a biracial household and has firsthand experience on the subject.

Isaac Mizrahi: What can we all learn as a society from a biracial household?

David Morse: *It's impossible to be "color blind" when you live in a biracial household, as the realities of race in America are such that when one is non-White, there is never the privilege of not thinking about race. For family members who look non-White, race is part of their everyday reality, and many suffer the same macro and microaggressions as their non-mixed, non-White counterparts. Other family members who might look "racially ambiguous" are continually being asked by others what race they are, which many find not only to be a constant annoyance, but actually offensive. Finally, for Whites like me, living in a mixed-race family, we get an opportunity to see up close what it is like to be a non-White person in America, though we still benefit from our White privilege when we are out and about.*

Mizrahi: From a business/marketing perspective, is a biracial household the same as one that is not?

Morse: *We've done much research with biracial Americans, particularly younger ones. We've found that so many embrace multiple identities, often identifying with both parents' ethnicities. On the other hand, parents, though tending to be more culturally and racially empathetic than those in single race relationships, also grew up as being one race or another, and often possess much of the mindset that they grew up with.*

In other words, each family member will be different, and for children, how they respond to an ad may reflect their physical appearance and how that child is treated by society. For instance, my children are half Asian, half Indian. One daughter is light and looks a lot like me. My other daughter is relatively dark, with Indian features. They get treated differently. Their young friends often ask how they can be "two different races." Not only are biracial households different—but also each member of a biracial family usually has unique challenges.

Mizrahi: How hard is it for parents of a biracial household to teach their kids about their multicultural heritage background?

Morse: *It can be challenging in a society that espouses "color blindness" and where race is often a taboo subject. But having discussions about race is very important, mainly when the children are male and might look Black or Hispanic. They need to be taught about racism, and particularly, to always be overtly cooperative with police officers and to keep their hands visible. They need to learn that they matter, although certain people might look down on them or hold lower expectations of them. And it's important to instill in all biracial children a sense of being proud of who they are and proud of their ancestors. It can be tough, particularly in a Black/White household where the children might look Black. However, one parent may be White and directly unfamiliar with how to navigate American racism safely.*

Mizrahi: Is multiculturalism good for the country? If so, why?

Morse: *I sure think so. Whereas race mixing has been common in some societies, for instance, in many Latin American countries, anti-miscegenation (race mixing) laws and hypodescent rules (like the "one drop rule" that defines who is Black) were the norms in the United States. Multiracialism helps us get over a racist past and our aversion to even talking about race. Multiculturalism will strengthen us as a country. The division is what makes us weak, and in the United States, race has been THE top divider. On the contrary, diversity and bringing different perspectives and experiences to the table will make us truly great. As the United States becomes increasingly multicultural, we need to become equally as multifaceted in our worldview in terms of its demographics.*

In terms of multiracial families, interracial marriage is often used by sociologists as a measure of social distance. In other words, the more interracial marriage there is, the more it can be said that racial barriers are diminishing. However, we have a long way to go. Interracial marriage, though high between Hispanics and non-Hispanic Whites and AAPI with non-Hispanic Whites individuals, is relatively low between Whites and Black individuals, due to White racism and pressure within the Black community to marry other Blacks. If we are to be truly multicultural, the lines between Black and White need to diminish.

As the country moves towards a minority-majority society, we expect further growth in multiracial families, which will increase the need for advertisers to understand that a one-size-fits-all message strategy won't be as effective as it used to be in the 1960s, 1970s, and 1980s. Developing in-depth knowledge when approaching the racial and ethnic nuances in America will be an essential skill set for marketers, today and in the years to come, since truly connecting with multiracial families may hold the key to unlocking future business growth.

Notes

1 U.S. Census Bureau, 2010 Census, 2020 Census.
2 Growth in Interracial and Interethnic Married-Couple Households BRITTANY RICO, ROSE M. KREIDER AND LYDIA ANDERSON JULY 09, 2018.
3 www.nytimes.com/2021/08/13/us/census-multiracial-identity.html

Chapter 16

The Tech World Faces a Reboot

When I started working on this chapter about the impact of the demographic changes we are facing in America from a technological standpoint, I quickly realized that the information was rich enough to fill, not just a small chapter but, rather, a whole book.

Without being able to fully grasp the impact of the post-COVID-19 era on consumers and technology, I have tried to summarize in this chapter some of the key trends impacting brands and marketers as a result of the convergence of technological advancements and changing demographics:

Minorities Over-Index in New Tech Adoption

What most people don't realize is that all minority segments over-index on technology usage, which makes some experts call these consumers "technology optimists." Furthermore, these minority users tend to be early adopters and influencers when it comes to setting the trends that may impact the broader marketplace.

I believe that, in the coming decades, the demographic changes in America will further accelerate this trend even more, and that the manufacturers and retailers that dedicate a disproportionate amount of resources to understanding their consumer target's needs and behaviors will be in a strong position to win in the marketplace.

The good news is that some leading tech companies have started to expand the concept of multicultural marketing, especially when it comes to their product development process. In order to get a better understanding of just what they are doing, I spoke with Annie Jean-Baptiste, head of Product Inclusion at Google, who described her company's approach to product development:

> Google's goal is to create products that reflect all of our users—no matter who they are or where they live. In order to do that, diversity and inclusion has to be a commitment both as it relates to an organization's culture and in its processes. Product Inclusion is about bringing

DOI: 10.4324/9781003348931-19

an inclusive lens to the product design process so that perspectives from underrepresented users are highlighted, leading to better outcomes for everyone. We've done research on the business case for inclusion, and both underrepresented and majority consumers prefer inclusive products.

The New Digital Divide

For many years we have heard about the Digital Divide, which describes a gap in internet access rates when comparing minority households, mostly from lower-income Black and Hispanic users, and the rest of the country. While we celebrate the fact that minority consumers have closed this gap through the adoption of mobile devices as their primary source to access the internet, it is important to recognize that some of these consumers will still lag when it comes to having access to high-speed internet, either at home or at school.

Closing this gap is extremely important since we are facing a job market that will be more impacted by automation. These technological advances will disproportionately impact individuals that work in jobs threatened by labor automation. This is an important discussion as we are in the early stages of 5G technology adoption in this country, which promises to unlock significant opportunities for more products and services that not only rely on heavy usage of technology but also may require a higher technological standard from an educational standpoint.

The Bipartisan Infrastructure Law passed by Congress in 2022 ensures that every American will have access to high-speed internet, but failure to close the so-called Digital Divide may further marginalize a significant share of our population, limiting the consumer market growth for some industries and categories while making our country's productivity more limited for decades to come.

Lack of Representation in Silicon Valley

Over the past few years, we have witnessed a rising awareness of the lack of diversity in Silicon Valley. Why is this an important topic? Because a business community that better reflects our country will have a higher probability of developing innovative products and services that can benefit the society it serves, thereby being more successful in the marketplace.

At the 2020 Davos convening in Switzerland, Goldman Sachs announced it won't take public companies that don't have at least one diverse board member. As part of this announcement, Goldman Sachs CEO, David Solomon, mentioned that companies with at least one diverse member on the board of directors have been performing much better when compared to those that don't.

Finally, in August 2021, the Securities and Exchange Commission (SEC) approved the Nasdaq Stock Market's proposal to amend its listing standards to encourage greater board diversity and to require board diversity disclosures for Nasdaq-listed companies. Starting in 2022, Nasdaq-listed companies will be required to (1) publicly disclose board-level diversity statistics on an annual basis using a standardized matrix template under Nasdaq Rule 5606 and (2) have, or disclose why they do not have, a minimum of two diverse board members under Nasdaq Rule 5605(f).

We expect to see more initiatives like these in the years to come, including the need for business leaders to focus more on overall employee diversity recruitment, better mentoring/sponsorships for diverse employees—so they can grow in their careers to senior levels in their organization—and more minorities working and owning VC firms to support a more ethnically diverse universe of startup companies.

Thankfully, many people are trying to accelerate this change.

To better understand how the startup universe is evolving, I spoke to Melissa Medina, co-founder and president of eMerge Americas, a Miami-based global technology platform and conference.

> One of the reasons I helped launch eMerge Americas was to foster a unique tech ecosystem in Miami, a city that already looks like the future of our country—minority dominant and built by immigrants. We launched this effort not to compete with Silicon Valley but, rather, to help create a launchpad of ideas that would welcome a diverse group of entrepreneurs. Although Miami is in the early stages of building a thriving technology hub, it certainly has all of the ingredients to become a sustainable, diverse, and inclusive ecosystem. Miami is consistently rated amongst the top entrepreneurial cities in startup activity in the USA and the top five U.S. metro areas for female entrepreneurship. As a female Latina in tech myself, it is extremely important to me to show the next generation of women that there is just as much room in the tech world for women than there is for men. No matter how we slice it, a more diverse workforce is always better for businesses and the economy. I think we are beginning to prove that great ideas and innovation need not be captive of Silicon Valley.

Is Artificial Intelligence Unbiased?

While we can't predict what the future will look like from a technological standpoint, I believe we can safely predict that we will see and experience higher importance and impact of Artificial Intelligence and Machine Learning in almost every aspect of our lives.

These trends beg a few hard questions as well: Are we better off when we trust machines to be bias-free? Will our society be better off because computers don't carry with them misconceptions about race, ethnicity, or sexual orientation? Or will machines only perpetuate preconceived ideas and biases because they tend to mirror the idea they are exposed to today, as imperfect they are?

Privacy Regulation Will Impact Marketing and Advertising

Last but not least is the topic of privacy. To avoid problems with consumer privacy, many browsers have been moving away from cookies for some time now. But when Google announced in 2020 that they would stop supporting third-party cookies, the advertising world freaked out. The phase-out of third-party cookies on Google will be complete by the end of 2024 and presents marketers with both challenges and opportunities.

A series of other privacy laws and regulations already block advertisers from targeting consumers based on their race or ethnic background. While brands will still have the ability to use language as a proxy, these changes will significantly limit the ability to directly reach bilingual and bicultural consumers.

A negative consequence of the changes in a marketer's ability to target their digital campaigns through cookies could be that marketers will treat these consumers as the general population perpetuating the false assumption of one-size-fits-all when it comes to messaging. However, some leading brands see these restrictions as an opportunity to build their own culture-based targeting strategies, with contextual relevancy and intent-based marketing. What does this mean? Even if you can't flag me as Hispanic, if you know my taste in sports, music, and food and if you understand my news consumption preferences, you will know that I am very close to the Hispanic culture. Research shows that messages that leverage these cultural cues are more effective than messages that treat me as a general market consumer.

Furthermore, building first-party data strategies that recognize the importance of cultural nuances will be more critical than ever before and brands that don't recognize culture as an integral part of their growth strategies may miss out on effective ways to increase their media investments' ROI.

It's time for the marketing industry to start having a debate about how technology will impact (and be impacted by) the demographic changes we are facing as a country. Corporations and marketers have a unique opportunity in the months and years ahead, to embrace this technological disruption and capitalize on opportunities in shifts of consumers' preferences and consumption patterns.

Chapter 17

It's Time for a New Script in Hollywood

The year was 2009, and Katie Elmore, then Communication and Development VP at a non-profit in Vermont, partnered with writers Carlos Portugal and Kathleen Bedoya to come up with a drama series focused on Latino teens living in East Los Angeles titled *East Los High*. Later in the process, she partnered with Brazilian producer Mauricio Mota to strategize how the show could be distributed.

They were passionate about the idea. After all, they felt that despite the demographic growth of the Hispanic community in the U.S., they were not seeing enough stories coming out of Hollywood that portray the dreams, lives, struggles, and aspirations from the perspective of the U.S.-born Hispanic youth.

With a creative take fueled by demographic tools, qualitative and quantitative data, and insights provided by partnering with nonprofits, foundations, and community leaders all over the country, Katie and Mauricio started knocking on every possible door. Meeting after meeting the response was the same—"interesting idea, but we're not interested in producing it." Some went a step further and suggested that they would consider producing it if the show was made to be "less Hispanic" and with an ensemble cast.

The *East Los High* team was facing a dilemma—either compromise on their vision to see their dream become a reality or continue the creative hustle, maintaining the artistic integrity of the idea. They decided to go with the latter.

Katie spent a long time raising funds through grants and donations, and they decided to write and produce 24 episodes of the show and many hours of digital content for the show's social media channels on a shoestring budget. After many conversations with possible buyers, Hulu emerged the most compelling one.

Hulu launched *East Los High* on June 13, 2013, and to everyone's surprise, two weeks later, it beat *Grey's Anatomy* on the platform. Sixty episodes, six Emmys, and a Cannes Lions later, the show is still watched by new audiences all over the world, despite ending its run in 2017.

DOI: 10.4324/9781003348931-20

The story of *East Los High* is probably similar to a lot of other stories that represent minority creators and producers in this country, albeit one that had the opportunity to be produced. I spoke with Mauricio Mota about the experience producing this extraordinary hit within the Hollywood system and here's what he had to say:

Isaac Mizrahi: Reflecting on your journey to produce *East Los High*, what were your key learnings?

Mauricio Mota: *That Hollywood, and many marketers as well, are still in the business of renting or buying audiences instead of developing them. That makes them ignore underserved audiences and become dependent on established media players.*

Another important lesson is that you should not create a compelling story without creating an ecosystem around it that will keep it alive by the connections it will make with fans. And when you partner with NGOs, foundations, community leaders, and activists, don't do that for lip service—they are more powerful and insightful than you can imagine. We owe a lot of our achievements to those partnerships.

Mizrahi: Do you think that today, you'd have a better environment to sell *East Los High*? Why?

Mota: *I don't know. Maybe with the sudden "awakening" of Hollywood and advertisers, yes. But I still think that Latino youth are still taken for granted or simply ignored. So, I would say 50/50.*

Mizrahi: How do you think Hollywood will adapt to America's new minority-majority in the years and decades to come?

Mota: *It will adapt slowly while other platforms and media like social media, gaming, comic books, publishing, and maybe brands catch up and design hundreds of Intellectual Properties and experiences that they will have to pay extra to tap into. But let's see. I hope I'm wrong.*

Our second protagonist in this conversation about Hollywood is Deniese Davis, co-founder and COO of ColorCreative Inc., and producer at Issa Rae Productions.

Deniese has been involved in several top shows, including HBO's *Insecure*, *The Misadventures of Awkward Black Girl*, and *A Black Lady Sketch Show*. Moreover, Deniese has been one of the country's leading voices pushing for the increase of diversity in films and TV. Here is an edited summary of our conversation:

Isaac Mizrahi: Are stories told from a diverse set of lenses attractive enough to all consumers?

Deniese Davis: *Absolutely. For decades, minorities in America have been watching and enjoying the content on large and small screens written, produced, directed, and acted by White Caucasian professionals. I believe content told from a multicultural perspective has significant relatability power, and this will make these stories more interesting.*

Mizrahi: Despite some recent progress on the inclusion of diverse storytelling in Hollywood, what's still missing?

Davis: *Diverse ownership. I believe we need to continue the evolution and have diverse creative minds sitting at the table not as "talent-to-hire" but as investors. We need more diverse ownership in production companies and studios as a way to increase the amount of diversity in our industry, on and off-screen.*

Mizrahi: How hard was it for you to succeed as a Black producer in an environment notorious for its lack of diversity?

Davis: *Extremely hard, even though I knew what I wanted to be and what I wanted to do, and I had very few role models to inspire me and guide me. That's why I take full responsibility to mentor and coach young diverse talent. I am a true believer in always leaving the door open for a new professional relationship as a way to counter an industry with so many barriers to entry.*

Mizrahi: Finally, how do you see the concept of "allyship" applied to Hollywood?

Davis: *I am a big believer in the idea of different minority groups working together. I believe we will see more of this type of collaboration in the years to come; first, because we will have strength in numbers, amplifying our voice. Moreover, when you're from a diverse segment, you bring a sense of respect and understanding from different angles and distinct stories.*

The challenge to make Hollywood more diverse is significant. It has several different dimensions, from creating the space for young talent to tell their stories with a distinct perspective to providing pathways for multicultural talent into the whole Hollywood ecosystem that includes producers, studios, and off-screen and on-screen casting that help make these stories feel genuine.

But progress is palatable; with more competition for content and fragmentation of media choices, consumers today have more access to different types of content than ever. And based on America's demographics and cultural trends that value the power of authentic stories, the demand for diversity creators in Hollywood will only increase in the years to come.

Like other areas of our society, there will be a competition for talent that can guide the industry to adapt and change. This is extremely important as decisions based on misconceived ideas will cost money and reputation. It's time for a paradigm shift, as minorities become the majority, Hollywood better be ready to change the script!

Chapter 18

For Sports Marketing, It's Game On

There is no denying the importance that sports marketing has as a brand/business-building tool for companies to connect with consumers. Not to mention the fact that sports have significant power to shape a society's culture!

For this analysis, I used data from MRI-Simmons, looking at the sports preferences of consumers under the age of 25, broken down by ethnicity—non-Hispanic White, Hispanic, Black, and AAPI respondents—in order to compare similarities and differences.

My analysis showed that when it comes to the relationship between sports preference and demographics in America, the picture is mixed. While there are some noticeable differences in preferences by different ethnic groups, there are also important commonalities. These differences and commonalities will be felt even more in the coming decades, since the impact of the choices demonstrated by minority consumers will increase exponentially, mainly the preferences of Hispanic and AAPI consumers, given their fast population growth. By contrast, the sports preferences of non-Hispanic White consumers may be less influential over time.

It's a Soccer World

Soccer has significant growth potential in the years ahead. Already the favorite sport among Hispanic Americans, soccer has a robust preference among AAPI fans as well, and it has been growing amongst non-Hispanic White fans too.

One challenge facing soccer is that unlike other major sports leagues in America, their fans are spread among different franchises, including Major League Soccer, the Mexican Fútbol League, and, growing in popularity, the European National leagues (mainly the ones from England, Spain, Italy, and Germany) as well as Europe's Champions League, making it harder to reach the whole spectrum of soccer fans with one sponsorship program. But this diversity among soccer leagues also offers a diverse set of options for marketers to align with.

DOI: 10.4324/9781003348931-21

I spoke with Ricardo Fort, former Coke's head of Global Sponsorships and founder of Sport By Fort Consulting, who is one of the authorities when it comes to sports marketing and is directly involved with the trends and opportunities when it comes to sports marketing. Here is his take on the growth of soccer in America:

> As the profile of the American fan becomes more international, particularly with Hispanics, soccer is likely to be the biggest winner. Thanks to the growth of the MLS, the increasing availability of international soccer content in open TV and, mostly, the incredible global success of the women's national team, new generations of fans will be as familiar with Mbappes and Alex Morgan as their grandparents were with Joe Montana and their parents are with Tom Brady.

The Three Major Leagues

From a demographic standpoint, America's favorite sports leagues—NFL, NBA, and MLB—face a mixed set of challenges for the decades to come.

- NFL, without a doubt America's favorite sport, has an excellent position with Black and AAPI sports fans, with a substantial appeal to Hispanic fans as well, which explains why we see more outreach efforts from the league playing games in Mexico City and increased availability of NFL games being broadcast in Spanish.
- Similarly, the NBA has also been investing in their marketing efforts to become more international, including efforts to connect with Latin American and Asian markets where basketball is very popular. These efforts, combined with their stronghold among Black sports fans, make the league another strong contender to benefit from the shifts in demographics in the years to come.
- For MLB, the challenge for the next decades is less about connecting with multicultural fans but more about how to make a game considered too long and played during too long of a season of interest to a generation of consumers who are used to "everything now."

Weak Spots

On the other side of the spectrum are Nascar and NHL, which significantly under-index in preference among sports fans from minority ethnic backgrounds, when compared to their non–Hispanic White preference levels. If these leagues don't become more relevant to minority fans, they risk experiencing declines in attendance at their events and in viewership, which could affect their broadcasting fees from media partners, and ultimately sponsorship dollars from corporations.

The Idol Factor

Idols are extremely important for building leagues, franchises, and brands. Having icons from the multicultural segment is a great step towards the path of making your brand more relevant to multicultural fans. Still, you don't need to be from a minority background to connect with minority consumers, as pointed out by Freddy Rolón: vice president and general manager of ESPN Deportes, "Kobe Bryant was a great example of an athlete that connected with multicultural consumers. He spoke Spanish, had publicly demonstrated his passion for soccer, which was a departure from the U.S. centric type of sports idol we are used to seeing," he said, citing Sports Poll data, a study about sports interest in America.

In spite of the fast changes we will face during the next decades, according to Rolón, a few things won't change:

> Despite all the future demographic changes, one thing that will stay the same is that there will be very few opportunities for brands to connect with a massive audience of fans like they do during a live sports event. Live sports bring scale because people want to watch sports live. Given the current (and future) media fragmentation environment we live in, expect live sports and news to break through the clutter and that's key in reaching a wider audience. However, brands should go beyond the game itself; marketers should also focus on the stories behind the game, the players, the stadiums, the ecosystem surrounding the games.

Watchouts

1 Almost every sports franchise, either at the league level or individual team level, will need a multicultural strategy for the next decades.
2 Similar to what we observe from best practices in multicultural advertising, sports franchises should focus on being relevant through authentic culture strategies, rather than depending on language or stereotypical approaches.
3 Sports franchises need to build their multicultural fan base with an approach that starts with the grassroots, from the youth connection, passing through the crucial high school and college steps in order to grow vertically to the professional levels.
4 Whether it's their video streaming consumption or the growing relevance of eSports, multicultural consumers are leading the pack when it comes to the fusion of technology and sports.

One thing is for sure. The impact multicultural consumers will have on the sports scene in the U.S. is bound to make it a whole new ballgame. Get ready!

Case Study—How a Brand Can Leverage a Sport Passion to Convey a Relevant Diversity Discussion

Coors Light—"Flores to Canton"

Executive Summary

Tapping into the passion for sports to communicate its message is not new news to beer brands (or almost any CPG brand for a matter of fact). However, with this campaign, Coors Light was able to tap into a growing trend among diverse segments: the issue of representation—the proper recognition of community idols and role models.

The Business Challenge

As the second largest light beer in America, Coors Light already enjoyed great brand awareness among the nation's 57 million light beer drinkers. To more memorably communicate its core benefit of being ice-cold, it had recently re-positioned its brand to champion "Chill" (i.e. relaxing, worry-free) moments and attitudes. As a result, it entered late 2020 having climbed to Number 2 in its category.

However, it found itself lagging behind category competitors in immediate consideration, therefore struggling to stay consistently "top of mind" among drinkers. To close the gap, the world's "chillest" beer saw a great opportunity: making a splash during the 2020–2021 season of America's most popular sports property: The National Football League.

Armed with a modest local partnership with the Las Vegas Raiders, their agency partners were tasked to do something that wouldn't just impact consumers in Raiders markets but snowball into a national impact that would reverberate across the entire category.

The Insights/Strategy

The brand core audiences shared a common grievance which spoke to a larger issue of representation. Raiders and Hispanic fans both feel disrespected by the football world: Hispanics see their contributions ignored, while Raider Nation feels persecuted by a "biased" NFL. But they discovered one grievance both shared, one which Coors Light could meaningfully champion. All they had to do was partner with an 83-year-old who left the league 25 years ago.

Enter Tom Flores, the overlooked Raider legend—A Hispanic ex-Raider who, despite being the first minority coach to win a Super Bowl (and winning four of them), had been denied from the Pro Football Hall of Fame for twenty years. Raider's fans blamed dis-taste for their team's "bad boy" image. Hispanics blamed racial bias, seeing this as a particularly glaring part of the larger problem of Hispanic underrepresentation in the Hall. Either way, discontent during "Hall Season" was its own twisted tradition.

Idea/Execution

- The hub: an online petition—A natural choice for channeling public pressure.
- A collectible "Iceman Can"—In key markets, Coors Light released a limited-edition can featuring Flores and our state-ment of support for the inclusion of Tom Flores in the Football Hall of Fame.
- Creative showcased Flores' chill personality—The brand had a spot featuring Flores with his can—shrugging when asked about his snub—and a celebratory spot ready if he made it.
- Experiential acts brought our cause to the Hall's home.
  - An Ice Bust of Flores, evoking the Hall's busts *and* Coors Light's ice-cold equity.
  - An LED truck displaying pro-Tom tweets.

All pieces had to balance—to different degrees—educating about The Iceman (including why Coors Light would support him) and driving people to the petition. Accordingly, all work called view-ers to "sign the petition of support at coorslight.com/iceman" (the first priority message). Meanwhile, the long-form TV was able to (efficiently) educate new fans about his accomplishments, and the Iceman Can was able to make the brand's connection to his chill personality truly explicit.

Results

- A total of 1.1 billion impressions—the brand hit a nerve and yielded national fame beyond all expectations, doubling their stretch goal.
- Despite the controversy, press mentions were 94% positive or neutral, above their 75% benchmark.
- Nearly doubled the brand's 2020 national recall average (tripled among Hispanic): +15% GM/+28% Hispanic ad awareness; +20.8% GM/+31% Hispanic brand recall.
- Additionally, these results helped Coors Light achieve a larger overall year-over-year brand ad awareness jump with Hispanic than any direct competitor: 75%, a 9-point rise that helped the brand pass Michelob Ultra and put them on par with Bud Light.
- The positive attention resulted in a 75% consideration increase among all U.S. 21+ drinkers.
- The campaign also contributed to a rebound in sales lift: 3.1% in January 2021, the best performing month since the pandemic began.

Author's Comments

One of the reasons I like this case study so much was its simplicity. A community hero who has been bypassed to receive the ultimate recognition of his career, being inducted into the Football Hall of Fame, despite all of his achievements. This is an example of stories brands can help amplify. There's an opportunity to move beyond representation in advertising from a casting standpoint, to relevant, authentic community stories.

Chapter 19

Multicultural Segments Top the Music Charts

When Disney launched its animated film *Encanto* in November 2021, based on a uniquely Hispanic storyline, the film did not break out at the box office. However, when the soundtrack of the movie, with songs written by Lin Manuel Miranda—inspired by both salsa and hip-hop music—reached No. 1 in the Billboard charts of January 2022, people were truly astounded, especially since it displaced Adele's new album "30," which had reigned the Billboard charts for six weeks in a row.

Welcome to the extraordinary power of Music.

Exhibit One: In February 2020 Super Bowl LIV was played in Miami and its world-famous halftime show featured an all-Hispanic line-up for the first time. With the iconic J. Lo and Shakira headlining the show, an estimated 103 million viewers tuned in, which was 4% more than the previous year's Maroon 5 halftime performance.

Exhibit Two: Popular K-Pop band BTS ended 2019 with three No. 1 hits in the U.S. and four top 10 hits on the prestigious Billboard 200 chart.

Exhibit Three: J Balvin's megahit "Mi Gente" was remixed by Beyoncé. That move brought her closer to her Hispanic fans and brought Latin music closer to non-Hispanic audiences, similar to when Justin Bieber did a remix of Luis Fonsi and Daddy Yankee's "Despacito" in 2017. Both examples illustrate a trend towards "reverse partnerships," with mainstream artists looking for in-culture and in-language collaborations with Latino artists.

The list of exhibits could go on and on. Music has long been at the forefront of setting trends in our society, with a strong track record for giving minorities a voice.

Here are some thought starters on how the minority-majority transformation can impact the music business in the years to come.

DOI: 10.4324/9781003348931-22

Native versus Imported

Minority artists will continue to discover and fall in love with artists and rhythms that come from countries and regions associated with their cultural background. However, I believe that given the demographic changes in America, we will start to see a steady growth of artists bringing a home-grown, bicultural perspective to their work.

Another trend that I anticipate is the creation of the reverse "Spanglish" songs by Hispanic American artists. While I believe we will witness a significant number of Hispanic artists singing in English, we also expect to see songs to be created in Spanish with some English incorporated into them versus English songs that have a bit of Spanish thrown in.

I spoke with Melissa Giles, founder of Soulfrito, an Urban Latin Music Festival and Culture Strategy Group, who pointed out that while U.S.-born Hispanics may be bilingual, they also have grown up listening to mainstream Hip Hop, R&B, POP, and other music genres outside of Latin. Giles said,

> There is a ton of Hispanic talent here in the U.S. that are making music other than Latin or Spanish Language. The music industry, both on the Latin and general market side, has just barely scratched the surface in terms of tapping U.S. born Hispanic talent who are pulling from various influences outside of Latin music.

Audio Revolution

In an age when technology seems to disrupt traditional media every day, the amazing resilience of radio is a story that needs to be underlined. Radio has not only stayed relevant over the past few years but in many markets, it has grown. Latin music has been one of the drivers of the medium's strong performance.

Despite its strength, the audio business is not immune to disruption. Services like Pandora, Spotify, and Clubhouse have become even more popular, and they will continue to leverage increasingly culturally sensitive AI technology to grow even more sticky. Those algorithms will help preserve unique cultural preferences for some groups. At the same time, they will introduce new musical choices to a broader share of the population.

A Smarter Sponsor

For marketers, the cost of partnering with the most popular music artists will only grow in the years to come, forcing brands to find alternative strategies to leverage music as a way to connect with consumers.

This may require a combination of better curation skills, searching for and identifying talent that fits a brand's strategy before they become too expensive to partner with, as well as the ability to look at music from a different angle, leaving the traditional sponsorship paradigms behind and adopting a more modern partnership approach with the artists. According to Jesus Gonzalez, vice president, Creative, Latin Broadcast Music Inc (BMI),

> Brands that invest the time and effort to properly research and curate their Latin music partnerships will truly benefit from building genuine equity with emerging as well as established talent and brand affinity with their fans and consumers. Nothing is worse than a shiny-object syndrome.

New Channels

In early 2019, more than ten million fans "watched" a live performance of EDM's artist Marshmello. What made his performance unique was the fact that it was not something fans could attend in person, nor was it broadcast on Network TV, Cable, YouTube, or any other video streaming services. The performance was available exclusively for Fortnite players while in the game.

This new way of experiencing music is paradigm-breaking beyond brand sponsorship. For young music consumers whose first concert was brought to them by one of their favorite brands, at zero cost, without ever leaving their screens, the bar for brand integration has officially been set. And the new frontier will be defined by gaming and the increased use of Augmented and Virtual Reality spaces, like the Metaverse.

There is no doubt that the demographic shift in America will accelerate the convergence of music, gaming, and technology because minority youth over-index when it comes to video game usage, and music consumption and are eager to adopt technology as early as possible.

Marketers need to be open to new and different ways for music to be consumed and distributed, significantly enhancing access to new artists and minority voices.

Music has been one of the most visible aspects of multicultural diversity in America for decades. As we experience an acceleration of our demographic diversity, brands will need to pay closer attention to how minority consumers influence and shape American culture as a way to move up the charts when it comes to relevancy. And advertisers should be all ears!

Chapter 20

For the Health and Wellness Industry, It's Time for a Check-Up

The idea to write about the impact of our demographic trends from a Health and Wellness "angle" precedes the extraordinary times we are facing under the COVID-19 pandemic. Given that the current crisis has accentuated and exposed some of the issues and opportunities we will face for years to come, here are the most relevant topics I believe we need to focus on.

The Healthcare Access Gap Is Still Large

While the number of Americans from minority backgrounds without access to healthcare coverage significantly decreased since the implementation of the Affordable Care Act in 2010, the gap between different segments is still significant. If you take into consideration the trend for the Hispanic segment, back in 2010, the number of uninsured was above 30%, and data from 2019 showed a significant decline in the number of uninsured Hispanics to approximately 19%. For the Black population, the number of uninsured individuals was around 20% in 2010, declining to 10% by 2019.[1]

Even at record low levels, the gap of uninsured Black and Hispanic individuals compared to the non-Hispanic White and AAPI segments is still significantly higher, as reports show these segments at only 7% uninsured.

Why is this important? If these trends stay the same in the next decades, we will face an increase in the country's overall uninsured rates, bringing with it a range of social and economic consequences, including the increase in healthcare costs and loss of productivity that can cost billions of dollars per year.

Culture and Language Can Impact Healthcare Outcomes

According to the study "Communication and Long-Term Care: Technology Use and Cultural Barriers Among Hispanics," conducted by the Associated Press-NORC Center for Public Affairs,[2] approximately 62% of U.S. Hispanics prefer healthcare-related resources and information in Spanish and

DOI: 10.4324/9781003348931-23

58% prefer to deal with a healthcare provider who speaks Spanish. Almost half of the respondents think that some of the info received in the past got "lost in translation."

When it comes to bilingual language skills, one thing is to feel comfortable enough to watch a movie and even be part of the workforce, but when the subject of the discussion is your health or the health of your loved ones, the complexity of the topic may push you back to your original language, where everyone feels more comfortable. This is not only true for Hispanics but for all Americans for whom English is not their first language.

But language is not the only barrier for minority segments looking for healthcare services. A 2018 research[3] conducted by the NBER (National Bureau of Economic Research) showed that Black males believe that when they are assigned to a Black doctor, they get better treatment and more preventive and screening services (like screenings for diabetes and cholesterol). Also, they are more open to discuss health-related and personal issues.

The Next Generation of Multicultural Health Professionals

Research conducted by the Association of American Medical Colleges showed that while Hispanics and Black segments represented approximately 33% of the U.S. population in 2017, they made up less than 13% of medical school students. According to the AAMC in 2018 less than 6% of active physicians identified as Hispanic.[4] When it comes to Registered Nurses, the numbers are a bit better, but still minorities are underrepresented. According to a study from the American Association of Colleges of Nursing, in 2018, Hispanics and Black students represented less than 25% of all nursing students.

With the costs of higher education skyrocketing over the years, it is important to understand that having a population of healthcare professionals that represent our minority segments is not a matter of equal representation but rather an opportunity for better services and better outcomes. But affordability is only one factor on a complex topic that also includes other aspects like mentorship and flexible study hours.

Eating Habits + Lack of Exercise

One of the biggest problems in our country's health as a whole comes from our eating habits. Minorities, especially Hispanics and Black individuals who are at a higher risk for conditions like diabetes and cardiovascular diseases, have perceptions and attitudes towards their diets that may further elevate their risks. For instance, both cultures have diets that are high in fat and carbs with sweet and salty dishes, mostly consumed among friends and family around a lunch or dinner table. Furthermore, members of these minority segments may also believe that food cooked from scratch tends to be healthier, regardless of what's in the food, which creates another cultural barrier from a perception standpoint. Beatriz Rojas, senior director of Multicultural Marketing at Kaiser Permanente, said:

> Another important consideration is that unfortunately, in many neighborhoods with a high index of Hispanics and Black individuals, there is a lack of availability of healthy food. In those neighborhoods, you find more small corner-style grocery shops, where they do not carry much fresh food. And also, fresh and healthy food tends to be more expensive.

While minorities don't have a good track record when it comes to their eating habits, they also tend to lag behind the White population with regard to their exercise habits. A 2020 report[5] from the Center for Diseases Control and Prevention (CDC) concluded that the majority of Hispanic and Black individuals covered by the study did not meet the guidelines for either aerobic or muscle-strengthening exercises.

The Gap in Marketing Investments

One additional indicator that aggravates the under-representation of minority consumers in the Health and Wellness industry compared to their population size is advertising. Studies conducted by the Hispanic Marketing Council have indicated that, historically, healthcare providers and pharma companies have invested approximately 2% of their advertising dollars in the Hispanic segment although this segment represents almost 20% of the population and over-index in certain diseases.

While some of these consumers are exposed to the industry's ads targeting the general population in English, there's still a significant number of Hispanic consumers who prefer to receive their information about health and wellness in Spanish. Most importantly, many ads tend to follow the one-size-fits-all approach and totally miss the cultural nuances and contexts that would make their messages more effective with Hispanics, even in English.

Moreover, when a brand advertises specifically to minority segments, they connect with not only the individual potential customer but, in many cases, with the whole household. Among the U.S. Hispanic population, where almost one-third of all households are multigenerational, it is common for healthcare decisions to be made more on a collective level rather than made by an individual. Again, here's Beatriz Rojas' take on the need for advertisers to reach and connect with minority audience:

> In addition to traditional advertising, I think it's important that we focus on new channels and content: this audience is very thirsty for content: digital, social, partnerships with trusted sources (like Telemundo,

Univision, CNN, etc.). This kind of educational content is critical, especially when talking about the importance of having health insurance options and also healthy habits and now super relevant topics like mental health are key.

The next few years and decades represent an opportunity for a shift in the way minorities in America are approached by the Health and Wellness industry. A healthier society is also a more productive society, and there are significant challenges as well as opportunities ahead of us to close the gaps mentioned in this chapter. This is not a matter of government policies only; it is an effort that will have to be tackled by all stakeholders. It's time for a check-up!

Case Study—Most Pharma Companies Have Historically Ignored Diverse Segments in Their Marketing Programs. One Company Is Changing That

Lilly—Trulicity "*Está en ti*"

Executive Summary

In 2019 Trulicity became the only brand to speak directly to Hispanics, despite a higher likelihood for them to die from Type-2 Diabetes (T2D) complications than non-Hispanics. The campaign had to inform and connect in a more relevant way since Hispanics lack the same disease knowledge as the general market (GM).

An in-language and in-culture campaign was developed, leveraging a key, culturally relevant driver to inform and motivate Hispanic patients: Their innate resilience and ingenuity to find solutions within themself for the collective good.

The Business Challenge

Hispanics are most in need of Type-2 Diabetes treatments but also the most resistant to using injectable treatments like Trulicity.

The Insights/Strategy

The same inner drive that motivates Hispanics to move family and community forward can be harnessed to take charge of Type-2 Diabetes.

Hispanics live a more collective, community-oriented lifestyle than non-Hispanics. They are motivated by a duty to help family and community—putting others' needs above their own. They do whatever it takes and Hispanics with Type-2 Diabetes are no different. They are motivated to always be there for their family.

We know that Hispanic Type-2 Diabetes patients may delay taking action, taking the advice of friends and loved ones instead of listening to their doctor. But by tapping into their resilience and ingenuity, these same Hispanic patients can be inspired and motivated to ask their doctor about Trulicity and begin to make important lifestyle changes that are required to manage their Type-2 Diabetes.

When taking Trulicity, patients are able to (re)activate the insulin that their body is still producing. Trulicity itself is *not* insulin but it releases what you already have inside to make you truly powerful against Type-2 Diabetes.

Tapping into the potential of Hispanics' inner drive to be better also clarifies our most important message: Trulicity is not Insulin. Rather, it activates the potential of the insulin still being produced by your body.

If they understand Trulicity's potential, it will amplify their own motivation to ask their doctor about Trulicity and start making lifestyle changes.

Idea/Execution

General market patients are better informed and more engaged with their doctor, usually long before being diagnosed as a Type-2 diabetic. Conversely, Hispanic patients are not as informed or engaged with their doctor; they're more likely to have advanced Type-2 Diabetes upon diagnosis, requiring insulin as their initial treatment. . . Our *"Está En Ti"* (It's within you) campaign is adapted from the General Market concept, *"Truly Powerful."*

The *"Está En Ti"* work is centered on the key motivations and barriers facing Hispanic Type-2 Diabetes patients and how Trulicity

can help in both motivating and helping to overcome key barriers. We connected their inner potential for better well-being with
Trulicity's ability to tap the potential of unused insulin inside their
body, with the tagline "*Está En Ti*," which has a positive double
meaning in Spanish:

- "It's within you" to do this. (motivational)
- You can do more with what's already "within you." (functional)

While the campaign idea is shared, the creative is uniquely Hispanic:
aspirational, empowering, emotional, centered on a successful Hispanic and invaluable moments spent with his family. The motivation
for Hispanic Type-2 Diabetes patients to get healthy is being there
in the future for their family long term. Their family and friends'
acknowledgment of their effort to get healthy inspires our Hispanic
to do more in managing their Type-2 Diabetes through diet and
exercise every day.

The key messages are presented in a straightforward fashion:

- Trulicity is *not* insulin, but rather activates the insulin your
  body still produces.
- Trulicity is taken once weekly (not daily).
- Trulicity is effective at helping to lower your A1C from the very
  first dose.

The scenes are aspirational, showing the kind of energy, motivation,
and active living that many Hispanic Type-2 Diabetes patients are
missing right now. Furthermore, the lifestyle scenes demonstrate
that Trulicity's once-weekly dosage means that treatment doesn't
get in the way of daily life.

Our hero and his family's story is told through direct-to-con-
sumer TV advertising, which focuses heavily on product awareness
and education.

Leveraging the creative and storyline from the TV ad, the campaign was further amplified through the following:

- **Social media** posts focused on individual reasons to believe
  that reinforce the broader story of hope and empowerment
  told through the TV creative.

- **Digital** banners focused on helping patients lower their A1C, the biggest challenge most Type-2 Diabetes patients face on a daily basis.
- **Search** focused on driving Hispanics looking for diabetes information to discover Trulicity.

All of the above is linked to the dedicated website, Trulicity.com/es. This website is different from the English version, with unique imagery and information in Spanish that echoes the Spanish creative campaign.

Results

The campaign successfully made the brand connection with Hispanic patients that inspired them to ask their doctor about Trulicity by name.

Overall, our efforts resulted in 41% more Hispanic patients filling their Trulicity Rx, 91% of whom intend to refill that Trulicity Rx, which signals a long-term commitment to stay on Trulicity and keep the lifestyle changes needed for Type-2 Diabetes management.

Author's Comments

This is a case I am very proud of as I was involved in the discussions with Lilly before this project was created. In my opinion this is a poster child case of how a brand can drive significant results with a program anchored on relevant consumer insights and authentic communication.

I applaud Lilly's efforts and hope that their example will be followed by other Pharma companies since Hispanics represent less than 2% of the industry's total measured advertising investments.

Notes

1 2010 American Community Survey, 2019 American Community Survey.
2 https://apnorc.org/wp-content/uploads/2020/02/APNORC_LTC_2018_Hispanic_report.pdf
3 "Does Diversity Matter For Health? Experimental Evidence From Oakland," by Marcella Alsan Owen Garrick Grant C. Graziani.
4 www.aamc.org/data-reports/workforce/interactive-data/figure-18-percentage-all-active-physicians-race/ethnicity-2018
5 Physical Inactivity is More Common among Racial and Ethnic Minorities in Most States (Posted on April 1, 2020, by Janet E. Fulton, PhD, chief of CDC's Physical Activity and Health Branch in the Division of Nutrition, Physical Activity, and Obesity).

Chapter 21

Multicultural Consumers Faced Distinct Challenges during the COVID-19 Crisis

During the first few days of this global COVID-19 pandemic, I attended a virtual meeting with colleagues from different locations across the world. In this meeting, I heard about how local markets like China, Hong Kong, Australia, UK, and Germany, among others, were tackling the challenges created by the disruption we were facing. After a few minutes of listening to the speakers, it was clear that this was a global crisis that saw no boundaries.

It also became apparent quickly that different communities were responding to this crisis in different ways, and most importantly, that culture had a significant impact on the way populations around the world faced those challenges. For instance, in Asia, past experience with other respiratory viruses created a culture of prevention, including the broad use of protective masks and gloves, followed by strict social distancing protocols that were widely observed; meanwhile, in places like Italy or Spain, people unfortunately suffered the consequences from close and frequent social interactions that are so culturally ingrained in those countries.

The same was true in the U.S., where we saw how some communities faced the challenges created by the COVID-19 pandemic differently. In order to track those cultural responses to the pandemic my colleagues at alma advertising conducted a study[1] using a combination of social media listening and secondary data from partners to highlight some of these cultural differences. Here is a gist of my summary:

Working from Home Is a Luxury for Minorities

Working from home quickly became a reality during the pandemic; however, for minorities in America, this also represented a significant challenge. As has been widely reported, working from home is much easier when you have a white-collar job. According to statistics from the U.S. Department of Labor,[2] approximately 47% of Non-Hispanic White Americans can work from home, compared to 39% of Hispanic workers and only 34% of Black workers in the job market.

DOI: 10.4324/9781003348931-24

Additionally, minority consumers represent a disproportionate number of people employed in the informal economy. Finally, Hispanic and Black entrepreneurs have been leading the creation of small businesses over the past decade, and these businesses have also been significantly impacted by the economic consequences of the COVID-19 crisis.

The Surge of COVID-19 Racism

Unfortunately, one of the negative consequences of the COVID-19 crisis in this country was an alarming increase in racism towards AAPI individuals, fueled by xenophobic rhetoric in parts of our society. However, on the positive side, minority groups in the U.S. quickly mobilized together to fight this negative trend. All over social media, messages of "minority solidarity" were shared, creating a pushback against this wave of hate against Asian Americans.

Information and Culture Gaps Exist

During the early days of the government's response to the COVID-19 crisis, it took three days for the official guidelines from the CDC website to be translated into Spanish. Online searches in Spanish for information on COVID-19 spiked, ranging from information about the virus, where and how to find grocery provisions, how to get unemployment benefits, to even research on alternative home remedies to fight the disease.

An analysis based on iSpot.TV data provided by TelevisaUnivision showed that while 117 brands from 22 industries developed COVID-19-related messages during the first quarter after the U.S. shutdown, only 13 brands from 7 industries developed messages in Spanish.

But minority disparities are not only driven by language gaps, members of the Black community across the country were struggling to get access to healthcare information and support as well. This was crucial and resulted in the Black community being more impacted by the COVID-19 virus relative to its population size. Now we know that lack of information and distrust coupled with a higher incidence of diabetes, heart, and respiratory diseases among the Black population have also contributed to higher infection rates and the devastating outcomes.

Grandparents Rule!

While our society as a whole struggled to convince young people to stay at home as a way to protect themselves and their family or friends from the contagion, we saw Hispanic youth leading the movement for youth to stay home. Why? Because they disproportionately live in multigenerational households (15% of Hispanic households vs. 8% of non-Hispanic White households are multigenerational[3]). The relationship between minorities and their elderly has always been extraordinary, and the bonds and stories that were created during these times will leave a legacy for generations to come.

The Power of Optimism Gets Stronger

During these difficult times, the Hispanic community's cultural trademark of optimism helped face its biggest challenges. All across the country, Hispanic users were using TikTok to share their favorite videos, and Pandora saw a marked increase in the consumption of Latin music as a form of relief during COVID-19 lockdowns. In essence, familiar culture is always comforting, especially during tough times.

And this sense of optimism is working again as we see the light at the end of the COVID-19 tunnel. Hispanic consumers already have a significant optimistic view of the months to come, with 51% feeling hopeful that their financial situation will improve in the next six months, compared to only 22% of non-Hispanics.[4]

I spoke with my colleague, Angela Rodriguez, SVP, head of Strategy at alma advertising, and who led the development of this report, and asked her how marketers should react to the insights presented, and this was her take on it:

> A common enemy doesn't mean a common impact on all consumers. Not only were many segments experiencing greater health and economic consequences as a result of the coronavirus pandemic, but their safety, life, and purchase decisions were made through the lens of their culture more than ever. Safety isn't only a matter of personal protection and job losses reverberated beyond the household. Marketers should recognize the importance of showing they understand and care about these consumers when showing up for their communities means more than ever.

After navigating the plethora of opinions from many subject matter experts and consultants about the consequences of the COVID-19 pandemic, one common conclusion was that life won't be the same when this crisis is over. It is also essential to recognize that these consequences won't be felt the same by different segments of our society, and this realization is significant since it can improve the way we support our communities in times of crisis.

Notes

1 Alma's Quarterly Cultural Digest—First Look COVID-19 Impact, Q1 2020.
2 Matthew Dey, Harley Frazis, Mark A. Loewenstein, and Hugette Sun, "Ability to work from home: Evidence from two surveys and implications for the labor market in the COVID-19 pandemic," Monthly Labor Review, U.S. Bureau of Labor Statistics, June 2020.
3 U.S. Census Bureau, American Community Survey 2008, 2018.
4 Alma's Quarterly Cultural Digest—First Look COVID-19 Impact, Q1 2020.

Chapter 22

The Future Tastes
Like Change

Food has long been a strong pillar of cultural identity—in particular, meals and the habits associated with family getting together around a table to break bread. Growing up in Latin America, I did not speak the language or understand the nuances of my grandparents' lives. But I vividly remember the fabulous dishes they prepared from their homeland for our family gatherings. The same is true in this country, where waves of immigrants over the years have celebrated their culture through food.

And with the accelerated growth of minority segment groups for the years and decades to come, those cultural celebrations will continue to contribute to America's rich and evolving food scene. Let's analyze some of the potential!

Ethnic Food on the Rise

The growth of the so-called "ethnic food" category has been significant over the past decade, driven not only by major food companies looking for ways to innovate and capitalize on the demographic shifts in America but also by the strong appeal "ethnic" food has with many non-Hispanic White consumers as well.

This trend can be related to the belief that these foods are more flavorful, and some are even perceived to be healthier, but most importantly, because they can also bring an emotional benefit as they are perceived as exciting, exotic, and unique—attributes that are essential in a society that seeks activities that feel more experiential.

According to the Bureau of Labor Statistics, the majority (58%) of head cooks and chefs working in restaurants in the U.S. are from the three main minority segments[1]: Hispanic, Black, or AAPI. These are the minds influencing America's palate and food preferences. And it's no coincidence that, according to the U.S. Census Bureau, almost 50% of start-up businesses under the "Accommodation and Food" sector are minority-owned.[2]

DOI: 10.4324/9781003348931-25

Cross-over Impact

It is almost impossible to write about the impact of demographics in changing this country's eating habits without mentioning the well-known fact that for the past 20 years, salsa has taken over ketchup as the most popular American condiment! But salsa is merely the tip of the iceberg. Over the past several years, the marketplace has seen significant growth in other items like taco shells and refried beans, and tortillas outselling American staples like hot dog buns.

The evidence is also clear in the highly competitive alcoholic beverage industry with the significant growth in the consumption of Mexican imported beers, Tequila, and Mezcal over the past decade.

In the breakfast business, we have witnessed the trend of Latin flavors infiltrating even the most all-American staples at iconic restaurants like IHOP, with their Mexican Tres Leches Pancakes or Spicy Poblano Omelet, and at Denny's, with their Dulce de Leche Crunch Pancakes.

The reality is that the consumption of what was once called "ethnic food" has outgrown the minority segments that introduced these new flavors to the country's mainstream. Today, it is almost impossible to find a food or beverage company in the U.S. that doesn't have an "ethnic food" item in their portfolio or as part of their innovation pipeline.

The Search for Authenticity

Some countries and cultures are intrinsically associated with food. When you think about Italy, you think about pasta or pizza. Mexico? Tacos. Argentina? Steaks (sorry, wine lovers). But the reality is that this is a very narrow view of a vast and rich food environment we live in. As our country becomes more diverse, we will witness a process whereby we will be exposed to more complex and less stereotypical cuisines we ever thought we knew. For instance, instead of thinking about Mexican cuisine in general, we may see more interest in some of Mexico's local foods from places like Oaxaca, Puebla, Yucatán, and Jalisco. Likewise, we may be able to learn more about Vietnamese food beyond Pho.

I also see a trend towards more spicy foods and condiments to add to America's palate with Middle Eastern food already becoming more mainstream, along with the introduction of dishes from Brazil and Portugal.

Food as Culture

Food has always been more than nutrition, and this is a universal truth that's everlasting. I believe that as America becomes more diverse and multicultural, food can bridge some cultural divides.

During the COVID-19 years, I believe food served as a short-term substitute for the traveling limitations we were all experiencing, so that people were able to explore and learn more about other countries, cities, and cultures through their culinary traditions.

Moreover, with the growth of multigenerational households in America—driven mainly by minority segments—we are looking at how grandparents influence the family's food habits and how what is called "multicultural grandparent food" can set new trends in this country.

Another trend I have been observing is the fact that younger consumers are feeling comfortable and unashamed of cooking dishes from the land of their grandparents and using food to forge closer and stronger bonds with these cultures.

A New Paradigm for Access and Distribution

Over the past few years, we have seen two trends in multicultural food distribution in America. First, the growth in the availability of ethnic food choices in mainstream food retail stores, and second, the expansion of specialized stores, ranging from mom-and-pop outlets to large chains like HEB and H Mart.

While I think these trends will continue, the pandemic showed us all that e-commerce will have a significant impact on the way American shoppers buy and discover new food options. For instance, now I can buy my favorite Mexican peanuts (Sabritas' Cacahuates—Japanese Style) on Amazon without the need to search for them at my regular food retail stores.

Imagine the possibilities for food companies who analyze e-commerce shopping of imported items before deciding to produce these items domestically. Or the ability that brick- and-mortar retailers now have to expand their offerings online without the pressure to find "space" for new SKUs on their shelves.

If you want to really understand the changes in this country's demographics, start looking at food consumption behaviors for the past 20 years. Food is, and will always be, one of the pillars of culture, and over the next decades we will all be able savor the delicious taste of change. Bon Appetit!

Notes

1 Labor Force Statistics from the Current Population Survey, 1/20/22.
2 www.census.gov/newsroom/press-releases/2021/characteristics-of-employer-busi-nesses.html

Chapter 23

Diverse Consumers Are Changing the Grocery Retail Business

After three years of living with the COVID-19 pandemic, there has been significant discussion about the steps retailers need to take in order to adapt to new limitations, and consumers' expectations. The grocery industry is no exception.

However, the COVID-19 crisis may obscure an exciting new trend happening in our country: more Americans are consuming more ethnic foods. According to the MRI-Simmons Fall 2020 NHCS Adult Study, almost 20 million adults reported shopping (in the past four weeks) at what is categorized as an "ethnic grocery store." The study also showed that 20% of all U.S. Hispanic adults shopped at a Hispanic grocery store, and when asked about shopping at "any" ethnic grocery store, that number grew to 22%.

You might think that's not surprising given the growth of ethnic communities in the U.S., but the report also showed that even non–Hispanic adults increased their shopping visits to "ethnic grocery stores." Almost 5% reported shopping at "any" ethnic stores in the past four weeks, the highest number recorded by this report since 2016.

To better understand the latest ethnic grocery store industry trends, I spoke with Gus Calabro, executive director at Abasto Media, a leading trade publication specializing in the Hispanic retail space. Here's a summary of our discussion:

Isaac Mizrahi: What are you observing in the ethnic grocery business?

Gus Calabro: *There have been a lot of different movements. Ethnic retailers are growing in size and geography. Mainstream grocery chains are increasing their offerings of ethnic products and even hiring specialized buyers to understand and cater to this growing segment. We also see a higher interest from companies in Latin America looking to expand their business in the United States. And finally, we are seeing higher interest and demand from all consumers for ethnic products, driven by the demographic changes in America and a more heightened sense of curiosity by younger,*

DOI: 10.4324/9781003348931-26

	non-ethnic consumers looking to explore new flavors and tastes. These are exciting times to be in the ethnic grocery ecosystem.

Mizrahi: Are national retailers "catching up" with the demographic changes in America? Do they have enough shelf space/footprint to offer more products that cater to ethnic consumers?

Calabro: *We know that national retailers are more than "catching up" with the demographic changes in America based on all the data available. There is a lot more work to do in terms of space, but we see positive changes overall. Most of the initiatives to increase the in-store ethnic footprint are in the metropolitan areas.*

Mizrahi: Do you think that brands have an accurate view of their sales in ethnic retailers? Is the lack of precise measurement a barrier?

Calabro: *It all depends on the size of the brand. Let's talk about some multinational corporations. Their metrics on sales are generally more accurate than for other smaller to medium brands. Many small to medium brands usually rely on their distributors to obtain sales metrics. So yes, measurement is a barrier among ethnic retailers. Cultural, language, and financial resources are some of the obstacles that contribute to the lack of proper metrics.*

Mizrahi: If you are a small U.S.-based brand catering to the ethnic segment, how does a brand breakthrough into the ample retailer space?

Calabro: *What we usually suggest is to start by targeting the ethnic retailer first. It is wise to penetrate the ethnic consumer and establish a comprehensive retail program attractive to the retailer. After showing a successful program and good results in sales in the ethnic retail space, approaching the corporate retail buyer will likely be more successful.*

To get another perspective on the ethnic retail business, I also spoke with Adam Salgado, chief marketing officer at Cardenas Markets, one of the largest Hispanic grocery chains in the country, with 59 stores across California, Nevada, and Arizona. Here's an edited version of our conversation:

Isaac Mizrahi: What is the current state of ethnic retailers and, in particular, your business?

Adam Salgado: *Cardenas Markets continues to show solid results and is poised for continuous growth as Hispanic customers continue to outspend their non-Hispanic counterparts in grocery purchases.*

Mizrahi: What are the key drivers for your growth?

Salgado: *Primarily, fresh and authentic products are available both in-store and through our e-commerce platforms. Our merchandising efforts* *around sourcing high-velocity items during the pandemic and our focus on the safety of our team members and our customers allowed us to continue to be there for the communities in which we do business.*

Mizrahi: How do you keep yourself updated from a merchandising perspective? How do you follow the trends of product preferences?

Salgado: *Our Merchandising team is constantly learning about their respective categories and what our customers are seeking. We have developed a comprehensive review process using internal metrics and external syndicated data points while seeking innovation from our supplier partners coupled with keen observation of the marketplace as a whole.*

Mizrahi: What role does the local Hispanic community play in your business? What do you do to support it?

Salgado: *Through our Cardenas Markets Foundation, we support the communities where we do business through four key pillars of need: education, children well-being, health and nutrition, and hunger relief.*

Mizrahi: Do you see non–Hispanics shopping at your stores? Why do you think they come to you?

Salgado: *We do see customers from all walks of life and diverse backgrounds come through our doors. We are constantly studying our evolving customer base and are using our learnings to understand ways to expand our base while staying true to our core customers. Our customers will find an exceptional variety of fresh and authentic product offerings that celebrate life, family and culture in a fun and festive environment.*

As we continue to experience a shift in America's demographic towards multicultural consumers, the growth of ethnic products and ethnic retailers across the country is expected to continue. To retain their appeal in the future, established brands need to reassess their appeal towards diverse consumers regarding product composition, flavor profile, packaging, communications, and community support.

Furthermore, we will see more multinational companies bringing successful brands from their international markets to the U.S., and other brands that are not currently in the U.S. will start targeting diverse consumers as an entry strategy to America.

Hence, we may expect more fragmentation of brand preferences and retailer choices as diverse consumers may feel their current options may not fully reflect their cultural background and identities. More than ever, it will be necessary for brands and retailers to have a deep knowledge of consumers' habits and trends since failing to understand them may cost them in a few years.

Chapter 24

The Large Role of Multicultural Small Businesses

One of the most fascinating business stories in the U.S. over the past couple of decades has been the growth of minority-owned small businesses and their contributions to our country's present and future economic health.

The importance of small businesses to our economy has been well documented. According to the U.S. Small Business Administration (SBA), small businesses in America represent 44% of the country's GDP, employ 47% of our private sector labor force, and represent a disproportionate amount of job creation, with 62% of all jobs created in America during the pre-pandemic period.[1]

In 2018, the SBA estimated there were more than 1 million employers (i.e. those who have paid employees) minority-owned small firms in America, including all ethnic groups plus female- and veteran-owned businesses representing, approximately 18% of all America's small businesses.[2]

As the country's minority population is growing faster than the non-Hispanic White population and we move towards a minority-majority society, the impact of these demographic trends on our small business landscape will be significant. But our society still needs to better understand the barriers and opportunities surrounding minority small business owners to fully unlock this segment's economic power.

First, it is important to recognize that the desire to own a business runs deep among minority segments. I looked at recent MRI-Simmons studies data for the question "I would like to set up my own business one day," and 63% of Hispanics agreed with that statement, followed by 63% from Black individuals. However, only 36% of non-Hispanic White respondents agreed.[3]

Entrepreneurship Runs Deep

Owning your own business or being your own boss is something that deeply connects with many immigrant families because they see it as one of the few paths they have towards wealth creation for their families, especially given

DOI: 10.4324/9781003348931-27

the perceived barriers they see for minorities to have a successful career in corporate America.

The path towards minority-owned business success, however, is hard for minority entrepreneurs. As reported by the 2019 State of Latino Entrepreneurship (SOLE) Report,[4] sponsored by the Stanford Latino Entrepreneurship Initiative (which is part of the Stanford Graduate School of Business), Latino Entrepreneurs tend to face significant challenges.

According to an article about the report, "How Latino Entrepreneurs Can Boost the U.S. Economy,"[5] published in January 2020, "Latinos are starting business at an unprecedented rate. The number of Latino-owned businesses has surged over the past decade to 34%, outpacing that of any other ethnic group."

However, the report also covers some of the challenges Hispanic entrepreneurs face that are worth highlighting:

- *Lack of Access to Capital:* A significant number of minority-owned small businesses still rely on sources like personal credit cards or home equity credit lines to finance their operations. This demonstrates the fragility these companies operate under and, most importantly, the limitations they may have regarding future growth.
- *Lack of Education:* Only 12% of Hispanic small business owners attended college before starting their own businesses. Furthermore, a significant number of minority small business owners would welcome support in running and helping to grow their businesses.
- *Lack of Access to Resources:* Lastly, a significant number of minority-owned small businesses still lack the knowledge of available resources such as minority certification, which is an essential tool to gain access to government contracts.

In addition to these, I'd also include one challenge based on my own observations in working with B2B marketing programs for minority-owned small businesses: the informal nature of their ventures, which are managed and organized casually between family members and are often not even formally registered as a business.

Besides the accelerated population growth, there are a few trends that may positively impact the formation of minority-owned small businesses in the years and decades to come, including a trend identified by many as "Gentefication," which describes the higher probability of minority-owned small businesses to invest in the same communities they come from. "Gentefication" is not to be confused with gentrification. The word "*gente*" means *people* in Spanish, so this is a play on words and specifically refers to Hispanics, but the same phenomenon can be seen in other communities of color across America. After all, as the author Anna Lappe once said, "Every time you spend money, you're casting a vote for the kind of world you want."

This is very relevant as we see the growth in the number of consumers who seek a higher level of consciousness in their purchase choices, including a higher demand for supporting minority-owned, small businesses.

Today there are relatively lower barriers of entry to starting a business and to competing in the marketplace. There is widespread access to simple and relatively inexpensive technology related to business management (payroll, taxes, banking management), distribution (e-commerce), marketing, and advertising. All you need is a good idea and the willingness to work hard.

As our country faces new challenges to our economic recovery for years to come, it is important to understand how minority-owned small businesses can play an important role in this process and, most importantly, what policies can the federal and local governments enact and what strategies can the private sector implement to unlock the full potential of this group of entrepreneurs.

They may be called small businesses in name, but minority-owned small business owners will have a large impact on our economy and our communities for years and decades to come.

Notes

1 https://cdn.advocacy.sba.gov/wp-content/uploads/2021/12/06095731/Small-Business-FAQ-Revised-December-2021.pdf
2 https://cdn.advocacy.sba.gov/wp-content/uploads/2021/12/06095731/Small-Business-FAQ-Revised-December-2021.pdf
3 2021 Fall MRI-Simmons USA.
4 www.gsb.stanford.edu/faculty-research/publications/state-latino-entrepreneurship-2019
5 www.gsb.stanford.edu/insights/how-latino-entrepreneurs-can-boost-us-economy

Chapter 25

For the Ad Business, a Much-Needed Relaunch

Over the past few chapters, I've been talking about the impact a more diverse America will have on different industries, and the advertising business is not immune to these changes.

Like all other businesses in the U.S., the advertising business must also adapt to a changing consumer and media landscape. Here are the five key trends that I believe are reshaping the ad business.

1 Messaging Strategy Will Be More Segmented

As general market agencies have (finally) woken up to the need of hiring more multicultural talent in their ranks, there's a perception that multicultural agencies may no longer be needed since this fresh pool of multicultural marketing talent will make their agencies' ideas more diverse and relevant for a more multicultural society.

However, there is one major problem with this reasoning. While there is no doubt that a more diverse workforce in the ad industry will create a more diverse set of ideas, those ideas will still try to connect with multiple and fragmented audiences through one single message.

What needs to happen is that the ad industry will need to evolve towards a more balanced approach, with a mix of general market creative ideas and media buys complemented by a robust set of segmented messages and specific channel choices.

These segmented strategies will address groups of consumers that provide the largest growth opportunities for advertisers and will grow beyond the traditional ethnic segments (Hispanics, Black, and AAPI consumers). They will also need to incorporate other groups like LGBTQ+, People with Disabilities, Baby Boomers and the over-65-year-olds, veterans, college students, and working moms, just to name a few.

This new approach will balance mass media and mass messages' efficiency with the effectiveness of the "mass segmented" approach.

DOI: 10.4324/9781003348931-28

2 Multicultural Marketing Will Evolve into a Broader Business Discipline

One of the most significant changes in our industry in the next few years will be the transformation of the multicultural marketing industry from a mostly advertising-related discipline to a broader and more business-oriented one.

This transformation will elevate the need for companies to consider the implications of the country's demographic changes in key business areas such as R&D (are you developing the next generation of products and services that fit the needs of a more multicultural consumer base?), distribution (does your company have the right geographical footprint?), and human resources (are you recruiting and promoting the right talent to reflect the changes in our society?), just to mention a few.

Addressing these needs will require a significant shift across all levels of your organization, from the C-suite to the board of directors to the entry-level recruits. multicultural marketing experts can play a significant role in helping organizations during this transition. Traditional consulting firms won't be able to help you since they are not equipped, at least today, with the talent and know-how to advise their clients in this area.

But not all multicultural advertising experts will be prepared for this leap in scope, which takes me to my next trend.

3 True and Proven Experts Will Be on Demand

Our industry will need a new cohort of multicultural professionals with a track record and real expertise. To be clear, simply being of Hispanic descent will not make anyone fully prepared to lead a Hispanic-driven marketing effort. It may help, but it has never been enough to succeed in your job (and the same goes for any other segment).

These multicultural professionals will have to be present among different stakeholders, including clients, agencies, media companies, and research organizations.

Moreover, they will also need to be represented at different levels of these organizations, including decision-making levels, C-suites, and board of directors. There will be a higher demand for training and development of multicultural marketing and business skills. In the next decade, we will be witnessing a significant increase in the offerings of training programs.

4 Brand Purpose Will Meet Social Justice

The younger generation of consumers don't just prefer brands to provide something more than just a service or product for their dollars, they expect it. This is one way brands will remain authentic and relevant in an environment where consumers tend to ignore and even avoid their messages.

This trend perfectly fits within the multicultural marketing opportunities since most of these consumers come from a multicultural background. There are opportunities to engage with causes that disproportionately impact multicultural segments, like access to health care and education, pay gaps, and representation in critical industries, especially technology-driven ones.

While it is natural for brands to be concerned with the country's political polarization, there are ways to commit to multicultural communities without fears of being accused of being partisan.

5 There Will Be a Reset on Resource Allocation

A more robust multicultural marketing approach must be made with a comprehensive reassessment of how resources are being allocated. Today, most companies still take an incremental approach, meaning they cover what they perceive as "mainstream" plans first and then look for ways to cover what they consider "peripheral investments," such as multicultural marketing.

The reality is that this current approach does not fit the demographic trajectory of America, and most importantly, it does not fit the real sources of growth for many brands. To put it in perspective, multicultural marketing efforts still get less than 10% of an average marketing budget while representing a much larger share of the marketer's business growth. Not only will the advertising and marketing industry be impacted by this country's demographic changes, it will also have the opportunity to shape a more diverse, inclusive, and, most importantly, a more effective business environment that will help to create a new wave of sustainable growth for brands for years to come. To do that, we have to be courageous, break with old paradigms, and use one of the most important assets we have to lead this reinvention—the power of creativity.

Part IV

The Right Approach to Your Hispanic Business Opportunity

Chapter 26

Hispanic Marketing in Ten Steps

By now, I hope you understand more about the Hispanic segment opportunity for your company. But a key question remains unanswered: How to move from understanding into action? This is a question I get a lot. The simple answer is that there's no simple approach or specific steps to be taken, as the answer would depend on the company, the industry, and many other factors to take into consideration. But in this chapter I attempt to summarize the most important steps most companies I've worked with, or seen in the market, have taken and led them to succeed in the marketplace.

1 Hispanic Marketing as a Long-Term Commitment

The first thing successful companies in the Hispanic marketing segment do well to understand that this is not just another "program" for a brand to execute. A "program" is something you can do one year and abandon in the following year. Rather, Hispanic marketing is a commitment; it is a continuous initiative that the company has prioritized, aiming to reap benefits over the years, so it must be part of your long-term strategic plans and not something you try out only over a few weeks or months.

2 Assign Accountability

It is important to have a clear leadership structure to guide the company on these efforts—ideally someone who is senior enough to develop and execute a business plan, have control of the budget/P&L and enough power to navigate corporate politics, build bridges, and find allies. Moreover, this executive should have a strong champion— ideally the CEO, CMO, or someone at the C-suite level, and even at the board of directors level of the organization.

DOI: 10.4324/9781003348931-30

3 Data and Information Audit

Before you try to understand where you should go with your Hispanic marketing program, it is fundamental to assess where you are. Few companies do a thorough job of this and tend to only focus on sales. But here are a few questions one should ask when starting this process:

- Do you know how much of your sales come from the Hispanic segment?
- Do you know how many of your customers are Hispanic?
- Do you know how much Hispanic clients contribute to your revenue and profitability?
- Do you know whether your Hispanic customers have different purchase behaviors when it comes to our products and services? If yes, do you know why?
- How do you track your business performance, and how do you know you are properly tracking your Hispanic customers?
- Do you have the right distribution channels to reach Hispanic consumers?
- Do you have the right pricing or credit policies to attract and retain Hispanic customers?
- Is your product or service optimized for the Hispanic segment? Do you need in-language support? Are you following in-culture opportunities/ needs?
- Do you need features or flavors in your products or services that better attract Hispanic consumers?
- Do you have the staff to support your Hispanic marketing practice?
- How many Hispanic employees do you have? How many of them have experience with Hispanic marketing programs?
- How many of your employees speak Spanish? How about other languages?
- When you do consumer research, are your samples fully representative of the Hispanic population? In size and cultural affinity levels?
- If you subscribe to third-party data or if you are building your own first-party data set, are you considering the Hispanic segment characteristics?
- If your business operates through third-party distributors, how much do they know about Hispanic marketing?
- Is your communication strategy relevant to Hispanic consumers?
- Do you know what Hispanic communities aspire/need in your key markets?
- Are your business-building programs adequately set up to reflect the current and future demographic changes in America?

Overwhelming? Probably, but the more time an organization spends trying to understand the answers to these questions, the higher the probability they will be able to develop a successful Hispanic marketing practice that will last over years and help the company's future growth.

Above all, these sample questions demonstrate that Hispanic marketing can't and should never be reduced simply to an advertising campaign, as tempting as it may sound. Hispanic marketing equals future business growth, and advertising is only part of a robust effort a company should take towards the segment.

4 Quantify the Business Opportunity

Once you have gathered all these information you will be able to answer the key questions: How are we doing with the Hispanic consumer segment today and what are the growth opportunities for the future?

One of the most popular approaches to these questions is to run a side-by-side analysis of the key performance indicators (KPIs) for each business, comparing the Hispanic segment behaviors and results with the non-Hispanic consumer's performance.

For instance, for CPG brands most companies compare household penetration, market share, sales, frequency of purchase, and average household expenditure in the category.

Service companies tend to compare gross adds, churn, net adds, average revenue per user, and market share, among other metrics.

More sophisticated companies can calculate a customer/segment lifetime value. The bottom line is that these metrics are important because they will help you to understand how the Hispanic segment trends when compared to the non-Hispanic segment.

One simple, but eye-opening comparison could be the analysis of sales of a specific product or service vis-á-vis its share of the population. For example, brand "A" takes 10% of its sales from the Hispanic segment, and we know that the share of the Hispanic population in the country is close to 20%; this under-index ratio may mean that closing this gap may be the business opportunity at hand. The next step would be calculating how much closing this gap to "fair share of the population" may represent in gross revenue. And that's your new business opportunity!

5 Understand the Challenges

Next, each company needs to have an honest assessment of what are the current business barriers that are causing the gap in your fair share of the Hispanic segment. The good news is that the questions mentioned in step #3 would probably automatically describe what the key issues are. Moreover, qualitative discussions can further enrich one's analysis. For instance, interviewing your sales force, your distributors, store managers, and customer call centers' employees can give you unique perspectives on what are the issues Hispanic consumers are facing when it comes to your product and services.

But what if there are really no issues? What if your business is overperforming with the Hispanic segment? Well, first of all, congratulations! Then the question you should be asking yourself is what is the cost of losing this advantage? Chances are your competitors are seeing this stronger performance and will eventually try to catch up. No competitive advantage is static, and you may need to consider investing to protect and sustain your edge with Hispanic consumers.

6 Create a Plan, Including Resources and Measurement Criteria

This is where the rubber meets the road. You need to develop a comprehensive plan that addresses all the challenges listed in step #5. Ideally it should be a three-to-five-year plan with specific measurable indicators per quarter/year.

These indicators should create a dashboard to be reviewed regularly and assess success. Also important is to discuss the proper level of resources needed to accomplish these goals, not only financial resources but also human resources (internal and external).

7 Assemble Your Team

As previously mentioned, it's important that you are clear on the human resources needed to support your Hispanic marketing efforts. This should include full-time resources dedicated to the Hispanic marketing team, external partners like research and communications efforts, but also, importantly, the internal and external allies you will have to recruit to support your initiative.

When I led Sprint's multicultural marketing efforts, I was able to identify and negotiate the support of members of other functional teams to support my team. They were experts in media, PR, customer service, web support, measurement, and so on. These resources are key to your success given that your goal should never be to create a "parallel" marketing organization dedicated to Hispanic marketing but rather to integrate Hispanic marketing throughout the organization. You will need to be strategic on where to draw the line between the resources that need to be under your direct leadership and the resources you will assemble through internal allies.

8 Execute, Measure, Learn, Improve, Execute

Now you're off to execution. Make sure you manage it as a cycle of constant evaluation: execution, measurement, learnings, and implementations of your learnings to make your plans stronger. Chances are you will face a significant number of "surprises" along your way, and your goal should be to create a resilient plan, a plan that adjusts quickly and evolves with the market conditions and your own learnings. A perfect plan does not exist! What does exist is your ability to constantly improve your plans based on the best available information.

9 Communicate

Once you start to get the results of your Hispanic business efforts, first, you will need to communicate them to all members of your team and your allies across the organization. It is amazing to see their satisfaction when they see their hard work paying off.

Second, you need to share these results with the company's senior leadership and department heads to demonstrate how their support is also helping their teams and the company as a whole.

Third, it is important that the company's employees and suppliers also receive a summary of the activities and results. This can be an important step in helping your company attract new talent through HR recruitments and increase your supplier's diversity targets.

Finally, don't ignore the importance of having your work recognized by your industry, through press coverage and financial analyst reports. More than ever, companies are being assessed by their ability to "read" the market trends, and effective multicultural marketing is one of these trends investors are tracking now.

10 Protect

Finally, a leader of a Hispanic business unit should always look for ways to protect the practice, either by constantly reviewing the business assumptions and results, making sure resources are allocated proportionally to the investment levels, or by making sure employee turnover doesn't negatively impact the practice in the near future.

Chapter 27

The Advertising Implementation Dilemma

When it comes to implementing multicultural advertising programs, most brands face an important dilemma: How much effort should be dedicated to multicultural audiences?

If the investments are limited, following a total market approach, they will probably not deliver any significant results to the business' bottom line, not only wasting most of the investments but also perpetuating the false narrative that multicultural marketing efforts "don't work."

On the other hand, some clients feel like they really can't afford to have a complete, parallel, marketing effort towards multicultural marketing. Where can one find a balanced approach between resources and effectiveness?

As always, it is important to recognize that there are no "right or wrong" approaches; however, based on my experience, I can tell you that today's most successful marketers gravitate towards a model that balances inclusiveness and specificity.

What do I mean by that? The inclusiveness comes from companies who are mostly focused on making their mainstream, general messaging efforts more multicultural in essence. That means making sure that the insights, the strategy, the stories, the casting, and the contexts of any creative execution delivered to the public incorporate elements of multiculturalism, carefully avoiding stereotypes and preconceived notions about diverse segments.

This can be achieved by bringing your multicultural marketing experts in early during the planning process, giving them a voice to collaborate with your other marketing experts to shape the elements of your plan from scratch through a multicultural lens.

Then, you complement your overall marketing plans with specific executions aimed at diverse segments. These efforts can be extensive, using mass media at the national/regional level, or can be very targeted, like a direct response campaign or a local market activity. The criteria to decide the magnitude and intensity of your diverse specific efforts should be based on the contribution/importance each diverse segment has to your overall business and the resources you have to effectively reach each segment.

DOI: 10.4324/9781003348931-31

For the Hispanic segment I always recommend having at least three to four specific efforts per fiscal year, given the importance of not letting the target forget your brand, which is what happens when you only "show up" in front of them once a year.

Remember, while Hispanic consumers may be exposed to your general market messages, as discussed in previous chapters, these messages tend to underperform in effectiveness and ROI when compared to culturally relevant messages. So specific marketing efforts allow your brand to deliver specific messages that tend to be placed in culturally relevant environments with much higher effectiveness.

Great opportunities to create Hispanic-specific messages (beyond the traditional Hispanic Heritage Month) are Holidays, Mother's Day, key cultural events associated with music, sports, and business-specific moments like the launch of a service or a line extension of your brand that you feel will resonate with the segment.

Furthermore, a marketer's intrinsic business dynamic can and should also be a reason for considering a specific effort towards Hispanics. For instance, when you have a business challenge where Hispanics underperform in some KPIs or when they overperform, your own business performance may indicate opportunities to create targeted Hispanic messages.

In the end, the balance between "inclusivity and specificity" is a delicate, fine-tuning exercise. Sometimes your multicultural marketing efforts converge towards your mainstream message, and at other times, they diverge. However, it is important to clarify that when they diverge, they should still follow a brand's positioning in the market and its overall strategy. The key to specificity is that brands need to recognize the market forces that may require a special approach towards a diverse segment, be that business conditions, specific insights and/or behaviors regarding your brand or service, or even for executional creative or media reasons.

Chapter 28

The Hispanic Market "Long Tail"

The "Long-Tail Economics" concept was created by Chris Anderson, former *Wired* magazine editor, and to this day, it's one of the best descriptors of the impact the digital revolution has had on the business world. Anderson defines the term as follows:

> Our culture and economy is increasingly shifting away from a focus on a relatively small number of "hits" (mainstream products and markets) at the head of the demand curve and toward a huge number of niches in the tail.

In my opinion, we could identify a similar pattern in today's U.S. multicultural market. What was once considered to be a "niche" opportunity—like the U.S. Hispanic population—was 62 million strong in 2020[1] with purchase power levels north of $2.7 trillion a year.[2] This is not a "niche" opportunity anymore.

While some advertisers still question whether it is worth having dedicated efforts towards this growing segment, progressive and innovative brands are already looking into new "niche sub-segments" within the Hispanic segment as well as other opportunities that have become attractive enough on their own, thus reinforcing the concept of "Long-Tail" marketing.

The risk of not considering these sub-segments in your marketing plans may be felt in missed sales and a decline in market share. A marketer that takes too long to engage these groups may have to spend more in the future trying to win them back when these consumers' preferences may already be fully established.

American CMOs looking for incremental growth this decade should consider these five sub-segments as they develop their marketing plans. Here is a brief description of the opportunities based on our analysis using MRI-Simmons research, and Census data.

DOI: 10.4324/9781003348931-32

Hispanic Millennials—Opportunity: 17 Million[3]

At 75-million strong, U.S. millennials represent one of the most coveted segments in today's marketplace. However, when it comes to ethnicity and cultural affinity, considering this segment as cohesive and uniform could be a costly mistake.[4]

Almost 25% of all U.S. millennials are Hispanic, and these consumers, while displaying similarities with other non-Hispanic millennials when it comes to attitudes and behaviors, also demonstrate a strong connection to the Hispanic culture.[5] When these cultural nuances are in play, unique marketing opportunities are created for marketers.

For example, Hispanic millennials tend to over-index non-Hispanic millennials when it comes to paying more attention to commercials: they over-index their non-Hispanic peers on their desire to have their own business one day, they tend to build a family and have kids at a relatively young age, and they also tend to over-index on purchases such as clothing, apparel, grooming essentials, and alcoholic beverages.[6]

Non-Mexican Hispanics—Opportunity: 24 Million[7]

While the majority of U.S. Hispanics are of Mexican origin, non-Mexican Hispanics represent more than one-third of the total U.S. Hispanic population, and this growth outperforms the Mexican-Hispanic population (13% vs. 4% growth in the past 5 years).[8]

This group is mostly foreign-born (61%), with 25% of them being from Puerto Rico, 10% from Cuba, and recently, this segment has seen significant growth from South American countries, including Venezuela, Colombia, and Brazil.[9]

This is an interesting sub-segment for many reasons, including its geographic concentration (mostly on the East Coast with additional population pockets in Illinois, Texas, and California[10]), their strong bilingual capabilities, and their strong consumption of digital media.[11]

According to MRI-Simmons data, this sub-segment has higher disposable income and tends to spend more than Mexican-Hispanic consumers, representing a significant opportunity for several categories. As an example of their slightly different behavior nuances, uncovered by studying the "Hispanic Long-Tail," when it comes to alcoholic beverages, non-Mexican Hispanics tend to prefer whiskey, wine, and cognac over tequila.[12]

The Hispanic 55-Year-Old+ Population— Opportunity: 10 Million[13]

While almost every demographic statistic about U.S. Hispanics over the past 40 years confirms that the segment is "very young," with the median age of Hispanics in the U.S. in the high 20s, most people forget that a

37-year-old Hispanic consumer who was enjoying Ricky Martin's "Living La Vida Loca" back in 1999, has celebrated her/his 60th birthday already.

Don't get me wrong, the U.S. Hispanic population will still bring down the average age of Americans based on its relative youth, but the number of U.S. Hispanics over 55 will keep growing, and marketers shouldn't ignore this sub-segment.

While concerned about their economic stability in the present and in the future, this is a group that has significant influence on young Hispanics when it comes to keeping the cultural connection to their Hispanic roots. They are also key influencers in multigenerational households.

Some relevant categories where this sub-segment tends to over-index vs. their non-Hispanic peers are casual dining and personal items, such as colognes and perfumes.[14]

Hispanics with Household Income above $100K/ Year—Opportunity: 12 Million[15]

One of the most common misperceptions about targeting U.S. Hispanics goes like this: "I understand the significant population growth, but this is a low-income segment, they don't have the purchasing power my brand is looking for."

First, the U.S. Hispanic household income has actually been growing over the past decade, fueled mainly by advances in education.

Second, one of the biggest kept secrets of this marketplace is that today there are more than 4 million U.S. Hispanic households with an annual income at or above $100K, representing almost 12 million Hispanic consumers.[16]

These Hispanic households have built their income with more household earners (2.4 vs. 2.0 earners when compared to non-Hispanic $100+/year households).[17] Interestingly enough, data shows that a Hispanic household with an income $100K+/year tends to mirror the shopping behaviors of their under $100K/year Hispanic peers (despite having much more income to spend), instead of displaying similar purchasing characteristics to their high-income non-Hispanic peers.

Regardless of their income, these households demonstrate significant opportunities for marketers to sell credit cards, travel, and automobiles (mainly more upscale models), as well as offer financial services support (including life insurance).[18]

Emerging Hispanic DMAs—Opportunity: 6 Million[19]

We assume that if you have a Hispanic marketing strategy in your Marketing Plan, you are probably already targeting Hispanics in Los Angeles, New York City, Miami, Dallas, Houston, and Chicago.

However, there are important markets that tend to be forgotten when plans are developed and resources are allocated. These are not your "traditional Hispanic markets," but over the past few years, they have demonstrated significant Hispanic population growth.

According to the 2020 Census data and as reported by the Pew Research Center,

> The Hispanic population grew by 50% or more from 2010 to 2020 in 517 of the 1,685 counties with 1,000 or more Hispanics in the 2020 census. The vast majority of these counties are not located in what have historically been Hispanic population centers.

In fact,

> growth *rates* were highest from 2010 to 2020 in counties located in states with smaller Hispanic populations. Among counties with 1,000 Hispanics in 2020, the top 10 Hispanic growth rates ranged from 234% to 1,002%—at least 10 times the national growth rate of Hispanics. There are three in Louisiana, three in North Dakota, and one each in Alabama, Georgia, Michigan and South Dakota. North Dakota, the state with the fastest Hispanic population growth (148%), has the two fastest-growing counties: McKenzie (+1,002%) and Williams (+794%). They are among the top oil-producing counties in the country and were the two fastest-growing counties for total population between 2010 and 2020, in part due to job growth.[20]

The problem is that since most of them are not on most marketers' "radar screens," proper investments in distribution, sales support representation, PR, local community efforts, and advertising are not taking place, leaving the door open to competitive brands trying to establish themselves in the hearts and minds of these consumers.

I'd also like to highlight markets like Sacramento, the Washington, DC, metro area, Denver, Atlanta, Salt Lake City, Baltimore, Nashville, Raleigh-Durham, Charlotte, and Columbus as non-traditional areas that have had incredible growth of Hispanics in the past two decades.[21]

While I understand that marketers have a limited budget to expand their Hispanic marketing reach, I'd like to point out that these markets can be targeted with a fraction of what marketers spend on the most traditional Hispanic DMAs, which tend to be large metropolitan areas.

In summary, the opportunities listed earlier represent the future of multicultural marketing. Instead of looking for a misconceived interpretation of Total Market, where a one-size-fits-all approach tailored to non-Hispanics is forced from the top down to create the perception of inclusiveness, progressive brands will further segment their marketing opportunities. This will,

Hispanic population growth rates from 2010 to 2020 highest in states that historically did not have large Hispanic populations

% growth of Hispanics

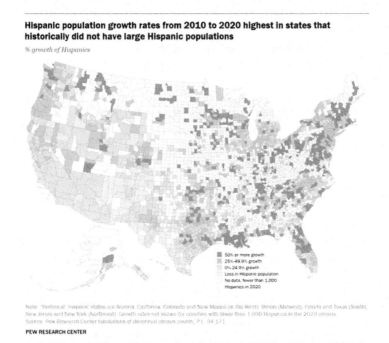

Note: "Historical" Hispanic states are Arizona, California, Colorado and New Mexico (in the West); Illinois (Midwest); Florida and Texas (South); New Jersey and New York (Northeast). Growth rates not shown for counties with fewer than 1,000 Hispanics in the 2020 census.
Source: Pew Research Center tabulations of decennial census counts, P.L. 94-171.

PEW RESEARCH CENTER

Figure 28.1 Hispanic population growth rates from 2010 to 2020 highest in states that historically did not have large Hispanic populations.

Hispanic population grew most in counties with large Hispanic populations and grew at fastest rate in counties with small Hispanic populations, 2010-20

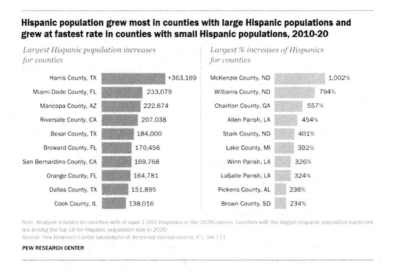

Largest Hispanic population increases for counties

Harris County, TX	+363,169
Miami-Dade County, FL	233,079
Maricopa County, AZ	222,674
Riverside County, CA	207,038
Bexar County, TX	184,000
Broward County, FL	170,456
San Bernardino County, CA	169,768
Orange County, FL	164,781
Dallas County, TX	151,895
Cook County, IL	138,016

Largest % increases of Hispanics for counties

County	% Increase
McKenzie County, ND	1,002%
Williams County, ND	794%
Charlton County, GA	557%
Allen Parish, LA	454%
Stark County, ND	401%
Lake County, MI	392%
Winn Parish, LA	326%
LaSalle Parish, LA	324%
Pickens County, AL	236%
Brown County, SD	234%

Note: Analysis is based on counties with at least 1,000 Hispanics in the 2020 census. Counties with the largest Hispanic population increases are among the top 18 for Hispanic population size in 2020.
Source: Pew Research Center tabulations of decennial census counts, P.L. 94-171.

PEW RESEARCH CENTER

Figure 28.2 Hispanic population grew most in counties with large Hispanic populations and grew at fastest rate in counties with small Hispanic populations, 2010–2020.

in turn, form smaller clusters of customers and prospects (which has always been the foundation behind segmentation) that can be supported by the current advances in marketing, based on data analytics tools, leveraging the improvements on addressable media opportunities not only on the digital and social media spaces but also with traditional TV.

So while some may be discussing the "end of multicultural marketing," pragmatic marketers will be acting on the hidden opportunities the segment offers for those seeking growth in 2023 and beyond.

Notes

1 U.S. Census Bureau, 2020 Census.
2 2021 LDC U.S. Latino GDP Report, www.LatinoDonorCollaborative.org
3 U.S. Census Bureau, 2020 Census + 2021 Geoscape Marketscape DataStream™.
4 U.S. Census Bureau, 2020 Census.
5 2021 Geoscape Marketscape DataStream.
6 2021 Fall MRI-Simmons USA.
7 U.S. Census Bureau, 2020 Census + 2019 American Community Survey.
8 U.S. Census Bureau, 2020 Census + 2019 American Community Survey.
9 U.S. Census Bureau, 2020 Census + 2019 American Community Survey +, 2021 Fall MRI-Simmons USA.
10 2019 American Community Survey (1 Year Data).
11 2021 Fall MRI-Simmons USA.
12 2021 Fall MRI-Simmons USA.
13 U.S. Census Bureau, 2020 Census + 2021 Geoscape Marketscape DataStream™.
14 2021 Fall MRI-Simmons USA.
15 U.S. Census Bureau, 2020 Census + 2021 Fall MRI-Simmons USA.
16 2021 Geoscape Marketscape DataStream™.
17 2021 Fall MRI-Simmons USA.
18 2021 Fall MRI-Simmons USA.
19 U.S. Census Bureau, 2020 Census, 2010 Census.
20 U.S. Hispanic population continued its geographic spread in the 2010s, BY JEFFREY S. PASSEL, MARK HUGO LOPEZ AND D'VERA COHN www.pewresearch.org/fact-tank/2022/02/03/u-s-hispanic-population-continued-its-geographic-spread-in-the-2010s/
21 U.S. Census Bureau, 2020 Census, 2010 Census.

Chapter 29

Multicultural Marketing Investments Deserve a New Resource Allocation Methodology

Every year, as companies kick off their business planning process, CMOs and their teams face a perennial challenge: allocating their limited resources among a variety of brands, projects, programs, and opportunities, while still achieving the necessary ROI and expected growth rates.

To complicate matters, especially after the pandemic, marketers face a constantly changing marketplace that challenges past assumptions regarding consumer behaviors, media choices, and demographic shifts.

Most organizations continue to allocate their resources based on antiquated models that, at best, provide room for some "fine-tuning" over what used to work years ago. Unfortunately, outdated resource allocation models based on the past are no longer good enough for most brands. Some marketers have started to realize there's an ever-widening gap between where most resources are being allocated versus where most of the incremental growth is coming from.

Nowhere is this problem more acute than in the multicultural marketing space. Most organizations have notoriously underinvested in the core targets of this segment (Hispanic, Black, and Asian American Pacific Islander consumers), so the gap between business importance and intentional investments only grows larger.

For example, according to Nielsen data, the industry's investment in measured Spanish-language advertising was only 5.9% of the total investment in 2020, despite the fact that the Hispanic segment, with almost 20% of the country's population, represents the largest minority ethnic group in the U.S. To make this gap even more critical, nearly 70% of this population has a high affinity for Hispanic culture, including media consumption in Spanish.

A few key factors driving this myopic behavior are listed:

Difficulty in Defining the Opportunity: Most marketers still see multicultural marketing programs as an extension of advertising, negating a more significant opportunity to positively impact the whole business.

DOI: 10.4324/9781003348931-33

Absence of Multicultural Key Performance Indicators: If you don't track your business performance by multicultural segment, you can't know a segment's contribution to your business. If you don't know this, you can never set proper objectives, strategies, and programs to grow it.

Lack of Understanding the Role Multicultural Segments Have on Long-Term Growth Plans: Most organizations ignore multicultural marketing efforts or treat them as an appendix of their mainstream marketing efforts. Consequently, multicultural marketing investments are often the first line to be cut when budgets need to be reduced.

In addition, even companies that tentatively invest in multicultural advertising do so based on stereotypical insights or creative ideas, and worst of all, merely translate existing messages to Spanish without considering consumer barriers or drivers.

The Illusion of Total Market: This is still prevalent because many brands believe they already connect with multicultural consumers via their existing mainstream investments (the spillover or halo effect of media). Several studies have already debunked the perception that this spillover is effective, confirming what experts have always said, "Reaching is different from connecting with multicultural consumers."

It still surprises me how some marketers continue to pour millions of dollars in multicultural media buys only to place sub-par, ineffective messages to air on these vast investments. The inability to invest in multicultural insights and relevant multicultural messages, which in most cases represent only 10%–20% of a marketer's investment, makes the remaining 80%–90% almost irrelevant. The irony is that precisely this 10%–20% range is called "non-working dollars" by many, but in reality, this is the part of the budget that makes the bulk of the investments work.

Misunderstanding the Way Multicultural Advertising Works: Most marketers still don't fully understand how highly effective multicultural messages work. Most of the recent studies that dissect the components of the effectiveness of multicultural advertising highlight elements that increase effectiveness, such as cultural fluency, nuances, relatability to everyday situations, use of dialogue, and humor.

In other words, the more specific you are in your approach, the more authentic your message will ring. That authenticity is key to building your brand in your consumers' eyes and driving disproportionately higher ROI. Brands that ignore multicultural consumers or merely translate their messages targeting Anglo consumers, hoping that some part of that message will connect with multicultural audiences, will likely suffer in the short and long term.

But there is some good news to report. Not all companies are trapped in past assumptions and are starting to put their money where the growth is. According to Nielsen, in 2021, 14 companies out of the top 20 Hispanic-focused advertisers in the country showed an increase in their relative Spanish-language investments vis-à-vis their total expenditures.

While most advertisers hesitate to openly discuss their resource allocation strategies, most do follow some or all of these best practices:

- Adopt a zero-based budget where past years don't influence future marketing investments.
- Consider a proportionality between investments by multicultural segment and their importance as existing customers or clients.
- Consider a relationship between sources of growth or incremental sales derived by multicultural segments and investments towards these segments.
- Surround yourself with experts (internal and external) who can help you with the allocation of resources and with the implementation of your plan.

It is time to revisit old assumptions you may have and place your brand on a growth path by allocating your resources wisely. Marketers should consider a constant rebalancing of their budget allocation criteria, similar to what investors do with their own portfolios.

Growth will reward companies with the courage to break up with old paradigms and fully embrace the new marketplace reality.

Chapter 30

How to Find the Right Creative Approach

Picture this: you're a senior marketing executive and your Hispanic ad agency has just presented a creative idea for your next campaign. You like the direction but suddenly you ask the question: "Have you seen what our general market agency presented? Why wouldn't that work for Hispanics? What's not Hispanic about it?"

Pressured to find synergies and budget efficiencies year over year, the temptation to adopt a one-size-fits-all approach that may not only save production and agency fees but could also save valuable time by reducing the number of meetings is a reality facing many marketers in America today.

And it's a challenge that general market agencies are more than eager to take on. Some help by acting as orchestrators of partner agencies and creating "synergies" by crafting single briefs based on universal insights and by coordinating double shoots. Others support the quest for efficiencies by offering fully integrated services which they achieve by hiring a few Spanish-speaking executives and presenting themselves as capable of also doing Hispanic marketing (which only demonstrates how ill-prepared these agencies are as they equate Spanish-language proficiency to Hispanic marketing expertise).

For their part, Hispanic agencies feel the burden to justify their client's investments but their recommendations are often received with a level of suspicion; after all, any recommendation for creative development may increase the agency's scope and compensation.

The reality is that the process of deciding whether a brand would benefit from a segmented creative strategy should be neither subjective nor driven by cost. Clients and agencies should instead come together using a rational, fact-based decision process that takes the emotion out of the process while working to maximize the brand's ROI.

Here is a summary of the process we at alma advertising have developed and successfully implemented with many of our market-leading clients. This model has been presented in industry meetings and has been adopted by other agencies and their clients with positive results.

DOI: 10.4324/9781003348931-34

A defining feature of our model is that, at its core, it does not aim to have a communication strategy that creates a different brand positioning, voice, or tone. Alignment on these elements is non-negotiable as the goal should never be to create a different brand to reach Hispanic consumers. Rather the goal of our approach is to identify whether there are opportunities to sell the brand's story in a more relevant way, and this is determined based on a series of planning stages.

The first stage is focused on the business opportunity. Based on our observations, it is amazing how many clients and agencies seldom start the debate around Hispanic-specific executions by analyzing the issue/opportunity the brand is trying to tackle. This is a fundamental step as the non-Hispanic side of the business and the Hispanic side of the business may be in very different business life stages. For example, some brands still see the opportunity to grow penetration and frequency of consumption with Hispanics, while for non-Hispanic consumers of the same brand the strategy should be more focused on market share protection and up-selling/cross-selling opportunities.

If your business challenge/opportunity is different between Hispanics and non-Hispanic consumers, your creative brief should probably be different too. Different creative briefs may require different creative executions and that has nothing to do with language or culture. It's just a smart business decision based on need-driven segmentation.

For example, a financial institution focused on selling life insurance to its customers may notice that Hispanics tend to have lower penetration when it comes to Life Insurance than other financial services. Understanding the reasons behind these behaviors may allow brands to craft a more effective message.

The second stage is all about consumer insights, and it is mostly associated with the industry or product in question. While the business opportunity may be the same between Hispanic and non-Hispanic segments, when launching a new product, the consumer insight could be very different and different insights may require different approaches.

One great example is the launch of McDonald's Mango-Pineapple Smoothie back in 2011. The general market agency's launch brief rightfully positioned mango and pineapple as exotic options for non-Hispanic consumers. However, mango and pineapple are anything but exotic among Hispanics; these are staples of our food habits that are highly associated with positive memories from childhood.

Because of this, McDonald's approved a different creative strategy for the smoothie launch to the Hispanic market, which proved to be a results-driving move. Sales among Hispanics over-indexed the national average by almost 27% and the Hispanic campaign achieved a staggering 73% over-delivery against its goals.

The third and final stage of our model is focused on creative execution. Let's assume that your brand has a business challenge and that your agencies may have found a universal insight based on common consumer insights. In theory you should be all set for the same creative execution, right? Maybe all you need is a voice-over in Spanish, or a double content shoot, with the assumption that the creative idea should be the same, right?

Not so fast, one of the biggest opportunities with the Hispanic segment lies in the fact that cultural nuances may impact the way the different consumer segments receive and process advertising messages.

The Nielsen study already referenced in this book specifically demonstrated that culture impacts the way Hispanics react to advertising as they may prefer a different type of storytelling. My colleague Angela Rodriguez, SVP of Consumer Insights at alma advertising, expands on this:

> Holidays, festivals, and traditions are the tip of the iceberg when it comes to the transference of culture. Those visible acts are the minimal cues we can use to show empathy. That's the easy answer to what's Hispanic about it? To truly understand a culture, we must understand the non-visible; the myths and legends that a culture values and the indirect ways that communication happens.
>
> Just like international business demands that we know when to bow our head and when to shake hands, culturally relevant marketing communications must reflect the non-spoken subtleties. Good marketers will speak Spanish to Hispanics. Great marketers will know that Hispanics prefer emotionally-driven narratives over rational appeals, that stories with lessons are less appealing than stories that bring folklores to life, and that telling why something matters is often more important than getting to the (price) point.

For example, back in 2004 when I had the opportunity to lead Nextel's Hispanic Marketing efforts we had some concerns that most of the situations featured in our general market messages were associated with construction, transportation, and other blue-collar jobs, given the high popularity of Nextel services among these types of jobs.

However, we knew from research that while Hispanics proudly worked disproportionally in these professions, a significant number of Hispanics preferred situations where they were portrayed in more aspirational jobs, elevating the image of Hispanics beyond the expected or traditional. Because of this learning, we shifted our creative approach to portray situations that were more aspirational, like white-collar or entrepreneurial jobs. This is just one, basic, example of many that can be given around situations, setups, dialogues, and other elements that could enhance or decrease creative effectiveness.

At this stage the combination of deep consumer knowledge and craftsmanship on creative storytelling can offer brands an opportunity to stand out. Any agency can translate an ad into Spanish and use stereotypical cues to try to create relevancy. This may create a false sense of efficiency to some clients, but mismanagement in the area of creative storytelling may decrease effectiveness and ROI over time while also damaging the brand's equity.

Now we know that the flipside of saving money by forcing less relevant insights to connect with Hispanics results in a significant reduction in ROI. The Nielsen study "The Secrets to Higher ROI in Spanish Language TV"[1] demonstrated that translated one-size–fits-for-all insights-driven ads may have an ROI equal or lower than its general market, English-language version. On the other hand, high effective ads based on original Hispanic insights can drive ROI from three or four times higher than their general market counterparts, meaning that any savings a marketer may have achieved on agency fees or production can be eliminated by a negative ROI from the media investment when creative is less effective.

If you're a marketer, it's time to break the barrier on the opportunity to create segment-specific creative executions. You must stop thinking about how much you're saving in the short term to how much you're missing in the long term by not doing it correctly!

I hope our model can help you and your partner agencies have an unbiased debate on such an important topic. After all, let's not forget that every marketer's job is to grow their business, and that mistaken decisions around Total Market are actually hindering the ability to capture the potential growth that the Hispanic segment can provide and can negatively impact your business' bottom line.

Note

1 "The Secrets to Higher ROI in Spanish Language TV," Nielsen 2017.

Chapter 31

The Multicultural Communications Challenge

Building a multicultural plan that genuinely integrates the creative and the media disciplines is one of the biggest challenges in today's multicultural space.

Why is this such a challenge? Mostly because there's still a significant gap in the way brands approach the multicultural opportunity. I want to shed light on this problem and suggest a few scenarios to overcome these barriers.

First, it's important to recognize that the multicultural marketing industry faces the same issues the general market has been facing for the past decades: a separation between the creative discipline and the media planning and buying disciplines, at both the agency and client's sides.

While this decision drove a significant amount of specialization and resources that made media agencies more accountable for their clients' investments, this move also helped the market "forget" that the true effectiveness of a communications plan is a function of the combined effect of an efficient media plan and a persuasive creative idea. In other words, when media and messaging work together, ROI greatly improves.

It is no surprise to realize that, if not carefully managed, creative and media processes can go down their separate parallel paths and only converge when budgets are put together. In most cases, the creative side is told what the media side has negotiated, and the media side becomes aware of what the creative idea will be only after all-important media decisions are made.

A media plan that's considered excellent from an efficiency standpoint typically attempts to "stretch" the brand's budget throughout the year, maximizing weekly reach while trying to lower KPIs' costs. But this approach means that the media plan only offers the brand "an opportunity to be seen" by prospects and customers; it does not guarantee that the message will be seen by viewers who now have a myriad of opportunities to skip advertising.

That's precisely why a strong and relevant creative idea can make a media plan better. A compelling idea increases the probability an ad won't be skipped and will ideally resonate with viewers who think and feel differently about the brand due to the exposure.

DOI: 10.4324/9781003348931-35

Why is this discussion relevant to multicultural communications strategies? Because some advertisers are facing a double challenge. They face the situation mentioned earlier, where multicultural media plans and multicultural messages are not coordinated and synchronized, and potentially also have to overcome the fact that a significant amount of the reach levels they acquired were based on spillover from non-multicultural media choices.

In other words, a significant number of multicultural media plans start from the premise that multicultural consumers are already exposed to the advertiser's "general market" media plan. This phenomenon is a well-known trend that is, thankfully, already dying as a result of its failure: the "Total Market" approach.

The spillover is real, but when counting the reach of general media plans into multicultural consumers' reach and frequency numbers, one may forget an important issue. This spillover media brings a spillover creative idea that has not been created to serve multicultural audiences. That does not mean these creative ideas are ineffective or wrong. They are just not created by thinking about the multicultural consumer at the core, thus not always the best message for a segment consumer.

The consequence of this thinking is that most advertisers nowadays assume that their media plans are reaching different segments, and while this is true from a technical standpoint, this reach, while efficient, is less effective than it could be since spillover messages tend not to build equity with multicultural consumers who are outside of their intended general market targets.

Imagine a hypothetical media plan targeting Hispanics, with an average weekly reach of 80%—on the surface, quite an impressive level. Most plans like this have two components. First, the spillover's reach level represents most of the weekly reach levels, then and only then, the plan incorporates the multicultural media choices.

That means that the 80% weekly reach plan may be delivering less than 40% of culturally relevant weekly reach, a new measure that combines relevant cultural media with culturally driven creative choices.

The real culturally driven reach level may be even smaller, given that many clients still use translated or transcreated messages to run in their multicultural media plans. In other words, not only are these clients counting on media plans that deliver the majority of the media via spillover but even the small share of reach that is dedicated to multicultural segments receives creative messages that are not culturally relevant. It's a misstep twice over.

I asked Gonzalo del Fa, president of GroupM Multicultural, a leading media planning and buying agency his opinion on the topic, and this is his take on it:

> We always support the idea of calculating the spill that a General Market media campaign has towards different audiences. However, we always encourage our clients to clearly understand the real impact those assets have on those different audiences. That's why we always speak about

straight spill and effective spill because the difference between the two of them sometimes is quite significant, mostly because many of the assets used on General Market media are not created with multicultural audiences in mind nor are they relevant to that audience.

The best way to accurately calculate effective spill is by applying a discount factor to the straight spill, which leverages proprietary and syndicated data that identifies and measures all the factors that impact relevance and effectiveness in advertising. It is important to mention that this analysis needs to be done for each multicultural segment since relevancy and effectiveness are not the same for all groups. In other words, your communication campaign is not supposed to just reach eyeballs but connect and engage consumers' hearts and minds, and that is only possible if you place relevant and authentic content in relevant and authentic contexts.

Leaders in this marketplace are starting to realize that there's an opportunity to treat their multicultural communication strategy differently. Here are a few suggestions that may improve the effectiveness of your plans:

1   Consider an integrated planning process where creative and media plans are developed simultaneously and the agencies share a standard set of insights and data under a shared calendar.
2   Establish that all communications must have a common goal of effectiveness, measured on whatever KPIs the client selects (e.g. sales, market share, consideration). Having a media plan to reach a percentage of consumers may not be enough anymore.
3   Understand what percentage of your multicultural weekly reach is from spillover from general market media and what percentage comes from native multicultural media choices.
4   Run an analysis of what percentage of multicultural media reach is filled with creative work that is dedicated to the segment. You will be surprised by how low this number can be!

Based on these suggestions, new approaches may emerge, either for allocating media and creative resources or for developing media plans. For instance, some may consider starting a plan with native multicultural reach and only then adding the spillover numbers at a discounted rate because the spillover reach can't be treated equally as the native multicultural reach.

This discussion is vital as clients may not be seeing the ROI for their multicultural marketing plans, making them more cautious about future investments. The low ROI may be happening because multicultural consumers do not see relevant multicultural messages often enough. Reaching is not the same as connecting. Beyond just reach, the focus should be on "reach of heart."

Chapter 32

Multicultural Consumers and Millennials Are Ready to Fuel the Next Cycle of Brand Growth

I believe that the multicultural marketing opportunity is one of the few remaining areas of competitive advantage and sources of growth for brands and corporations for years to come.

From time to time a study produces data and insights that shed light on this topic, and Kantar Consulting did just that with their 2018 Monitor Study,[1] a comprehensive quantitative analysis on the state of the U.S. consumer marketplace, including essential perspectives on the multicultural segment.

The study concludes that strategies based on culture and language, when well executed, can unlock areas of opportunities for brands that are seeking to accelerate their business performance further.

Here are a few key learnings from the study:

1 Hispanic Cultural Identity and Community Sentiment Are at an All-Time High:

Hispanic consumers lead and over-index all other ethnic segments in cultural connection elements such as family, history, food, language, recipes, and music.

- More importantly, 59% of Hispanic consumers believe that their cultural heritage or background has a significant influence on their purchasing decisions, a 174 index versus all other segments.
- Moreover, 59% of Hispanic consumers said that they actively seek out brands that acknowledge their culture's unique traditions, a 164 index versus all other segments.

2 Multicultural Consumers Think Brands Are Not Listening:

Despite these substantial numbers, Hispanic consumers (and multicultural consumers overall) still feel that there are not enough brands doing a good job connecting with them.

DOI: 10.4324/9781003348931-36

- A total of 72% of Black respondents, 62% of AAPI respondents, and 59% of Hispanic respondents believe that brands are not doing enough to be representative of people like them in their campaigns.
- Interestingly enough for Hispanic consumers, these numbers get worse the younger the target gets, with 66% of 12–22 years old Hispanics not feeling adequately represented by most brands.

However, connecting is not a matter of representation in advertising only.

- Sixty percent of Hispanic consumers (43% of non-Hispanics) believe that companies do not make an effort to be active in their local communities.
- Sixty-six percent of Hispanic consumers (70% of 12–22-year-old Hispanics and 76% of Spanish-dominant Hispanics) believe that very few brands genuinely care about the state of the Hispanic communities.
- Sixty-six percent of all Hispanic consumers said they were frustrated by brands that treat them like an afterthought (versus 56% of all consumers).

3 Forget the Concept of Cultural Assimilation, and Embrace Biculturalism:

Most Hispanic consumers do not want to assimilate. This is a concept that was relevant in the waves of immigration in the 19th and 20th centuries, which is irrelevant today.

- According to the study, 92% of Hispanic consumers believe that it feels natural to live in the U.S. and connect to its culture, yet still, retain the culture of their country of origin.
- Furthermore, 80% of Hispanic consumers feel entirely comfortable being the only person of their ethnicity in a large group of people. This number reaches 86% among millennial Hispanics and 93% among younger Hispanics.

4 The Spanish Language Is Experiencing a Resurgence:

- Fifty-seven percent of Hispanic consumers believe that the Spanish language is more important to them today than it was just five years ago.
- Surprisingly enough, and contrary to what most believe, younger Hispanic consumers are becoming more interested in the Spanish language, with 62% of millennial Hispanics reporting a higher interest in the language.

	2011	2018	Difference
Spanish	16%	25%	+9 p.p.
Both Languages Equally	28%	30%	+2 p.p.
English	56%	45%	−11 p.p.

Source: Kantar 2018 Monitor Study

Still, on the topic of the importance of the Spanish language, Kantar made a comparison between 2011 and 2018 on the Hispanic consumer-preferred language in every situation and found that the importance of Spanish continues to increase over time, as you can see in the following table:

5 Hispanics Impact and Influence a Broader Demographic Spectrum:

Kantar's study asked millennials from every ethnic background about areas of their lives where their preferences were impacted by their interaction with people from other races and ethnicities.

- The results: 75% of their "Food & Cooking," 68% of their "Music," 61% of their "Movies," and 59% of their "Fashion & Clothing" choices were impacted by someone from a different ethnic group.

Finally, as expected, when asked about whether "Cultural Diversity is one of America's major sources of strength," consumers from diverse ethnic backgrounds lead the pack when it comes to agreeing to the above statement. Percentage of Consumers that Agree "Cultural Diversity is one of America's major sources of strength":

- AAPI—88%
- Hispanic—87%
- Black—83%
- Non-Hispanic White—79%

However, when analyzing the answer from the entire country, 81% agree with the statement as well, which is a robust response. Among all U.S. millennials, the response was at 83%, clearly indicating the direction the country is taking in embracing our country's multicultural fabric.

I spoke with J. Walker Smith, Kantar's chief knowledge officer, Brand & Marketing, about his take on what was the most significant learning from the study. He said,

Two things really struck me. One, there is a lot of talk in marketing these days about penetration as the cornerstone of growth. There is no group bigger than Hispanic consumers for this kind of growth strategy. Second, and perhaps most interesting, Hispanics are leading the market. Every single one of the trends driving the total market is significantly higher among Hispanic consumers—experiences, services, diversity, technology, and cultural expressiveness. You name it, Hispanics are the first among equals when it comes to the future.

When I started working with multicultural marketing in the U.S., as an advertiser more than 20 years ago, one of the most significant barriers in our industry was the lack of reliable data and insights. Nowadays, I believe that while it is always great to have more information, we already have a healthy amount of research that can guide advertisers navigating their multicultural marketing programs, and this Kantar study is proof of that. The question is whether today's marketers will be open to changing their existing mental models and embracing the new opportunities they are facing. Multicultural consumers and millennials are ready to fuel the next cycle of brand growth. Are you ready for them?

Note

1 www.kantar.com/Inspiration/Consumer/The-Hispanic-consumer-thinks-your-brand-doesnt-care

Chapter 33

Storytelling Is a Different Story for Each Culture

Recently I was talking to a friend about Alfonso Cuarón's Oscar-winning movie *Roma*, and we were debating the narrative's pace and style. My friend, who is Anglo-American, thought it was too slow, too visual. But for me, it was a beautiful movie that reminded me of my upbringing in Latin America. I realized this was a discussion not only about just film but, rather, about different styles of storytelling.

This exchange is reflective of how culture can impact people's reaction to a story, not just the content of a plot but also the style of the narrative storytelling. That minor nuance is significant in film and books, and it is also meaningful to how marketers approach their communication strategies when it comes to marketing to Hispanics.

For example, back in 2004, I joined the Nextel organization, famous for their two-way walkie-talkie services, as their director of Hispanic Marketing Communications. One of my first assignments on the job was to review the new marketing campaign that had been developed for general market and to lead the adaptation of that campaign for the Hispanic segment.

The new creative idea, brilliantly created by the TBWA/Chiat team, had the tagline "Done" and was focused on the fact that Nextel's two-way push-to-talk technology allowed businesses to run smoothly and accomplish more, faster.

However, when we tested this idea with Hispanic consumers, known for being big fans of Nextel's services, they were not as receptive to the "Done" campaign because they thought it depicted personal relationships as too cold and lacking in empathy and a more human connection. I remember listening to comments from focus groups such as:

> I don't want to connect with someone from my business or social circle (which for many Hispanics consumers is one combined circle), ask for a question, get an answer, and that's it. I would ask them first how they are doing; we would probably talk about sports or something we watched on TV, about our kids and family, and only then, will I bring

DOI: 10.4324/9781003348931-37

up the business issue I was reaching out about. That's how we do things; we are Hispanics!

Long story short, we decided not to translate the "Done" campaign to "Hecho," and rather shifted the benefit derived from the service from "fast problem solution" to the "power of immediacy." The walkie-talkie would connect Hispanics to their needs quickly, hence our new Spanish tagline "Ya" (Right Now). The Hispanic campaign change was a success and became a case study for the industry. This was the beginning of a marketing shift that moved from simple creative translation to culturally driven advertising that is so prevalent in our industry today.

I asked my colleague Angela Rodriguez, SVP head of Strategy at alma advertising, and an expert of culturally driven marketing, to further expand on the impact culture can have on storytelling.

> "Storytelling is at the core of culture. It is how histories are passed down, how customs are shared and how traditions become endemic to a group. Shared culture is rooted in a shared tradition of communicating. The stories a group tells, meta communicates what a culture values," said Rodriguez. "But it's not just what stories they choose to tell that transmit culture, it's how they choose to tell them. Do they go to the point? Do they linger over details? How important is context vs. outcomes?"

"When I reflect on the differences in some of the classic stories from different cultures, it is easy to see what Rodriguez means. Considering great children's novels of the late 19th century from two distinct Anglo cultures—*The Adventures of Tom Sawyer* from the U.S. and the English *Alice in Wonderland*—gives us insight into the very different things that these two groups who speak the same language value. *The Adventures of Tom Sawyer* presents a distinctly American approach, demonstrating cause-and-effect outcomes through lessons and ultimate moral resolution. In the end, Tom has grown up, and things he doesn't like are deemed to be just how things are done."

"Meanwhile, *Alice in Wonderland* has no such ambition. It leaves all teaching behind and creates a fantastical world meant only for young readers to enjoy."

"Both those examples contrast significantly when we consider Latin American literature, which presents no "classic" works just for the young. Rather its novels are read equally by the young and old. One of Latin America's great works is *One Hundred Years of Solitude*, by Gabriel García Márquez, a story which ends in an abrupt and rather meaningless resolution after pages and pages of metaphors that meander in much the same way that Latinos communicate."

The Latin American penchant for metaphor aligns us neatly with our culture's inverted pyramid communication style. That is, presenting all the context and relevant facts before ultimately getting to the point. This communication style is opposite from most Anglo cultures that believe that "time is money" and, as such, demand getting to the point first.

This brings us to the point that it is crucial that marketers understand the most effective communication methods for their customer segments and the need to hire professionals who can talk not just in a group's language but also in their style.

After all, the biggest marketing challenge nowadays is not about reaching people but rather how to connect authentically with them. For us Hispanics, the bridge to grabbing our attention is not via our brains but instead via our hearts. As Nelson Mandela once said: "If you talk to a man in a language he understands, that goes to his head. If you talk to him in his language, that goes to his heart."

Chapter 34

Multicultural Market Experts Recommend

Unlearn Your Biases

America is more diverse than ever and minorities themselves are diverse as well. They come from different places, backgrounds, and socioeconomic levels. They can even be Supreme Court judges or sit in the Oval Office.

Unfortunately, this very diversity leads to one of the most difficult and subjective aspects of working in multicultural advertising: dealing with the prevalence of stereotypes. What makes it challenging is the fact that most of these biases are unconscious, meaning marketers can be unaware, and worse yet, many stereotypes are perceived as harmless.

It is important to recognize that these biases go beyond ethnic background, as we still see stereotypes in advertising about women, people from the heartland states, those 55 or older and people with disabilities. No one is immune from these biases, and I will admit that even I have recognized biases in myself about people who are different from me. But learning about stereotypes can be extremely useful to advertisers who are trying to increase the relevancy of their brands in the eyes of a consumer that is becoming both wary and critical of the way they see themselves portrayed in the media.

To better understand this subject, I spoke with a few experts in the field of multicultural advertising: Aaron Walton, founding partner at Walton Isaacson, a leading U.S. multicultural agency; Matt Tumminello, CEO of Target 10, an LGBTQ+-focused expert marketing consulting agency; and Luis Miguel Messianu, chairman at alma advertising (full disclosure—he is also my boss, but most importantly, he's one of the most respected and awarded creatives in the Hispanic advertising). The following discussions ensued:

Mizrahi: What are the most common stereotypes in advertising when it comes to minority consumers?

Walton: *First, that African Americans can be reduced to skin color. In other words, casting a Black actor checks the box for representing African Americans or other Black consumers in advertising. Second, the misconception that all Black consumers are African American—and all African Americans are the same. The community is not homogeneous. There are Africans, West Indians, and Black*

DOI: 10.4324/9781003348931-38

Latinos—even African Americans are not completely monolithic—their experiences are shaped by geography, family history, socioeconomics, etc. Lastly, this notion that African Americans are all about music and dance—mostly hip hop.

Messianu: *There are several: the typical family supposedly reflecting the Hispanic audience, the casting, and looks (dark skin and mustache just for the sake of it); fútbol (soccer) as the default sport; the use of music and dance (without the proper understanding of the genre or category). These are only a few examples, but the list is much longer and there have been many blunders over the years. When reaching Hispanics, nuanced cues and subtle hints are the right approaches. The metaphor I use is that like in a good suit, you cannot afford to see the stitching. It takes cultural expertise and know-how to address this growing segment with respect and the right tone and execution.*

Tumminello: *A persistent stereotype is the false notion that LGBTQ+ equals White, gay, wealthy, and male. This narrow portrayal can come across as dated and uninformed on behalf of the advertiser and make LGBTQ+ consumers feel like a check-box. It's also boring. The rich diversity of the community and its different races, ethnicities, gender identities, and gender expressions make advertising interesting, relevant, and impactful.*

Mizrahi: What's your take on a general market ad agency working on your segment-specific creative?

Walton: *The reason general market agencies were ever called general market agencies was because they didn't have a cultural specialization, and, frankly, history shows us that they didn't care about celebrating the Black consumer until they started feeling the pinch of losing budgets to specialized agencies. So, while on the one hand I don't like to rule out the possibility of great creative coming from anyone, regardless of their own cultural background, I do believe in centering the Black experience and that can only be done effectively through the lens of creatives who are deeply immersed in the community, people who are tapped into its history and its present and its future—I know "general market" agencies that have hired Black talent. I don't know very many of those agencies that know how to let Black perspectives lead the creative conversation, from strategy through execution.*

Messianu: *If I were a client, I would ask myself why it took thirty or forty years for general market agencies to start talking about diversity and try to set up multicultural capabilities. Even when general market agencies go out to "buy" Hispanic talent they normally don't empower them or place them in decision-making positions that demonstrate a true commitment to the Hispanic segment. Furthermore, unlike multicultural shops, most of those agencies don't live the culture on a daily basis and don't even expose themselves to Hispanic media content. Would you go to a general practitioner to treat a heart condition? Multicultural shops are experts in emotion, and in most instances, better reflect today's population composition in a new America!*

Tumminello: *Great advertising originates from a deep understanding of the target consumer that you are trying to motivate and that is why advertisers and their agencies spend countless hours on consumer research. Few, if any, general market agencies have these insights and depth of knowledge when it comes to LGBTQ+ consumers and culture. At a minimum, having segment experts work with the general market agency can be the difference between an ad that is forgettable and an ad that is unforgettable. It also protects advertisers from getting it wrong, which happens often.*

Over the past few years, we have witnessed brands damaged by their lack of cultural intelligence. In a marketing environment where specialty and expertise are becoming more important than ever, there's nothing that can replace the value of a seasoned expert. This expertise should be represented across all key steps of a marketing program's development—from data collection, insights analysis, strategic recommendation, creation, production, to deployment. A wrong move can mean months of work and millions of dollars, wasted by a lack of cultural sensibility. It's time to learn how to unlearn our biases and move beyond the stereotypes.

Chapter 35

The Right Approach for Your Multicultural Agency Pitch

Hiring an advertising agency is an art. No matter how scientific one is during a search process, there is always a significant degree of subjectivity associated with it. This is especially true when hiring a specialized agency, where one may not be a subject matter expert.

During my marketing and advertising career, I have participated in hundreds of RFPs, either as a client or, currently, as an agency executive. What I've learned is that the process of finding a multicultural agency sometimes brings its own set of idiosyncrasies. If marketers don't understand these particularities, they may engage with an agency that is not a good fit, and that can be an expensive mistake.

Here are a few learnings I compiled over the years, together with a few relevant questions that may help marketers during their search for a multicultural agency.

1 Thought Leadership

A great multicultural creative agency starts with strong consumer insights capabilities. The reality, though, is that many agencies have deprioritized their investments on talent and sources of data and insights. As a consequence of this deprioritization, I often see agencies presenting data as if they were consumer insights, or I hear the same old insights about multicultural segments from the 1980s and 1990s being "recycled" and served up again with new packaging.

The multicultural segment in America is rapidly changing before our eyes, and agencies need to not only keep up with those changes but also anticipate them.

Relevant Questions:

* How big is the agency's planning group compared to the creative and account services teams?
* How experienced are the most senior members of this team?

DOI: 10.4324/9781003348931-39

- What services and secondary research sources does the agency subscribe to?
- Do they have a proprietary thought leadership program?
- What kind of unique consumer insights did they offer to clients in the past 12 months?

2 Business Consulting

Great multicultural agencies offer services to their clients above and beyond advertising. I have worked with clients whose scope of work for many months was mostly for launching a multicultural marketing initiative, including the development of a business case, assessment of the client's current multicultural capabilities, and distribution footprint, among other areas.

This is not the type of service that most creative agencies focus on. Still, some multicultural agencies have understood that if they don't help their clients in figuring out their multicultural business opportunities and strategies, they may not invest in multicultural business strategies at all. Hence, the need for agencies to develop a strong "business consulting" skill set.

I am not suggesting the type of consulting services that last years and cost millions of dollars (you know the type), but rather, a business support that can help clients figure out the proper brand strategies before even considering writing their first multicultural creative brief.

Relevant Questions:

- Can they share two to three examples where the agency served as a business consultant to clients?
- Does the agency have a proprietary methodology that can help clients when building their multicultural business plans?

3 Cultural Upbringing

This one may sound obvious, but it is incredible how often this is overlooked during search processes. To be considered a cultural expert, the agency's team needs to live the culture they sell. More often than not, marketers are exposed to people who don't consume the media they sell, and they don't know the artists their agency team recommends. Clearly, they are not plugged into the culture they represent.

Relevant Questions:

- What artists are your agency team listening to these days?
- What kind of entertainers and culture creators are shaping the culture in this country?

- How is the agency connected to trends in culture for your segment?
- What kind of culture creators are there inside the agency?

4 Creative Excellence

Most prospects ask to review a creative reel to assess a multicultural agency's creative strength, but very few engage in a dialogue with the agency's leadership about their creative philosophy. Every great creative agency has a creative philosophy, a signature.

Relevant Questions:

- How many ads did you produce in the past 12 months? How many were originally created by your agency versus adapted from someone else's concept?
- What are your production capabilities? Do you use your internal teams or freelancers?
- What kind of production capabilities do you have in-house?
- How do you find new directors?

As America continues to experience significant demographic changes, clients will be required to adopt a new approach towards selecting their ad agencies. I hope these questions will help you look for authentic multicultural elements that can distinguish the creative agency you're hiring to prepare your brand for the changing American consumer, rather than just looking for a diversity of talent. After all, future sales growth will come mostly from the multicultural segments.

Chapter 36

Six Ways CMOs Can Bring Equality to Their Multicultural Agencies

In general, many multicultural ad agencies are relegated to a secondary place on a client's agency roster, behind all their "general market," creative, media, Public Relations, digital, and shopper marketing agencies.

Until recently, the role of the multicultural ad agency has been that of translating or adapting what the mainstream agencies have created, with limited access to the client's leadership and restricted impact on the client's strategy and plans.

Unfortunately, for many marketers, their multicultural ad agencies are seen as an appendix to their organization, funded by whatever resources were left over from their "mainstream" plans.

However, as more advertisers begin to increase their investments in multicultural marketing to fuel their growth, they are starting to realize that managing a multicultural ad agency may require a different approach from the way they have historically engaged with them.

To illustrate this shift, I invited four multicultural ad agencies leaders to provide their perspectives on how to improve your relationship with your multicultural agencies; Marina Filippelli, CEO of Orci Advertising; Flor Leibaschoff, chief creative director at BeautifulBeast and president of the U.S. Hispanic Circulo Creativo; Lewis Williams, EVP, head of Brand Impact at Weber Shandwick; and Dabo Che, CEO and chief creative officer of Che Creative.

Here are six areas of opportunity for marketers to enhance their relationship with multicultural ad agencies.

1 Resources

Make sure your multicultural agencies get appropriate budgets for creating/producing ideas similar to the ones approved for their other general market agencies. It's common to see multicultural agencies receiving a fraction of the production or media budget to deliver the same results as their general market agency counterparts.

DOI: 10.4324/9781003348931-40

Moreover, multicultural plans tend to have a more modest media mix, with lower number of creative updates, less continuity, and lower levels of reach and frequency than the client's general market plans.

Dabo Che: *Often, engaging with multicultural audiences can be quite nuanced and may require additional strategy, research, and creative exploration. This pays off in dividends when the marketing is successful due to the multicultural audiences often having more loyalty to brands and also having an influence on the general market.*

Flor Leibaschoff: *Clients are used to expecting the same level of ideas from an agency that has a quarter of the people working on a campaign for the multicultural market. And here we are now, delivering amazing work with a quarter of the people and suffering the consequences financially. Only multicultural experts can do the work. The market is shifting, and brands need us more than ever before. If we are to change anything, now is the time to do it.*

2 Timing

Another challenge faced by multicultural agencies is that they tend to have less time to create and produce their work, even when working on an integrated idea with general market agencies. This puts the quality of the multicultural agency's work at risk, which directly undermines creative effectiveness and marketing ROI.

Marina Filippelli: *Many companies have been operating under the direction that the general market starts first and multicultural creative follows. However, when a brand starts by briefing all agencies together, everyone wins and they will undoubtedly be happy they did.*

Che: *We all understand that marketing moves at the speed of sound these days but allocating time to your communications plan early gives runway for great ideas and great execution. Black History Month is the same month every year. We shouldn't be rushing to do something in January.*

3 Creative and Production Limitations

One of the most significant limitations to multicultural agencies when it comes to creative production happens when clients request a "double shoot" to maximize their budget. That assumes that the creative ideas are close enough to maximize the location set and production companies.

Even when this is not the case, multicultural agencies have other limitations compared to their general market counterparts, like the amount of time they have for pre-production, production, and post-production, and their choices for director, which are sometimes much more limited.

Leibaschoff: *It's all part of the same big problem: fewer people, less time, yet the same expectations on execution and delivery. I like the analogy of a restaurant: If you go to a restaurant, the slice of pizza is the same for everyone. They don't change the price of the slice based on your ethnicity; they don't give you a smaller slice because you are Hispanic. So why is it that clients believe they can have a general market production for $700k and then expect the same level of amazing results when giving a Hispanic market agency $150k?*

Lewis Williams: *In this current climate, the multicultural agency's role should be more important than ever. Unfortunately, it has become more difficult for multicultural agencies to be seen, heard, and integrated because many brands are afraid of alienating the non-multicultural audience or consumers.*

4 Lack of Testing/Research

Having a client who invests in research, consumer insights, and data mining can be a blessing for any ad agency, but unfortunately, there's still a double standard for the availability of these assets to multicultural agencies.

From lack of sales data to limited sample sizes that don't truly reflect the marketplace, marketers tend to undermine themselves by not correctly securing research/testing investments to truly understand the new and more diverse marketplace landscape.

Filippelli: *In the same way that marketers have to analyze their sales to see where their sales and growth are coming from, they also need to be prepared to mine for insights properly and track their multicultural efforts in the same way they do for the general market.*

5 The Spillover Fantasy

One of the most common ways marketers undermine multicultural agencies is by believing that their general market messages are enough to persuade multicultural consumers to buy their products and services.

This approach, known as "total market," is based on a one-size-fits-all creative strategy supported by media consumption spillover analysis.

As already discussed at length in this book, this approach has been debunked by research as it fails to understand that reaching a consumer does not mean you're creating a connection with them. A one-size-fits-all approach negates the idea that brands should adopt narratives that reflect these diverse consumers' lifestyles and idiosyncrasies which can only be achieved by creating relevant messages to multicultural consumers.

Filippelli: *Believing in the "spillover fantasy" makes life easier for marketers and their general market agencies. In an era of "do more with the less," the idea that you can reach more people in the same place and with the same message is music to people's ears. However, it is a dangerous game to play with your media and creative strategy.*

Che: *This is a failed theory on its face. It was created as a ploy for general market agencies to swallow up the multicultural budgets, and they fed into the fear and apathy of many clients. The exact opposite is true. Multicultural markets are the most influential and powerful audiences globally, and they move the needle in the general market. Advertising is not an island unto itself. It follows the same trends as music, fashion, film, language, dance, and cultural innovation.*

6 Compensation

Finally, one of the ways multicultural agencies can be undermined is when it comes to the way they are compensated. Some marketers still expect to pay multicultural agencies a lower rate, despite the fact that great multicultural marketers may have a deeper understanding of the market, as they better understand both the mainstream marketplace and the multicultural one.

Failing to create a modern approach that integrates multicultural ad agencies into a brand's roster may hinder a brand's ability to effectively grow its business through relevant messages to a more diverse marketplace.

Furthermore, multicultural agencies are still small compared to mainstream agencies and may struggle with extended payments and other requirements that may put significant pressure on their cash flow.

Leibaschoff: *As a Hispanic woman working in advertising, I found myself thinking about how to break the glass ceiling often. I see how some multicultural agencies cannot compete with general market agencies in their compensation game for their teams. This is due to the way they are most often paid by the clients. Why are truffles so expensive? How about caviar? Because they require an expert to find them, to process them. Unique expertise usually costs more, not less.*

Over the next few years, we will see a higher demand for multicultural marketing experts, and multicultural ad agencies are well-positioned as they are used to work with limited budgets, following tight deadlines, under a hyper-collaborative environment, and most importantly, they are used to the assumption that every single idea requires deep cultural insight to support it (otherwise clients won't invest).

It's time to rethink how you may look at your multicultural agencies and upgrade them to the major leagues.

Chapter 37

When It Comes to Multicultural Marketing, Effectiveness Eats Efficiency for Breakfast

Over the past couple of years, we have been reading about how advertisers are increasing their investment commitment towards minority-owned media companies. While this is a critical movement, missing from the debate is an important discussion around what kind of messages these advertisers are planning to use in these new and more diverse media plans.

Understanding the relationship between multicultural creative messages and multicultural media choices is an essential premise of modern multicultural marketing strategy. It can determine whether a brand will reap the benefits of its investments or waste them without knowing why they failed.

Studies conducted in past years help us unlock the nuances of this relationship by comparing the ROI of campaigns based on multicultural consumer insights and ideas versus campaigns based on generic insights.

The conclusions from these studies are clear and the ROI difference is significant, yielding higher effectiveness levels when compared to campaigns that follow the one-size-fits-all approach (aka Total Market or campaigns translated into Spanish).

However, most advertisers still either don't invest in multicultural marketing, underinvest in it, or settle for the now-defunct "Total Market" approach, making me question, Why would a CMO consciously choose to invest in a campaign with lower ROI?

Unfortunately, most of them still believe that investing in authentic multicultural insights, ideas, research, and specialized production is not good because these investments are considered non-working dollars or "sunk costs." They believe their expenses should be minimized to leave more room for investment in what they call "working dollars," i.e. their media plans.

And that's precisely the irony of this approach. What we call "non-working dollars" is exactly what can directly increase your ROI. Pouring dollars into "working dollars" based on messages that don't truly resonate with multicultural consumers simply won't work!

As a matter of fact, we should start calling investments in multicultural experts "super-working dollars" since they can significantly influence and increase the overall effectiveness of marketing campaigns.

DOI: 10.4324/9781003348931-41

Here's a simple illustration with two hypothetical brands, both with the same Hispanic marketing budget of U.S.$ 5 million.

Brand "A" decides to translate its general market ad into Spanish, creating the illusion of saving budget on agency fees and production.

That allows them to invest 90% of their budget on media (U.S.$ 4.5 million) and the remaining budget on whatever adaptation costs are necessary. Their campaign yields a 1:1 ROI rate, so their U.S.$ 5 million investment gets Brand "A" a return in sales of U.S.$ 5 million.

Brand "B" starts with the same U.S.$ 5 million budget but decides to invest them following a slightly different mix. Brand "B" wants to maximize their multicultural marketing ROI, so they invest in the right insights, the most culturally authentic ideas, and the suitable production craft, thus investing 80% (instead of 90%) on media and the remaining 20% (instead of 10%) on agency compensation, research, and production.

According to industry studies, like the one published by Nielsen, the ROI could be up to 30% to 40% higher for brands who understand multicultural marketing drivers (Brand B) than those who translate (like our hypothetical Brand "A").

At a 30% ROI the Brand "B" campaign yields a return of U.S.$ 6.5 million, a whopping U.S.$ 1.5 million difference when compared to Brand "A" while using a smaller media investment.

Just to be clear, not every Brand gets a higher ROI since not all brands have the same set of parameters, not every insight is a great insight, not every agency is a great agency, not every idea is a great idea, or not every production is a great production.

Nevertheless, for most CMOs under the constant challenge to increase sales with ever-so-limited budgets, properly investing in multicultural marketing campaigns can represent a revenue opportunity. Sadly, in today's advertising environment it seems like most decisions around multicultural marketing are made by prioritizing media investments over investing in the necessary insights, ideas, research, and specialized production to achieve higher ROI.

Leading brands like P&G and McDonald's already understand that when it comes to multicultural marketing, growth is achieved when media choices and messaging are considered equally important investments.

As CMOs and chief growth officers do their business planning for the next year, I encourage you to begin treating the debate around effective multicultural marketing as a priority. After all, adapting a famous Peter Drucker phrase, "when it comes to multicultural marketing, effectiveness eats efficiencies for breakfast."

Chapter 38

Where Do Multicultural Marketers ·Come From?

As the multicultural marketing discipline grows in importance in today's business environment, I am frequently asked how to build the necessary skills to become an effective multicultural marketer, and my first answer is that not all experts are created equally.

Historically there hasn't been a robust, formal educational system to adequately prepare the new generation of marketers in America for a new multicultural consumer marketplace but this scenario is slowly changing.

Most executives involved in multicultural marketing are either marketing professionals who came from a minority ethnic background or executives who came to the U.S. from markets like Latin America or Asia, bringing with them a deep understanding of these markets from a cultural perspective that could be useful in the American market.

A positive development in our industry in recent years has been the creation of several programs focused on multicultural marketing offered at some of the higher education schools. I want to highlight a pioneer among these programs: the Center for Hispanic Marketing Communications at Florida State University (FSU), which was founded in 2004.

I reached out to the center's founder, and professor emeritus, Felipe Korzenny, Ph.D., and asked him about how the industry has been evolving when it comes to building the next generation of multicultural marketers, and this is what he said:

> I started the Center for Hispanic Marketing Communication at Florida State University to educate young people on how to reach this important marketing constituency. One of the fallacies common in our industry is that one's cultural background is key to knowing how to reach a specific cultural group. Unfortunately, that is not accurate. Having experience with the culture definitely helps but is far from sufficient in understanding the nuances involved in marketing to a unique cultural group.
>
> Members of a particular cultural cohort are not necessarily aware of their cultural components because living a culture is not the same as understanding it. The Center at FSU educates students on the nuances

DOI: 10.4324/9781003348931-42

of Hispanic/Latino culture and how to apply that knowledge in the generation of insights to connect with consumers. A central element of the program is the process of account planning to better establish a connection with the Latino consumer and to make a specific brand more relevant and emotionally engaged.

In my experience, being from a specific ethnic group significantly increases the chances for an executive to understand both the challenges and opportunities associated with that particular segment, but it may not guarantee it. To put it in a more direct way, for example, being a Hispanic doesn't automatically make a professional an expert in U.S. Hispanic marketing.

Assuming that someone who is Hispanic automatically makes them an expert in Hispanic marketing could be a risky business proposition, as this person may bring with her/him assumptions and experiences that are particular to them as individuals and not the broader segment.

Likewise, executives who come from different countries also may not fully understand the challenges and dynamics of the U.S. Hispanic market. While a Hispanic consumer, let's say from Mexico, has many similarities when compared to a Mexican-American living in the U.S., i.e. same language and culture, they also live a completely different reality when it comes to social and economic institutions, such as the way health care operates in Mexico, for instance.

I also spoke with Doris Aguirre, a well-respected executive recruiter with expertise in the multicultural marketing industry, and got her opinion on the evolution of the multicultural marketers' skills and experience over the past decades:

> In the past, when identifying a candidate to manage multicultural efforts, ad agencies and corporations had a requirement that the candidate comes from that particular cultural background. Today that is no longer as important. While it always helps to identify with that particular cultural market, what is important is that the candidate has the sensitivity to the issues of the multicultural markets they are targeting. In a few years, the general market will be the multicultural market, and that means that current general market marketers will need to understand the sensitivities that go along with each of the diverse markets they are targeting, or they will be left behind. My recommendation to all marketers is to "roll up your sleeves," put your education cap back on, get in the trenches of the various markets, become a social scientist and digest as much as you can about each diverse market in the U.S., so you will not be left behind.

In my career, I have faced similar challenges, coming to this country decades ago from South America. In my particular case, I developed my own crash course on Hispanic marketing in the U.S. (and later expanding to a broader multicultural opportunity) by reading and listening to some of our industry experts like Felipe Korzenny, Isabel Valdes, Chiqui Cartagena, David Morse, and many others. Their books and thought leadership at conferences helped open my eyes to the multicultural opportunity in the U.S., but also to the dangers of stereotypical thinking.

If you are looking for multicultural talent but are struggling to understand how best to vet them, here are some suggestions I have learned over the years that you can use before you partner with a multicultural marketing expert:

- Fully understand their background, their life story, what relevant experiences shaped their life, and how these experiences made them better experts.
- Ask for specific examples of where they led/participated in building multicultural marketing strategies and tactics, and about their roles on these projects, what insights were unearthed during the project, and most importantly, what tangible results these projects achieved.
- Inquire about what conferences, seminars, or training programs on multicultural marketing they have attended in the past 12 months. Moreover, ask what work influenced their professional life such as case studies, benchmarks, or books. These serve as a reference point on how curious the expert is and how much the expert invests in growing her/his intellectual capital.
- Most importantly, explore whether the potential candidate understands her/his ethnic background, knowing that it doesn't automatically make them a multicultural expert.

Over the next few years, we will hear more about how brands need to shift their approach towards the "new minority-majority." However, this process will only be effective if its foundation is based on a talented pool of marketers who fully understand how to create effective multicultural marketing strategies.

I predict that for the next few years, we will see a significant increase in demand for educational programs on multicultural marketing at every level (from college students to C-suite and board of directors levels) and specialized recruitment services. In the post-COVID-19 work environment we already know that competition for talent is fierce as high-quality experts are even more difficult to find.

Chapter 39

Time to Add Hispanic Marketing to Your Shopping Cart

In 2017, several business media outlets reported that U.S. retail sales were diminishing due to a decline in Hispanic consumer visits, driven mostly by the political environment and fear around the immigration debate. The perception was that a sizable number of Hispanics were shopping less because they were afraid of leaving their homes and risked being approached by immigration officials.

This story snowballed and unfortunately put into motion a false sense of instability around the purchasing power of today's Hispanic consumer. After all, on paper, the story seemed reasonable, mainly when it comes to the markets with a sizable number of immigrants like some of the markets in the southwest region.

Although the story wasn't accurate, it demonstrated the power of the U.S. Hispanic market and the importance of this consumer to the U.S. economy! Hispanic consumers in the total U.S. are spending, thriving, and more powerful than ever. Grounded in data, a 2018 Nielsen study called "Fact or Fiction—The Current State of Hispanic Market" conclusively showed that the narrative around the massive decline of Hispanic consumer purchasing power in 2017 was fiction.

Using data from thousands of retailers across the country, Nielsen was able to disprove the premise that the majority of Hispanics were buying less and bringing down sales in general. Here are some of the study's findings:

- Hispanics' spending was growing faster than non-Hispanic expenditure. Hispanics led CPG sales growth in 2017 with +1.0% in dollar change versus a year ago, versus only + 0.3% growth from non-Hispanics (per Nielsen Target Track, Total U.S. x AOC, 52 weeks ending December 2017).
- In 2018 this trend continued with a +1.8% increase in Hispanic spending YTD versus +1.3% from non-Hispanics, a 33% difference! (per Nielsen Target Track, Total U.S. x AOC, YTD ending 4/28/2018).
- Out of 15 different departments within a regular retail store, 13 experienced growth from Hispanic consumers versus. only 8 that saw an

DOI: 10.4324/9781003348931-43

increase from non-Hispanic consumers (per Nielsen Target Track, 37 markets, 52 w/e 4/28/18).

- In 11 of these 15 departments, sales growth with Hispanic consumers outpaced non-Hispanic consumers' sales (per Nielsen Homescan, Total U.S., 52 weeks ending 4/21/18 versus YAGO).
- From a geographical standpoint, Nielsen tracked sales performance in 37 markets. In 76% of these markets, Hispanic consumers' sales growth was equal or stronger than non-Hispanic consumers' sales (per Nielsen Target Track & Homescan, Total U.S. x AOC, 52 weeks ending December 2017).

I spoke with Molly Juers, vice president of Nielsen's Multicultural Growth & Strategy practice, and asked her what her biggest surprise from the study was and she said: "The biggest surprise has been the clients' excitement to hear that the Hispanic market is still strong, still growing, and still attainable."

Moreover, the study also helped to debunk the popular marketing myth that Hispanic consumers tend to purchase products that are on sale only, with little loyalty to brands. The actual numbers couldn't be more different. According to Nielsen, less than 1 of every 5 Hispanics spend are on sale items. This is the lowest level of any other ethnic group. Asian Americans led this group with 27% of their expenditures for items on sale; followed by non-Hispanic Whites with 23%. Black consumers bought items on sale at a rate of 20%.

What does this mean? If you are marketing your CPG products to Hispanic and Black consumers, price discount and value message alone will not be enough. Hence it is essential to focus on branding and advertising as tools to create relevant associations between the brand and the prospects.

Nielsen also looked into the untapped opportunity brands are leaving on the table when it comes to targeting the Hispanic segment. The answer in 2018 was more than $5 billion. Every single year. They reached this number by comparing the relative size of Hispanic households in America, 13.2% of all the country's homes, with the relative size of Hispanic consumers' CPG sales, estimated at 12.4%. The difference of 0.8%, equals more than $5 billion a year.

Nielsen's study not only debunked the idea that Hispanic consumers were spending less due to the political and social environment but showed Hispanic consumers were driving CPG sales at a faster pace than non-Hispanic consumers and they continue to do so even now after the pandemic! Furthermore, it also helped to demystify the perception that Hispanic consumers are mostly value driven and it hinted at the significant amount of revenue brands are leaving on the table.

In my experience the main reasons for this gap are the following:

1   Lack of a Hispanic marketing plan that goes beyond advertising.
2   Lack of understanding on the difference between Spanish-language advertising and Hispanic marketing.
3   When it comes to advertising, creative work that is not based on segment insights and are mere translations or adaptations of Anglo-driven communications.
4   Media plans that do not reflect investments proportionally to the size of the segment and the size of the growth.
5   Hispanic marketing and advertising decisions being made by non-experts and supported by non-experts partners at media and agencies.

Clearly, the Hispanic segment becomes one of the few opportunities that are still delivering growth and positive ROI for those who know how to invest smartly. Winners and losers in the highly competitive retail and CPG industries can be defined by the simple decision to invest in this segment or not.

Chapter 40

For Some Brands, It's Time for a Multicultural Comeback

Over the past few months, I've spoken to several multicultural marketing executives, and they were almost unanimous in sharing their excitement with the strong demand for their business.

Hidden underneath this higher demand lies an exciting trend, as this growth isn't only fueled by higher advertising investments from existing customers and demand from new advertisers. Some of it comes from brands that are reactivating their plans after years of hiatus. I call them "multicultural comeback brands."

I find it extremely interesting when executives from these multicultural comeback brands approach me because they represent a very accurate picture of the arch of the evolution of many multicultural marketing programs over the past few decades.

It's like a vicious cycle: Starting with nascent advertising-driven programs, growing in scope and importance, then being replaced, or canceled for countless reasons, to once again, planning to become an active player in the segment. Unfortunately, in this process, millions of dollars are either wasted or "left on the table," meaning unfulfilled sales that should have happened with the multicultural segments but were not realized.

Moreover, these brands are fascinating to study. By fully understanding why their original multicultural marketing programs failed, one can build a new, revamped, and more resilient multicultural practice with a higher probability of success and, most importantly, a higher likelihood of longevity.

Here are a few suggestions to consider if you are a brand or an organization that is planning to invest back in multicultural marketing after a few years of hiatus.

Understand the "Story" behind the Hiatus

Every unsuccessful multicultural market effort fades out for reasons beyond the market opportunity itself. This is true because (1) the multicultural segment continues to grow year over year, and (2) there are plenty of consumer

DOI: 10.4324/9781003348931-44

insights and ROI studies that confirm that younger, diverse consumers expect more culturally authentic programs and messages from marketers.

Fully understanding the reasons behind past failures may help build the foundation of new programs and avoid the missteps of the past: e.g. executive turnover, lack of leadership support, the misconception of "Total Market" (when multicultural marketing efforts were being diluted into integration efforts for efficiency gains), or even inadequate resources to support the initiative.

Trace Back Relevant Data/Plans

If your previous multicultural marketing efforts happened in the past 10–15 years, you might find vital KPIs like sales and market share data, as well as consumer research and maybe budget breakdowns.

All of this could be very useful as you build your new plans since it may give you a sense of realistic targets to set. For instance, if your current market share among Hispanics is around 15% and in the past it used to be at a significantly higher level, that indicates that at one point, the Hispanic consumer segment had a higher acceptance for your product or service. Hopefully, you can reach these levels once again.

Engage with "Corporate Survivors"

Chances are that some employees directly or indirectly involved with past multicultural programs are still working for your organization, or if they are no longer working there they may still be reachable for a chat. Consider spending some time talking to them, mainly the ones responsible for leading the efforts. Their anecdotes/input can be valuable.

Another potential path is reaching out to the ad agencies, consultants, or research companies involved in past programs to get their perspectives.

Benchmark

Marketers managing multicultural comeback strategies should take advantage of aggressive benchmarking, given that the number of brands active in the marketplace is growing. First, benchmark your competitors within your own industry, and then expand the benchmarking to other industries. There is a tremendous opportunity to benchmark best-in-class organizations, mainly those with longevity behind their support.

Get the Latest ROI Studies

Over the past few years, we learned more about what drives successful multicultural marketing programs, mainly in the field of communications and advertising. I strongly recommend starting with the Nielsen, Kantar, and the ANA/AIMM studies released over the past three years.

I spoke with industry expert Ida Chacon, senior solution strategist at the Collage Group, who was part of P&G's Multicultural Marketing Center of Excellence between 1999 and 2012. Here's her take on this subject:

> This comeback trend is definitely something we are seeing often lately. While the demographic shift has been happening steadily for decades, this moment of cultural impact in America reflects a tipping point that is fundamentally changing the country and, consequently, the way brands and companies need to "show up" for consumers. Now more than ever, consumers want brands to get "back in the game" to better understand how attitudes, values, preferences, and needs are changing. They also expect increased representation and support of diverse identities. Doing nothing is no longer an option. Fortunately, this doesn't have to be a zero-based approach as a lot can be learned by understanding what has been done in the past, what has worked and what has not, benchmarking with competitors and non-competitors from similar industries, and simply immersing in the wealth of insights and knowledge that are available today with a click of a button. Even though this might seem hard for some, especially as brands navigate sensitivities of race, ethnicity, gender, and other identity factors, the ROI is there more than ever. Hence, it is absolutely worth it!

Brands that are planning or executing their comeback in the multicultural marketing space will be more common in the years ahead. While their challenges can be many, they don't need to start from scratch if they carefully plan their steps and surround themselves with the right internal and external partners.

Case Study—An Example on How Brands Can Grow Their Business Even after a Hiatus on Hispanic Marketing Investments

Cheetos—"Deja Tu Huella"

Executive Summary

Despite ten years without Hispanic-dedicated efforts, the Cheetos brand was able to reignite its relationship with Hispanic Superfans by inspiring a celebration of their cultural identity and the impact they are having on the U.S. cultural landscape.

The Business Challenge

Increasing fragmentation across the snack category has flooded grocery aisles with new products, flavors, and brands. As a result, consumers are embracing variety to fulfill their snack appetites, leaving brands struggling to stand out and drive repeat purchase. This has taken a bite out of Cheetos brand's household penetration across most key cohorts, and the most pronounced declines have occurred among Hispanic households—who are also tempted by the influx of imported ethnic snacks into mass/grocery channels that have created even more competition for their share of basket.

The Insight and Strategy

In recent years, the Cheetos brand has become a champion of self-expression, inspiring creativity and liberating playful mischief. By connecting the brand's purpose with the cultural tension surrounding Hispanic identity, we unleashed a purposeful insight that delivers the kind of authenticity our Hispanic Superfans demand.

Idea/Execution

By openly embracing their cultural heritage, Hispanics are rewriting the rules and leaving their mark on the world around them. This idea is deeply rooted in the U.S. Hispanic experience and represents a celebration of progress. Their impact on the American landscape has become a source of pride, a sign of achievement, and a homage to the struggles of previous generations.

Our rallying cry, "DEJA TU HUELLA," captures the sentiment of "leave your mark" and the literal translation, "leave your fingerprint," brings a dual meaning for all the Cheetos dust-covered fingers that literally and figuratively leave their mark on everything they touch.

Harnessing the power of social media, a series of teaser posts from the brand's iconic spokes-cheetah, Chester, created speculation about a potential collaboration between the brand and Puerto Rican Superstar Bad Bunny. The news spread quickly and was picked up by notable media outlets, further fueling rumors of this unprecedented endeavor. Within a week, a formal announcement from the brand confirmed that Bad Bunny and Chester would bring the heat to the American Music Awards (AMAs). Press coverage across leading pop culture and music outlets helped spread the word and build positive sentiment.

In the weeks leading up to the event, our duo came together to keep the AMAs top-of-mind through owned social channels, paid support across Spotify, and sponsorship of the AMA voting process. On awards night, Chester and Bad Bunny were on the scene for a 360 integration. In-show segments announced the Latin Music category expansion, reinforcing the Hispanic influence on music. Our rallying cry lit up the stage at the presentation of Latin awards, and our Spanglish TV spot debuted featuring Chester alongside Bad Bunny and his hottest new track, "Yo Visto Así." The song represents the artist's unapologetic attitude towards his identity and how "if you don't like it, you don't have to look."

We sustained momentum post-show by broadening paid support across linear, digital, and OTT platforms, and a robust social presence kept the conversation fresh. The campaign launch phase wrapped up in late Q4 with a wildly successful TikTok hashtag challenge. Influencers with a range of specialties, including art, fashion, and dance, called on others to show the mark they are making. This initiative provided a peek into future efforts—signaling an expansion beyond the music passion point.

Results

Year-over-year Hispanic household penetration increased +3pts in Q4, surpassing the +1pt goal and outpacing GenPop growth by 4X. Secondary brand and media performance metrics demonstrated an overwhelmingly positive response to the campaign, indicating increased cultural relevance and its impact on achieving topline business growth. Positive social media sentiment (>90%), above-average engagement benchmarks (across all categories) on Spotify and TikTok, exponential growth in social followers (+26K), and an astounding rate of participation in the TikTok hashtag challenge (>3 billion views!) are some of the highlights proving the flame has been reignited with our Hispanic audience.

Author's Commentary

Besides the strong insights, clever execution, and strong results, what caught my attention in this case study was the fact that this is a brand that was absent from actively marketing to Hispanics for a decade, and despite this significant gap, it was able to deliver strong results.

That makes me reflect on how much revenue and profits were left "on the table" by the brand in those ten years, and unfortunately, how many other brands follow the same pattern. As discussed throughout this book, the time has come when brands (and mainly CPG brands) can no longer afford *not* to market to diverse segments.

Part V

Additional Considerations

Chapter 41

Multicultural Marketing Investments Expected to Grow

As we come to the end of my book I want you to know that there's a sense of optimism regarding the expectations around multicultural marketing investments. To give you a better sense of what to expect in the near future, I connected with a few industry leaders representing different segments and discussed the trends for months and years to come.

Here's an edited version of my conversations with Albert Rodriguez, president and COO of SBS (Spanish Broadcasting System), one of the country's leading Hispanic radio networks; Nita Song, president of IW Group, a leading AAPI-focused advertising agency; John Kozack, executive vice president of Multimedia Sales at Univision; and Michael Roca, managing director, DE&I Investment, Omnicom Media Group.

Mizrahi:	Do you see a higher demand for multicultural media/creative services?
Michael Roca:	*Yes—I see it for Hispanic, Black, AAPI, and LGBTQ+ communities. We will see typical spikes of increased culturally relevant creative during the heritage month celebrations (February for Black History, May for AAPI Heritage, etc.), but with the stronger potential of expanding into more moments throughout the year.*
Nita Song:	*Yes, I believe there will be increasing demand for multicultural creative and media. We also see increased multicultural casting in "general market" creative, which I predict will also continue to grow. A key question will be: Will clients effectively support the growth of both strategies?*
Albert Rodriguez:	*It's fascinating that many advertisers seek innovative, culturally engaging media campaigns/creatives that truly speak to the multicultural audience. As it relates to the Hispanic community, the fingerprints of our culture can be found across all forms of media. Whether through bilingual audio campaigns, the rise of Latin music, and the growth of diverse talent representation within the general market and Hispanic campaigns—nuestra*

DOI: 10.4324/9781003348931-46

	gente, our people are everywhere. The message couldn't be clearer, especially with the latest census results. The minority community is on the rise and if you're not growing with them, you're hurting your business.
John Kozack:	*Yes, I do. In fact, we already have more new business clients laid in with our Upfront sales event than ever before. Advertisers are seeing that running a generic spot on English language is not enough to deliver meaningful results that truly connect and build affinity with this audience. The simple fact is that in-language and in-culture creative drives higher recall and return on ad spend for advertisers. Combine that with the fact that brands know what a powerful growth segment Hispanic consumers are, and it's hard to overlook Hispanic-targeted media.*
Mizrahi:	Why do you think this is happening now?
Roca:	*The progressive cultural narrative is pushing all brand decision-makers to be more inclusive, and the reason behind this is because they are now accountable from Wall Street to their C-Suite.*
Song:	*The racial and social justice issues of the pandemic required brands to take a critical look at their DE&I strategies to drive impact and prioritize their efforts. Additionally, the 2020 Census results confirmed the growth of multicultural populations. And finally, I believe the pandemic moved brands to focus on future-proofing strategies, including Gen Z, the most racially and ethnically diverse cohort for advertisers.*
Rodriguez:	*It's a combination of many factors: the social justice movement, the growing minority population, and their spending power; the influence Black, Hispanics, and Asian-Americans have on mainstream culture and their ability to tell if brands are making a concerted effort to foster a deep, meaningful connection. Frankly, the higher demand for multicultural media shouldn't be considered a trend but a necessity.*
Kozack:	*This is twofold. First, the recognition by brands and marketers of the need to be more inclusive in their marketing plans. There has been a real effort over the past year to invest in minority-targeted media to reach multicultural audiences authentically. Second, with the demo shifts and new census data, marketers are waking up to the fact that not only is minority media investment the right thing to do, but it's also an investment in their future growth.*
Mizrahi:	Is this driven by existing brands, "comeback brands" (decreased or canceled past multicultural plans due to Total Market that are now back), or new entries?

Roca:	It's from all brands, the multicultural heavy hitters, the brands who have been dormant, as well as newcomers who are now dipping their toes in the waters.
Song:	Both. Brands that have come back stronger and new brands/categories including pharma, streaming services, and entertainment.
Rodriguez:	We're seeing existing, major brands step up and take the lead through powerful multicultural campaigns that address real issues that impact all people of color at the forefront. They are changing the game and are forcing other brands to follow. While it's become quite the domino effect, and we see the results in our year-over-year revenue growth, there is still a lot of work to be done. Brands need to do more than multicultural marketing; they must also invest in the community and businesses.
Kozack:	It's a combination of both. We've seen brands come back because they saw their business results suffer after deemphasizing our audience. On the other hand, our new business pipeline with new entries into the market has never been stronger. In fact, categories like pharma and direct-to-consumer brands have stepped up and are seeing meaningful business results.
Mizrahi:	Do you have any other comments about your expectations for the future?
Roca:	Many marketing plans are riding the DE&I wave, so we need to make sure we continue to educate brand decision-makers on the difference between multicultural marketing and DE&I; they both need each other but have very different swim lanes.
Song:	I anticipate this year will be another wild ride, but we'll all be stronger than ever, given what we've all gone through in the past few years. We'll all be figuring out that in a post-pandemic life, community/society will be more important than ever, and we'll all need to stay fluid during this "great reshuffle" of talent.
Rodriguez:	We embraced the challenges of 2020 and 2021 with ingenuity and innovation. Our passion for propelling through the tough times has set our foundation for the future. We're open for business and working closely with brands on developing innovative cultural marketing solutions that reach our loyal audience.
Kozack:	I expect this trend to continue and accelerate beyond 2022. Brands and agencies will want to continue to make sure that they are delivering on their promises to reach underserved audiences. And the acceleration will come from advertisers realizing firsthand how their investments pay off, especially when it comes to building their brands and driving affinity and consideration with growing, loyal, and spending consumer groups.

While the higher level of investment in multicultural marketing is good news, marketers should understand that investments alone may not deliver the expected results if other steps are not taken. Here's my advice:

- Make sure you have an adequate level of investment, based on segment size and growth expectations.
- Make sure that any investment in multicultural media is part of a comprehensive multicultural business plan.
- From a communication standpoint, the creative messages are based on relevant segment insights and authentic messages instead of generic versions that follow a one-size-fits-all approach.
- Surround yourself with true segment experts.

This year and for years to come, diverse segments will become increasingly important for marketers looking for growth, and this will also impact the level of sophistication and attention dedicated to multicultural marketing. It's an exciting time to work with this segment, but it's also time to develop better, deeper, and stronger capabilities in the multicultural ecosystem.

Chapter 42

Minority-Owned Media Gets a Boost with Nielsen's New Study

The movement for racial justice over the last few years has empowered diverse communities to raise their voices and call for action and advocacy from brands and businesses. The marketing and advertising industry met the call to action by committing to increase investments in minority-owned media. But as ad agencies and brands were prepared to invest, they hit some bumps in the road.

Which media companies are minority-owned beyond the major players? How do we evaluate the power of diverse-owned media in delivering audiences? What about diverse-targeted and diverse-operated media companies?

With record amounts of dollars set to be spent every year during the media upfronts, Nielsen, one of the largest media research companies, sought to answer these questions and more in a new report called "Diverse-owned Media—Audience Reach and Profiles."[1] In the study, Nielsen aims to clarify the issues and provide a view into the reach and impact of diverse-owned media—in order to support an increase in investments in these media suppliers in the coming years.

I spoke with Stacie de Armas, SVP, Diverse Insights and Initiatives at Nielsen, about the report:

Isaac Mizrahi: Why did Nielsen decide to release this report now?

Stacie de Armas: *The social justice movement inspired us to expect more from brands and businesses who want to support social causes, including investing in and supporting diverse-owned media. Brands and agencies made commitments to increase their investments in diverse-owned media and Nielsen is answering the call to facilitate those investments.*

Our diverse-owned media program aims to help grow diverse-owned media by breaking barriers to measurement, offering tangible support, and proactively surfacing performance data and complementary metrics in the Diverse Owned Media report. We recognized how important it is that we deliver these tools to the marketplace to facilitate the planning process for the upfronts

DOI: 10.4324/9781003348931-47

and help diverse-media owners maximize the record investments in the market.

Our report provides an aggregated view of the value of investing in diverse-owned local TV and radio. We hope to resource planners, buyers, and diverse media owners to use these metrics to validate investments. In the report, we've chosen to focus on Black-owned media as part of our celebration of Black History Month. With the rise of the Black Lives Matter movement, many marketers have also made specific commitments to increase their investments in Black-owned media. As we continue to grow our program, we will include more diverse media suppliers and plan to release another updated report in the latter part of the year.

Mizrahi: What's the most significant learning our industry will get from the report?

de Armas: The performance metrics of diverse-owned media underscore their power in the marketplace to deliver overall audiences and targeted audiences too. Our report offers both quantitative and qualitative ways to evaluate the audiences reached by diverse-owned media as well as targeted and total audience metrics. For example, Black-owned television stations reach as much as 41% of all adults in markets where they are present, and Black-owned radio has a reach among Black listeners that's six times higher than their total market reach during key weekday drive times.

We hope that this guide will help advertisers/agencies see the need to include diverse media suppliers in their future ad buying plans and will resource suppliers to validate the impact of their entities.

Mizrahi: What are the differences between the state of diverse-owned media across the three most significant multicultural segments, Hispanic, Black, and AAPI?

de Armas: The composition of diverse media ownership varies across the spectrum. For example, there are around 800 local ad-supported diverse-owned suppliers in the radio ecosystem with Black, Asian American, Hispanic, and Native American ownership. Local TV ownership varies but has representation from Black, Asian American, Hispanic, and Native American ownership. The significant opportunity is to support more ownership in the national TV space, where only a fraction of networks are certified as diverse-owned. There is very little ownership that is Asian, Hispanic, and Native American.

To support the suppliers at the local level, this report focuses on local, full power, ad-supported TV and local ad-supported *radio with a snapshot of Black-owned National TV. We worked with expert partners like Media Framework's MAVEN and ANA's Alliance for Inclusive Multicultural Marketing (AIMM) to identify commercial, ad-supported media suppliers with minority owner certifications.*

There are unique ownership trends across communities where broadcasters have found opportunities to serve both broad and targeted audiences. For example, our analysis in this report focuses on Asian American-owned, full-power local TV. But we know that Asian American-owned local television has a unique profile, with greater ownership in low-power TV, offering tailored opportunities to engage Asian Americans in both rural and larger markets.

Mizrahi— The report draws a vital distinction between diverse-owned media and diverse-targeted media. Could you tell us more about this and why this is relevant?

de Armas— *Diverse-owned does not necessarily imply diverse-targeted. As an example, several Spanish-language local affiliates have Asian American ownership. In some cases, diverse-owned media delivers strong targeted audiences, and in other cases, they deliver beyond their identity group. Still, there are non-diverse owned stations and networks that deliver targeted audiences, like Univision and Telemundo.*

The truth is that the industry's long-term spend commitments can transform business for diverse owners. Investment can directly support local communities and bring authentic brand partnerships to their audiences. But this will only happen if the suppliers are on the receiving end of the investments. We want to encourage and facilitate that.

That's why our program includes a diverse-owned media certification reimbursement fund. In collaboration with P&G, we are seeding a $130,000 reimbursement program with the National Minority Supplier Development Council (NMSDC) to help cover the certification fees for diverse-owned media suppliers who qualify. This fund aims to support the certification process, expanding the pipeline of diverse-owned media officially defined as a Minority Business Enterprise (MBE). The more diverse media owners that are designated as an MBE, the more opportunity for ad spend to flow to them.

Mizrahi: What are the challenges Nielsen faces when measuring the audiences, media reach, and frequency of Diverse Owned Media?

de Armas: *Measurement is only one aspect of our diverse-owned media equity program. We aim to support these entities all-around.*

Some stations are on the path to publicly shared measurement, but they may not be ready yet to surface and share that data today. Our goal is to help grow diverse-owned media suppliers and ensure they are best positioned when they are ready to surface their data. As an example, we revised policies allowing us to proactively monitor entities at our expense, ensuring we have a complete landscape of data for all diverse owners in the National TV space.

As we started our work to remove barriers to measurement and revise legacy policies for diverse owners, we recognized the need for clarity around who qualifies as diverse owners. Some have national-level certifications like NMSDC, and others have certifications from local municipalities, the Small Business Administration, or the Federal Communications Commission. The landscape is complex, and our collaboration with Media Framework and ANA AIMM was instrumental in understanding the complexities. We worked with them to identify with discipline the suppliers in the media ecosystem we aim to support and will continue to collaborate with them to surface more diverse-owned media.

Mizrahi: What else is Nielsen planning regarding its support of diverse-owned media?

de Armas: *Nielsen's first step is to turn on monitoring for diverse-owned stations allowing us to provide the aggregate performance metrics that can be used by buyers, whether those stations' data surface in systems or not, and by sellers to validate their performance. This report focuses on National TV, Local Radio, and full-power TV—not a landscape report of all diverse-owned media. It is purposely designed to create equity for smaller owners to ensure they are not excluded from media buys. A future report will cover streaming, satellite, digital, and syndicators.*

This effort to include more suppliers will take time. For example, starting in June of 2022, the annual revenue threshold for reporting minority-owned radio stations regardless of subscription status will increase from $7 million to $10 million for the sum of the stations in the group. This increase is expected to allow more individual stations to qualify for reporting making their data visible to planners and buyers. We will also host workshops for diverse owners who want to learn more about the benefits of certification and offer pro-bono consulting opportunities via our Next Level Suppliers program to diverse-owned media who qualify to help increase their visibility, educate them about the options for measurement, and work directly with them to enhance their sales materials.

It is fundamental for our industry to keep investing in studies like Nielsen's. It is also essential that the discussion about minority-owned media incorporate the perspective of diverse-targeted and diverse-managed companies to create a fair assessment of our marketing and advertising ecosystem.

Note

1 www.nielsen.com/us/en/insights/resource/2022/winning-for-the-long-term-investing-in-diverse-owned-media/

Chapter 43

Minority-Owned Companies—Important Observations for Marketers

Investing and supporting minority-owned marketing businesses is important; however, there are a few important observations every business executive should consider when developing its minority-ownership programs.

It is important to understand that the marketing ecosystem is way more complex and rich than a binary view of minority-owned and non-minority-owned companies.

There are organizations that are minority targeted but are not minority owned that are extremely good at what they do. For instance, in the Hispanic content market, the leaders in TV and video are Univision and Telemundo. Neither of these companies is minority-owned, but both are essential to any marketer interested in investing in the Hispanic segment. Moreover, both organizations invest millions of dollars in Hispanic-relevant content, strengthening the Hispanic culture and supporting Hispanic communities across the United States.

Organizations like Univision and Telemundo also employ thousands of employees, a significant number of them from minority backgrounds. And, last but not least, these two media companies combined provide significant reach and frequency to advertiser media plans, at a relatively efficient rate.

The reason I am mentioning this is because my early observations about this debate uncover a concerning trend: that advertisers may increase investments in minority-owned companies by cutting resources from existing multicultural targeted budgets, without increasing the total amount invested in multicultural marketing segments. This may bring the risk of the creation of less efficient and effective plans, which may trigger a cycle of disinvestments in the long run as these plans may deliver a lower ROI.

Would an advertiser be open to a less efficient or less effective program in order to allow a shift towards minority-owned alternatives? Should marketers be guided by what content and media choices minority consumers are making based on their preferences? Should a company that is not minority owned but is managed by minority executives be penalized and excluded from a marketing plan or an ad agency search because of its status? In other

DOI: 10.4324/9781003348931-48

words, is a minority-owned company more equipped and prepared to suc-ceed in the marketplace just because of its ownership structure?

Another concern is that while in the short-term these minority-owned companies may benefit from larger investments, their exit strategy plans to sell their business and cash out after many years of hard work may be under-mined. Simply said, if being a minority-owned company is a source of com-petitive advantage, investors that are not from a minority background may shy away from acquiring majority stakes in minority-owned companies. At best they may consider a smaller ownership share which may represent a much smaller return to their hard work.

Finally, we may also risk seeing the advent of some doubtful minority-owned companies that may use minority shareholders on paper only to achieve the minority-owned certification.

All of these questions and concerns reinforce the importance of seri-ous discussion in our industry to create proper mechanisms of control and reporting, and most importantly, protect and grow all multicultural market-ing investments, because that's what marketers need in order to grow their businesses now and for years to come.

Chapter 44

It's Time to Rethink the Hispanic Heritage Month Celebration

From an official standpoint, the U.S. started celebrating Hispanic heritage back in the late 1960s, when President Johnson established Hispanic Heritage Week. Decades later, President Reagan expanded this celebration to last a whole month (from mid-September to mid-October). In the late 1980s, it became a tradition for U.S. presidents, starting with President George H.W. Bush, to have a yearly proclamation celebrating the rich history and tremendous contributions Hispanics have brought and continue to bring to this country.

With the growth of the Hispanic population in the U.S. and its increasing importance as a business driver, Hispanic Heritage Month (like those months celebrating Asian Americans, Blacks, Women, or the LGBTQ+ community) became a staple in marketing calendars. However, among industry experts, there's a perception that marketers haven't updated their approaches to adapt to the evolving diversity in the U.S.

Take, for instance, Hispanic Heritage Month. While in the past the focus has been on immigrants and the diverse contributions Hispanics bring to American culture, it is important to recognize that the Hispanic segment today is significantly larger than any other ethnic segment and that the majority of Hispanics that live today in the U.S. were born here.

Hispanics, like other diverse segments, should be celebrated every day not just during one month of the year. The impact of this misguided approach has been the perpetuation of traditional stereotypes that end up alienating a significant share of the Hispanic population, mainly the younger generations. From a marketing perspective, the idea that brands should limit their Hispanic marketing investments to one Hispanic Heritage Month initiative per year is not smart and feels like "checking a box" and being satisfied with a pseudo-commitment to the segment.

I asked a few industry leaders from diverse backgrounds to share their perspectives and suggestions on how the business community should celebrate Hispanic Heritage in a fresh and contemporary way. Here is a summary of their thoughts:

DOI: 10.4324/9781003348931-49

Carla Eboli—EVP, Energy, BBDO

If this is your only effort focused on the Hispanic population, then, please think three times before you execute it. . . . It might look opportunistic and, in the end, cause more harm than good. However, if you plan to launch your long-term program during Hispanic Heritage Month, make sure your efforts are aligned with the community's needs and that the community is at the center of your initiative. Moreover, make sure your team is diverse and inclusive, reflecting the community you are serving. To get real insights about the Latinx/Hispanic community, we need to have people that are part of the community and truly understand (from within) their specific needs and struggles.

Victor Paredes—Executive Director, Multicultural Strategy,
Collage Group

How can marketers truly celebrate Hispanics in the U.S.? Marketers can invest in playing a role in the lives of the most influential cultural sector of the U.S. population. Invest in unearthing erased Hispanic history and celebrate our contributions to this country year-round. Invest in Hispanic endemic content environments and creators because your current marketing plans are incomplete and inefficient without these investments. Take notice and participate in the culture Hispanics have been creating for centuries right here in this land because that may also be the genesis of your next innovation.

The population of the U.S. is already majority non-White in many of the country's most populous regions. The health and prosperity of the U.S. Hispanic population is inevitably imperative to the success of any enterprise in the nation. Brands that are part of fomenting everyday prosperity in our communities, addressing the inequities that plague us, from immigration centers to health centers, will own the future.

Aldo Quevedo—CEO and Creative Chairman, BeautifulBeast

Just like mothers during Mother's Day celebrations, Hispanics should be celebrated every day of the year. When our clients ask us how to maximize their Hispanic Heritage Month efforts, we often recommend using it as the launchpad for their year-long community outreach programs. We have the data showing that Hispanics see through superficial efforts like adding flags or showing stories of successful Hispanics. Doing just that could (and will) backfire. They want to know more about your company beyond the products or services they buy from you; they are also interested in the way your employees are treated or if you are helping their community in any way. That's what ultimately creates brand loyalty.

Isabella Sanchez—VP, Media Integration, Zubi Advertising

Marketers can truly celebrate Hispanics by providing resources to individuals and organizations that are making a difference today. While the historical perspective is important and valuable for awareness and context regarding Hispanics' tremendous impact across all aspects of culture and progress in the United States, supporting current and future contributions can be more relevant and impactful.

Going beyond the obvious recognitions of historical figures and celebrities and supporting Hispanics that are currently making a difference in their communities will strongly resonate with these consumers. This can be done in the form of donations, grants, or scholarships which can provide the necessary resources to ensure that Hispanics can continue to thrive. An enhancement could be creating a new source of support, such as a customized educational forum or mentorship program.

To maximize the authenticity of the efforts, marketers should expand their support from just Hispanic Heritage Month to a consistent effort all year long."

Donna Speciale—President of Advertising Sales and Marketing, Univision

Connecting with the Hispanic community is all about authenticity and consistency. If you want to engage with this brand-loyal audience in a truly meaningful and credible way, you must stay connected to their passions throughout the year, every year. Celebrating Hispanics should be an everyday aspiration. This is a vibrant, growing community that contributes so much to this country. So, for brands, it needs to be a continuous journey of learning and commitment.

The growth and impact of the Hispanic community in terms of size and purchasing power will continue, and brands must get in the game now. It still astounds me that more than 1,500 brands advertise in English and do not advertise in Spanish. By not engaging with this audience, they are not giving them the respect, value, and information they deserve.

Lee Vann—Executive Chairman and Co-founder, Captura Group

The best way to celebrate Hispanics in this country is by rightsizing the level of resources committed towards marketing to this segment. It's not just the size of the media buy; it's the human capital, research, agency partners, production. Show a genuine long-term commitment to this growing segment.

Unless you're willing to commit for the long run, don't just show up during Hispanic Heritage Month. Instead, spend a full month immersing yourself and your team in understanding the size of the opportunity. It'll be eye-opening.

Marketers should take note of some of the foregoing comments to rethink and reinvent their "Heritage" Month celebrations. For example, one idea is to take advantage of the Hispanic Heritage Month to better connect with employees, prospective employees in colleges and career fairs, customers, and even suppliers. Expand your take on Hispanic Heritage Month, consider all stakeholders that touch your business, and leverage this time as a springboard for your efforts, not your short-term destination.

If there's one thing Hispanics are very proud of it is our ability to create and to reinvent ourselves in the face of adversity. Marketers can use Hispanics as an example and work on truly innovative ways to celebrate and honor the largest minority group in the United States.

Chapter 45

Multicultural Marketing and Employee Resource Groups— An Alliance That Can Drive Growth

Over the past two years, corporations have become more aware of diversity, equity, and inclusion (DE&I) related opportunities. As a result, there has also been a surge of interest around Employee Resource Groups (ERGs) as organizations have turned to their employees for information that could help them build more robust employee retention and engagement strategies.

During my career, I have had several interactions with ERGs, as a member, as an executive sponsor, or even as a speaker in ERG-sponsored events— often discussing multicultural marketing trends. But there's one interesting experience that taught me a good lesson about the convergence between multicultural marketing and ERGs.

In 2004, when I was hired by the Nextel Corporation to work on their Hispanic marketing efforts, one of my first projects was the adaptation of a general market campaign for the Hispanic segment.

After conducting extensive consumer research, we concluded that the original idea required changes and that a mere translation of the creative concept to Spanish would not be effective with the target. We needed to create an adaptation that preserved the essence of the creative idea while tapping into the segment's cultural insights. Once the campaign had launched, I got a call from my CMO saying that the company's Hispanic ERG had concerns about the new campaign, saying that "we did a bad job translating it from English to Spanish."

I offered to meet with the ERG team and explained to them that translation was never our goal. I told them why a translated strategy would not succeed, presented our research study results, and shared the positive research results from the new, adapted concept. Their reaction was unanimous, as they all understood and supported the proposed changes. More importantly, they felt that the company's Hispanic marketing was being handled by professional subject matter experts (both at the corporate level and with our partner agencies) on marketing to Hispanics.

The lesson I learned was that it was important for me and my team to bring the ERG closer to our efforts, even though they were not fully versed in marketing and advertising. From that moment on, we continued sharing

DOI: 10.4324/9781003348931-50

our work with them and the positive internal word-of-mouth gave our team even more support that culminated in significant results for the corporation.

I believe this anecdote is still relevant today because, until recently, the fruitful collaboration between your internal multicultural marketing experts and your ERGs may not be apparent. In fact, in some cases I have seen people try to merge these efforts, which could endanger your companies' business efforts with diverse markets.

To learn more about ERGs, I spoke with one of the country's experts on DE&I, Robert Rodriguez, president of DRR Advisors, who is a frequent speaker and consultant when it comes to building and nurturing ERG groups and recently published a new book exclusively focused on ERGs called *Employee Resource Group Excellence*. Here is an edited summary of our discussion:

Isaac Mizrahi:	When was the first ERG created?
Robert Rodriguez:	*It is hard to pinpoint precisely the moment the first ERG was created. Still, experts in this field believe it was in the late '60s, early '70s by Xerox, and the first ERG group was an African American group.*
Mizrahi:	What should be the primary goal of an ERG?
Rodriguez:	*It all depends on the corporation's vision, but most of my clients use a model I created to guide them. I call it the "4 Cs" model, representing four pillars: Career, Community, Culture, and Commerce. Some companies prioritize one pillar versus others, but most companies I work with gravitate around a few of them.*
Mizrahi:	Could you expand a bit more on each pillar?
Rodriguez:	*Sure. Under Career, the goal is to help the ERG members gain professional opportunities, advancements, and experiences. For Community, the idea is to help the corporation make a stronger impact in the communities they serve. On Culture, the goal is to elevate the awareness of the ERG's main focus inside the organization, mainly by celebrating events like the "Heritage Months." Finally, under Commerce, the idea is how the ERG can support the corporation's business with that specific group.*
Mizrahi:	Is there a risk when ERGs also are responsible for multicultural business strategies?
Rodriguez:	*ERGs were not created to replace multicultural business experts, but they can be allies, as you described in your anecdote. Besides the fact that the ERG members may not be fully experts in the multicultural marketing field, one significant risk is that they may be biased towards their organizations and their own business.*

Mizrahi:	Who are the leading corporations when it comes to implementing an integrated ERG Strategy?
Rodriguez:	*Each industry has its leader, and B2C companies tend to fare better than B2B ones, but if I have to name a few, I'd probably mention McDonald's, IBM, J&J, Facebook, and Sodexo.*
Mizrahi:	What are the latest trends regarding ERGs?
Rodriguez:	*One of the biggest trends I am observing is around the idea of intersectionality, when two or more segments get together, not necessarily to create a new ERG but rather to motivate discussions that may be common to multiple groups. For example, some Women-centric ERGs and Hispanic-centric ERGs can host discussions about Latinas' professional challenges.*
Mizrahi:	Are ERGs restricted to employees that represent the group it focuses on?
Rodriguez:	*Actually not. Most modern ERGs adopt an open concept, meaning any employee can be a member, regardless of their background. This helps to increase awareness and education of crucial DE&I topics and enhances the idea of allyship.*

We are experiencing times of strategic convergence between external communications to customers and prospects and the internal communications' efforts to employees and potential recruits. A brand's promise and narrative can no longer be distinguished between these two dimensions.

For companies committed to building an environment where DE&I and multicultural marketing are supported, tapping into your own employees' voices may be a source of ideas and suggestions one may not have considered before, and ERGs can be great allies in this process. However, it is also important to understand their limitations and how ERGs can interact, support, and amplify their multicultural marketing efforts.

Chapter 46

Multicultural Marketing Hard at Work Can Enhance Minority Employment Recruitment

As an executive at a multicultural ad agency, I am often part of discussions with clients or prospective clients that want to recruit Hispanics as potential customers.

However, over the past few years, an unusual pattern has occurred, which makes me think we could be witnessing an interesting new cycle in multicultural marketing business: where corporations are asking their agencies to work on campaigns targeting Hispanics as potential employees.

The country is currently experiencing a very low unemployment rate; therefore corporations are competing more than ever for talent in a market where Hispanic, Asian American, and Black talent represent the majority of the workers entering the marketplace. So, it makes sense that visionary companies have decided to deploy smart marketing strategies, regularly used to reach customers, in order to lure these potential employees to their organizations.

Even before the Pandemic hit and the Great Resignation began, HP launched the industry acclaimed "Reinvent Mindsets" program, with a series of social media videos, with community-based Public Relations support. These efforts were targeting African Americans, LGBTQ+, Hispanics, and Women segments based on the fact that these groups are underrepresented in the technology labor force. (Full disclosure—the ad agency I currently work for, alma advertising, was responsible for creating HP's Latino video.)

I spoke with Karen Kahn, chief communication officer at HP Inc., and asked her about the reasons HP decided to embark on this initiative:

> We have an obligation to ensure our workforce reflects the communities we serve, so we had to first look within and recognize that we can do better. The Hispanic installment of the Reinvent Mindsets film series was inspired by the misconception of what a "Latino Job" is and addresses stereotypes of Hispanic workers, then replaces them with positive truths about professional growth, hard work, and commitment to achievement. Our message with all of our Reinvent Mindsets campaigns is unwavering: HP is hiring and talent is our only criteria.

DOI: 10.4324/9781003348931-51

However, this is not a phenomenon seen in high-tech companies of Silicon Valley only. Across our society we can observe concerning gaps in recruitment in critical sectors that may have a negative impact on our economy, like for instance the deficit in truck drivers or nurses in America.

While recruitment advertising always has existed, what makes these recent efforts remarkable is that they are borrowing from conventional multicultural advertising and marketing tools to not only reach the multicultural segment but also connect in a meaningful and emotional way to prospective Hispanic employees, presenting their organizations as a great place to work.

Out of the many best practices I've seen from the several employee recruitment projects I've been involved with, here are the ones that seem to be a constant in almost every best-in-class companies:

Community Support: Corporations that lead in diversity hiring tend to have an active and continuous presence in the minority communities they focus on, and also have established programs to give back to these communities, like college scholarships, for instance. It is important to note that these efforts tend to complement traditional advertising and marketing programs to diverse consumers, not replace them.

Role Models and Mentorship: Successful companies that attract diverse talent tend to have various role models in high-level positions of their organizations and have in place coaching or mentorship programs for diverse young talent.

Employees Resource Groups: ERGs, as they are known, tend to be a great way to understand your employees' concerns and listen to their suggestions. Similar to what we see in the consumer marketplace, a happy employee can be an effective way to convince potential recruits to join an organization and ERGs are starting to play an important role in corporations' diversity recruitment.

Take A Stand: We all know that we live in a highly divided society, and this fact makes corporations extremely uncomfortable when taking a stand on key social or economic issues, because they are concerned about alienating a significant number of customers. However, studies show that a significant number of consumers, especially millennials and Gen-Zer's, appreciate brands that stand for something that is in alignment with the company's values, which they believe is meaningful. Leading companies understand these issues and act according to its core set of values and beliefs, regardless of potential short-term risks.

Robert Rodriguez, the DE&I expert and author, confirms that minority recruitment marketing effort is a trend that we will be seeing more and more of in the years to come:

Upwardly mobile Hispanic professionals with a proven track record of high performance and demonstrated leadership capabilities are in high demand. This means they have numerous choices as to where they can work. Companies that have an employment branding approach that appeals to top Hispanic talent in a culturally appropriate way will have a competitive advantage in the war for Hispanic talent. Additionally, companies that are having success in the Hispanic consumer market, but have little to no Hispanic representation in senior management, run the risk of being seen as exploiting the Hispanic community. Companies that want to avoid this distinction are wise to leverage a multicultural approach in their Hispanic talent acquisition strategies.

The time has come for CMOs and Human Resources leaders to start working together to integrate their multicultural marketing consumer strategies with their talent acquisition and retention plans. A representative Hispanic workforce can be a great addition to companies and also a great bridge to expanding your Hispanic customer base.

Chapter 47

Effective Multicultural Businesses Should Start at the Board Level

One of the questions I often get about my experience as a multicultural marketing expert is: What do the most effective companies in this field have in common? My answer is always the same: Consistency is probably the main characteristic they share in common. Some people seem surprised because they think that the amount of investment is perhaps the defining factor for multicultural programs.

Don't get me wrong; financial resources can be a huge help. Still, successful companies in the multicultural marketing space are ahead of their peers because they no longer waste time debating whether they should support minority segments or allocate a significant share of their budgets towards segments that represent the lion's share of their current and future growth.

These companies have developed a "mental muscle," and this consistency starts at the top, with the most senior leaders. Seldom does a multicultural marketing program last longer than a few years without solid support and championship from the whole C-suite and the company's board of directors.

That may explain why so many companies are still lagging in such a significant consumer trend. Today, America's boards of directors are considerably behind when it comes to minority representation.

When the board of directors and senior leadership of an organization are disconnected from the multicultural marketplace in this country, there can be a risk of stagnant or negative growth and financial losses.

The fact is that less diverse boards and C-suites may not fully understand the business implications that the game-changing demographic shifts are having on the country and, most importantly, how these changes could impact consumer behavior for years and decades to come.

A recent study commissioned by the Latino Corporate Directors Association (LCDA), an organization that I support as a member, called "Sounding the Alarm: Latino Board Trends 2010–2020"[1] sheds some light on the challenges American corporations face when it comes to diversity.

DOI: 10.4324/9781003348931-52

Here are a few highlights of the study:

- While Hispanics represent almost 19% of America's population, they only hold 2% of the Russell 3,000 (R3K) company board seats.
- White Caucasian executives represent 87% of the Russell 3,000 board seats (but only 60% of the country's population), Black directors represent 5% of all board seats (and 13% of the population), and Asian American directors represent 3% of those board seats (and 6% of the population).
- The situation is even worse when it comes to gender breakdown. Latinas represent only 1% of Fortune 500 companies' board seats, the least of any gender or ethnic group.

I spoke with Esther Aguilera, President, and CEO of the LCDA, about the report and what is being done to address this challenge/opportunity.

Isaac Mizrahi: What's the most significant excuse that justifies the lack of diversity in America's Boards of Directors?

Esther Aguilera: *First, no excuse justifies the lack of diversity in America's corporate boardrooms. Boards are dangerously disconnected from the new American marketplace and workforce. Latinos are two in ten Americans, and the Latino market share is growing 70% year-over-year. Plus, Latinos contribute 70% of new entrants to the workforce.*

Our organization has written letters to every Fortune 1000 company listed by NASDAQ with the business case and the talent case. There is ample Latino talent for American boardrooms, with over 4,000 current or retired Hispanic C-suite executives in public companies and many more in private companies.

We have engaged dozens of Board Chairs and Lead Independent Directors. We still hear the excuse that they can't find Latinos qualified for their board roles. This is only one of the many misconceived reasons used.

Mizrahi: What are organizations like the LCDA doing to help change this situation?

Aguilera: *LCDA is the only organization that prepares Latino individuals to potentially serve on boards and teach them how to make an impact. LCDA's BoardReady Institute brings a comprehensive approach to preparing and positioning Latinos for the boardroom.*

Mizrahi: Can having a more diverse board of directors directly impact the company's performance?

Aguilera:	*Yes, a growing body of research connects business performance with diverse teams and decision-makers—you can search reports by McKinsey on this topic.*
Mizrahi:	Do you think investors may use the diversity (or lack of) of a board as one of the criteria for investment recommendations in the future?
Aguilera:	*With boards dangerously disconnected from the customer and employee base, large institutional investors are advocating for boards to better reflect these stakeholders, not only as a good governance but also as a good business practice. Furthermore, Nasdaq, Goldman Sachs, as well as proxy advisors, including Institutional Shareholder Services (ISS) and Glass Lewis, have guidelines promoting board diversity and are engaging companies.*

For many corporate executives, the multicultural business opportunity is almost a foreign concept because the multicultural consumer is "invisible" to many of them. It is time to make them "visible" again and make them present at all levels of a corporation's structure, starting at the very top, with the board of directors.

Note

1 https://files.constantcontact.com/aeb69085601/49ea8105-60af-4bcf-bee1-f32c9bba71c2.pdf?rdr=true&fbclid=IwAR1T_PtMJ8daCXS1w0-ENF7_3RJ3f_X43Li6fWcmPJs-OQm94btdTOsrEPA

Chapter 48

Is Marketing to Latin Americans and U.S. Hispanics the Same?

Over the past few years, advertisers have realized how ineffective it was to use general market creative ideas to target U.S. Hispanic consumers. The strategy, also known as "Total Market," ignores specific segment's nuances and cultural insights that are proven to increase the probability of higher advertising ROI.

Abandoning this old one-size-fits-all approach is a step in the right direction. However, one additional question still looms in several advertisers' minds. How about a creative idea developed for Latin American countries? Can it also be effective with U.S. Hispanics? How about the opposite? Would an idea created here in the U.S. for the Hispanic segment also be effective in Latin American markets?

This is a fascinating question. After all, Hispanics in the U.S. and Latin Americans share a common culture and language. However, advertisers must be highly cautious in assuming that creative strategies may work perfectly in both markets.

I have had the opportunity to work in both geographical markets during my career, both on the corporate side and as an advertising agency executive. Based on my experience, there are a few differences that will influence how a Latin American consumer or a U.S. Hispanic will react to a brand's message.

First, external factors must be considered, including the state of the economy in markets an advertiser is considering to launch their campaign, the overall social and political mood, and whether the country is facing a moment of optimism, instability, or crisis. The Latin American region is also considered very volatile from an economic and political perspective, so creative campaigns must "live" in a context that is relevant and authentic.

Second, internal factors may impact the way consumers perceive brands. For instance, how extensive is the local competitive set for a brand and how easily can a consumer find the brand in local distribution channels? For example, in several Latin American markets, online shopping is not even close to being as pervasive and reliable as it is in the U.S., a fact that may drive a different distribution strategy for certain brands.

DOI: 10.4324/9781003348931-53

To further discuss this topic, I have reached out to a few industry colleagues with vast experience in both markets and asked for their perspectives. Here you can read an edited version of their comments:

Mike Roca—Managing Director DE&I Investments, Omnicom Media Group

There are over 20 Latin American countries that have their own distinct culture, heritage, and dialect of the Spanish language. Given that over 65% of the 62 million U.S. Hispanics are U.S.-born, this adds an extra layer of complexity and lived experience that Latin Americans can't identify with unless they spent a large amount of time in and out of the States during their upbringing. The fact is that U.S. Hispanics want to see authentic reflections and representations of their U.S. lived experiences from marketers who want to sway their purchasing behavior. If you want to connect with almost 20% of the U.S. population, you need to invest in making sure the storytelling is authentic. Marketers need to ensure that their efforts in reaching U.S. Hispanics are equipped with the proper resources to nail down the details that truly distinguish a dedicated campaign versus a one-size-fits-all.

Victor Paredes—Executive Director Multicultural Marketing, Collage Group

I've seen CPG brands positioned from a pricing standpoint as either mainstream or even value-oriented in the U.S., while they were positioned as premium brands in Latin America. In the U.S., given the size and strength of the economy, CPG products are everyday staples of the average middle-class consumer. In Latin America, the same products are a premium treat for affluent consumers. That's why a brand like Lux from Unilever is a premium self-care product in Latin America, yet comparable products in their U.S. portfolio are value-driven products in the U.S. market.

Marialejandra Urbina—Executive Planning Director, Dieste

One first stop for marketing to Hispanics is soccer (or fútbol for us). When connecting a brand with the fútbol passion, be aware of the differences, because not all fútbol fans are the same; for Brazilians, it may be more important than life, compared with Venezuelans, where fútbol is only a national theme every four years when the World Cup is played. For instance, the Mexican National Team is a device for the U.S. Hispanics to cheer for their roots in balance with being Americans. On the other hand, the national team is a unity device for Colombians.

Cerveza Aguila rallied for one nation with the campaign during the World Cup qualifiers and in a polarized political context. Its message, Cuando Juega La Sele Juega Todo Un País (when the national team plays, a whole nation plays), reminded Colombians that everything is better when they come together. In contrast, the Mexican National Team brand celebrates how fútbol connects U.S. Hispanics with their Mexican cultural roots while keeping their American pride. The brand's Somos Locales (we are locals) campaign convokes U.S. Hispanics to reconcile their strong bonds with both nations.

These examples confirm that marketers should run a thorough assessment before seeking short-term synergies by using the same strategy and creative elements for campaigns targeting Latin Americans and U.S. Hispanics.

Nowadays and in the foreseeable future, effective marketing strategies should be anchored in deep, relevant, and specific cultural insights. Developing an understanding of the nuances and differences between these two markets is needed.

Chapter 49

McKinsey Report Brings Focus to the Business Opportunity of the Hispanic Segment

Over the past few years, the economic potential of the Hispanic segment has been influencing business strategies across America, and in December of 2021, a new report released by the consulting firm McKinsey & Company added additional insights to the topic. The report, "The Economic State of Latinos in America. The American Dream Deferred," was authored by Lucy Pérez, Bernardo Sichel, Michael Chui, and Ana Paula Calvo.

The report focuses on four key areas associated with the Hispanic segment's economic activity: Hispanics as workers, business owners, consumers, and business investors. The outcome? In all four segments of the analysis, the Hispanic segment demonstrates its continuous growth. However, the study also reports an existing economic gap in all four areas, which negatively impacts the Hispanic community and undermines the whole country's economic growth.

I spoke with Lucy Pérez, senior partner at McKinsey & Company and co-author of the report, and here's an edited version of our discussion:

Isaac Mizrahi: Why did McKinsey decide to invest in this study?

Lucy Pérez: *We're deeply committed to working on sustainable, inclusive growth and, more specifically, identifying ways to create a more inclusive economy. We've had a long history of working on the topic and recognize the importance of research and data to the discussion. By 2050, we know that one in four people in the U.S. will be Hispanic—a significant population that can have an even greater impact on the U.S. economy. It's critical for us to ensure that access to services, leadership roles, capital, opportunities, and more are equal for all.*

Mizrahi: Let's start discussing each of the four segments covered by the study. Starting with Hispanics as workers, your study reports a $288-billion gap when compared to the non-Hispanic population. However, it also says this gap is mainly due to certain professions where Latinos are severely underrepresented.

DOI: 10.4324/9781003348931-54

Pérez: *Latino labor-force participation is significantly higher than the other labor-force participation rate. However, Hispanics are concentrated in low-paying occupations, less likely to have non-wage employer benefits, and strikingly underrepresented in higher-paying occupations, compared to their share of the U.S. labor force. Collectively, Hispanics are underpaid by $288 billion compared with non-Hispanic White workers. Fifty percent of this gap is concentrated in 4% of professions, including academia (including elementary and middle school teaching, postsecondary teaching), management, professions requiring postgraduate degrees (such as law and medicine), and STEM professions like software development. In a scenario of parity, wages for Hispanics could be over 35% higher, and there could be 1.1 million more Hispanic families in the middle class.*

Mizrahi: When it comes to Hispanic business owners, your study estimates that an incremental 735k new businesses could be created, employing almost 7 million more Americans. What are the barriers driving this gap? Hispanics have the highest rate of entrepreneurship of any group in the U.S., but they face significant barriers in starting and scaling their businesses.

Pérez: *First, Hispanics face challenges securing financing; they have the lowest rate of using bank and financial institution loans to start their businesses compared with other racial and ethnic groups. Even once established, Hispanic-owned employer firms continue to depend on personal sources of funding, making them potentially vulnerable to personal financial risk. Second, Hispanic entrepreneurs tend to have narrower professional networks and are less likely than their White counterparts to seek support and mentoring from professional advisers and colleagues instead of turning to family to support running the business and making decisions. Finally, Hispanic-owned firms are less likely to have a digital or online presence.*

Mizrahi: When it comes to the consumer segment, your estimate is a gap in consumption of $660 billion. In your study, you say that one aspect of this gap is that "Many Hispanic communities have lower or inadequate access to key product and service categories, including food, housing, banking, broadband, healthcare, and consumer goods." Why do you think this is happening?

Pérez: *Many companies across sectors have underinvested in having a presence in areas with a high density of Hispanics. Additionally, many companies have not aligned their offerings with the needs of Hispanic communities.*

Mizrahi:	Regarding the fourth segment, Hispanic as investors, is the household income gap the only factor for creating an estimated $380 billion gap versus non-Hispanics?
Pérez:	*The largest driver of the gap is intergenerational transfers. Hispanics are four times less likely to receive an inheritance than non-Hispanic Whites, and when they do, it's more than three times smaller. The concentration of Hispanic workers in lower-paying jobs and the lower participation of Hispanics in wealth creation vehicles like the stock market further contribute to this U.S. $380 billion gap.*
Mizrahi:	It's been almost five months since the release of this study. What has been the reaction to this study so far?
Pérez:	*That is a great question. As you know, we released the report in collaboration with the Aspen Institute Latinos and Society Program and have had many public and private sector conversations on the report. One overwhelming reaction is that the magnitude of the opportunity for a stronger American economy is massive, and folks want us to do more—go deeper into specific categories to get a better understanding of what outcomes could be achieved if we come together. The other piece is on building bridges across the Hispanic and non-Hispanic communities to find how we can move the needle and make a real impact. Let's take, for example, Hispanic entrepreneurs—Hispanics are highly entrepreneurial even with their limited access to capital. Imagine what we could do together if we could open doors, not just for capital to help companies scale. And as a preview, we will be releasing our second version of the report later in the fall—so definitely much more to come.*

Reports like this from McKinsey & Company bring an extra layer of attention to the Hispanic segment opportunity, given their credibility and the tremendous visibility they bring to this discussion. Moreover, companies like McKinsey connect to a management level that most Hispanic agencies and media companies have limited access to, like CEOs and board of directors.

Building a "more inclusive economy," as described by Lucy Pérez, benefits all of us and makes America stronger. We hope this report can accelerate the discussion on how to move from identifying the gaps and opportunities the Hispanic segment faces from an economic standpoint to the time of action to close these gaps.

Conclusion

When I started my journey as a multicultural marketing executive in this country many years ago, one of the most significant barriers for companies to consistently and effectively invest in the Hispanic segment was the lack of measurable ROI, the lack of meaningful insights, and the lack of best practices or benchmarks.

I hope this book helps to refute this old-fashioned way of thinking, by shedding light into the latest demographic trends, by discussing specific insights from several different industries and categories, by presenting the latest studies on marketing effectiveness associated with the Hispanic segment, and by sharing case studies from leading brands that are achieving growth through successful Hispanic marketing programs.

So why do we still have brands that are either not investing or underinvesting in the Hispanic segment? I assume that these brands may be operating under the wrong insights and assumptions, mainly the one that casts U.S. Hispanic consumers as assimilating to the Anglo culture and therefore not worth being targeted with culturally relevant strategies.

Another reason I have observed in my interactions with marketing and business leaders across America is their aversion to change. In many marketing organizations there is a resistance in adopting new practices, new segmentation schemes, and new resource allocation strategies. Most companies in America plan each year using the past few years as their benchmark. But we all know that today's market is different from the pre-COVID-19 market and certainly much more different than the market from 10 or 20 years ago.

Furthermore, multicultural marketing is barely a topic discussed in colleges and higher education centers; this is unfortunate because a new generation of marketers is leaving schools unprepared to work in a marketplace that is very different and diverse from the one featured in their books and case studies.

Most brands still place the White Caucasian consumer at the center of their business plans, but these brands have a hard time acknowledging that this segment is shrinking in size—every year!

DOI: 10.4324/9781003348931-55

This is not a political statement. This is not a judgment. This is not a Republican, Democrat, Liberal, or Conservative statement. This is a reality. This is what's happening in communities across America.

The demographic changes in America are already significantly affecting most businesses operating in this country. From their consumer marketing programs to their R&D investments, product formulation, distribution footprint, hiring and promotion practices, financial and pricing strategies, in order to keep on growing in the U.S., companies must change the way they do business.

Here is a summary of the thoughts shared in this book:

1   America is becoming more diverse each year, and the White Caucasian segment is starting to decline yearly.
2   The Hispanic segment is the largest and one of the fastest-growing population segments in the country.
3   If your growth plan doesn't include a significant Hispanic segment plan, you're probably not set for growth in the years and decades to come.
4   The Hispanic segment is not assimilating into the mainstream Anglo culture; on the contrary, younger generations demonstrate a stronger sense of cultural identification, and the Hispanic segment is influencing changes in the broader society.
5   Translating your general market messages from English to Spanish does not work to drive sales. The fact that Hispanics may see these translated messages means only you're reaching them, but it does not mean you're connecting with them. These messages may only be considered unsolicited distractions and represent a waste of resources.
6   Advertising is an essential aspect of a Hispanic segment plan, but to be truly effective, you need a comprehensive marketing and business plan.
7   Investments need to be proportional to the segment's size and the opportunity's magnitude. Consistency of investments over the years is the key to success with the segment.
8   Effective Hispanic marketing plans are developed by true experts that understand the market and have a track record of specializing and success.
9   Any company and brand can have a Hispanic marketing plan, regardless of budget size.
10   Effective Hispanic marketing requires breaking away from old marketing methods and reallocating resources, and the payoff will come as Hispanics tend to be loyal to brands that support the segment and the community.

I hope that marketers and business leaders across America start thinking about the answers to this question: What is my Hispanic business strategy? Because the time to start thinking about these answers was "yesterday."

Finally, I hope that business leaders understand that the key to their future growth depends on developing and implementing consistent Hispanic marketing programs based on genuine culturally relevant insights in partnership with seasoned and authentic subject matter experts. This is the only way to tap into the Hispanic market power, achieve accelerated business growth, and support the development of a more just and inclusive marketplace.

Index

Printed in the United States
by Baker & Taylor Publisher Services